Microsoft®
Combat Flight Simulator 2
WWII Pacific Theater

Microsoft®

PUBLISHED BY
Microsoft Press
A Division of Microsoft Corporation
One Microsoft Way
Redmond, Washington 98052-6399

Library of Congress Cataloging-in-Publication Data
Van West, Jeff.
    Microsoft Combat Flight Simulator 2 : WWII Pacific Theater : Inside Moves / Jeff Van West.
        p. cm.
    Includes index.
    ISBN 0-7356-1176-9
    1. Microsoft Combat flight simulator. 2. Computer war games. 3. Computer flight
games. 4. World War, 1939-1945--Aerial operations--Computer simulation. I. Title.
    U310.V33 2000
    793.9'2'02855369--dc21   00-057858

Printed and bound in the United States of America.

3 4 5 6 7 8 9   MLML   5 4 3 2 1

Distributed in Canada by Penguin Books Canada Limited.

A CIP catalogue record for this book is available from the British Library.

Microsoft Press books are available through booksellers and distributors worldwide. For further information about international editions, contact your local Microsoft Corporation office or contact Microsoft Press International directly at fax (425) 936-7329. Visit our Web site at mspress.microsoft.com. Send comments to *mspinput@microsoft.com*.

Direct3D, DirectSound, DirectX, Fighter Ace, Microsoft, Microsoft Press, MSN, SideWinder, and Windows are either registered trademarks or trademarks of Microsoft Corporation in the United States and/or other countries. Other product and company names mentioned herein may be the trademarks of their respective owners.

Illustrations from the Airplane Spotter Card deck reproduced by permission of U.S. Games Systems, Inc., Stamford, CT 06902. Copyright 1998 by U.S. Games Systems, Inc., Stamford, CT. Further reproduction prohibited.

Unless otherwise noted, the example companies, organizations, products, people, and events depicted herein are fictitious. No association with any real company, organization, product, person, or event is intended or should be inferred.

Acquisitions Editor: Casey Doyle
Project Editor: Devon Musgrave
Technical Editor: Brian Johnson

Dedication

To Jenny Van West & Company

Acknowledgments

My thanks to the folks at Microsoft Press for all their patience and hard work. Specifically, I'd like to thank my editors: Sandra Haynes, Brian Johnson, Rebecca McKay, and Devon Musgrave. I also thank Casey Doyle for all his work, assistance, and his faith in my ability to do the job.

Thanks also to all the people on the Combat Flight Simulator team. Without their willingness to help, this book would not have been possible. I'm indebted for the time they took out of a busy development schedule to help with this project. The people I must thank by name are Michael Ahn, Hal Bryan, Kevin Griffin, Tom McDowell, Roy McMillion, Jon Seal, Bruce Williams, and Michael Zyskowski. I'm especially grateful to Rob Brown, Mike Lambert, and Tucker Hatfield for answering my endless e-mail questions promptly and with good humor. I'm also indebted to Tucker for a lunch.

Finally, thanks to Kevin Lane-Cummings for his help getting the project rolling, Ken Williams for his hardware expertise, Jim Musgrove for his airplane insights, and Jenny Van West for her support and patience with my schedule, even while she was working on a couple of important projects of her own.

Contents

PREFACE

Within the world of computer games, simulation games stand in a class by themselves. The difference between flying a World War II–era fighter in combat and, say, running around in a spaceship blowing aliens into little moist pieces is that the fighter combat really happened. Some of the people who lived it are still here to tell us about it, and some of the airplanes are still up and flying. (I suppose some people would claim the alien thing really happened too, but that's beyond the scope of this book.) Those real experiences and real airplanes provide an objective standard that the development team for Microsoft Combat Flight Simulator 2 tries to match. They put a huge amount of time and effort into making the game's airplanes look, sound, and fly as much like the real thing as possible.

Flying a realistic airplane isn't always easy. Sometimes when you pull back on the stick to go up, the realistic airplane goes down. When the engine powers up for takeoff, tailwheel warbirds seem to have a mind of their own as they zigzag drunkenly across the runway. Although you have the option of adjusting the game's realism so that the airplanes are easier to fly, there's a serious satisfaction in taking to the sky in a realistic airplane, claiming victory in combat, and then bringing the warbird safely back to earth, all while adjusting for the quirks and subtleties that make it real.

The goal of this book is to give you information, strategies, and techniques to make your Combat Flight Simulator 2 experience as rich as possible. Some chapters of this book focus on understanding how the Combat Flight Simulator 2 game works so that you can get the most out of your computer system. Other chapters focus on understanding the theories of flight and combat that apply to both real-world and virtual airplanes. The book is designed to complement the Combat Flight Simulator 2 manual and the online documentation that come with the game. If you find there's something missing from this text, look in those other sources. You'll probably find it there.

In my own study of flight and air combat, I've been frustrated by books that give me plenty of specific moves and diagrams but no overall concepts to use to organize this information in my mind. In this book, I've tried to organize the ideas of flight and combat around a few core ideas. These ideas are then put into practice with flight examples and cockpit views so that you can see something demonstrated from your own point of view. Wherever possible I have kept the discussion focused on the pilot's point of view. Hopefully, this technique will help provide a foundation for you to build your own understanding of what it means to be a fighter pilot. Your experience flying the airplanes is the best teacher. General Chuck Yeager once said that if he had to choose between flying against a less experienced pilot who flew a superior airplane and a more experienced pilot who flew an inferior airplane, he would choose the less experienced pilot every time.

Some of you might be totally new to aviation or combat flying; others of you might be veterans of Combat Flight Simulator who are looking for the next challenge. It's my intention for this book to offer something to a simulator pilot of any level. The chapters are written so that they don't necessarily need to be read in order. Pick the chapters that are most useful to you. Whether you came to Combat Flight Simulator 2 as a gamer, a pilot, or a World War II enthusiast, the game will offer something new and exciting for you. The skies of the South Pacific are waiting. Let's begin.

Chapter One

FIRST LOOK

What's New in Combat Flight Simulator 2?

The latest version of Microsoft Combat Flight Simulator is not simply the original Combat Flight Simulator set in the Pacific Theater. The new version is based on the next generation of Microsoft's flight simulation software. Microsoft Combat Flight Simulator 2: WW II Pacific Theater sports improvements in the way the airplanes look and fly, in the realism and intricacy of missions, and in the intelligence of the computer-controlled pilots.

New Aircraft

Combat Flight Simulator has seven new player-flyable aircraft: three Japanese and four American. You'll find two versions of the Japanese "Zero" fighter: the A6M2 and the A6M5. These aircraft were the staple of the Japanese Navy throughout the war and are arguably the best-known fighter aircraft of the Pacific Theater. The Japanese Kawanishi N1K2-J *Shiden-kai* (Allied codename "George" or "George-21") is also available. This fighter is less famous than the Zero but is a tougher opponent for any of the four American aircraft. The U.S. fighters include the heavily used Grumman Wildcat (F4F-4) and Hellcat (F6F-3), as well as the better-known Vought Corsair (F4U-1A) and the twin-engine Lockheed P-38F Lightning. For complete descriptions of the aircraft, see Chapters 10 and 11, "Player-Flyable Aircraft" and "Non-Player-Flyable Aircraft."

New War Theater

Fighting in the Pacific was a whole different animal from fighting in Europe. Landmarks and runways were few and far between. In fact, the area of the Pacific mapped out in Combat Flight Simulator 2 is four times the size of the European Theater. The game developers used actual Landsat satellite data to produce the base map for the simulation. If you are en route on a mission and you see some unnamed little atoll off your right wing, that atoll really exists at the same latitude and longitude in the Pacific Ocean.

Too Slow

Figure 1-1 *Carrier landings are one of the big new challenges in Combat Flight Simulator 2.*

Finding a place to land in all that water can be difficult, especially when the airports don't stay in one place! As Figure 1-1 illustrates, carrier takeoffs and landings are now required skills for successfully completing missions.

Improved Aircraft Details

The resolution of the aircraft textures is four times greater than in the first version of Combat Flight Simulator. As you'll see if you compare Figures 1-2 and 1-3, the improved level of detail is especially clear in chase view.

Moving Airports

Creating the carrier landings was quite a challenge to the game development team. They had to account for the relative motion of the airplane to the water, the ship to the water, and the airplane to the ship. Sometimes after the airplane touched down, the varying speeds and courses of the airplane and ship would cause the aircraft to suddenly depart the carrier in a new direction. Other times, the airplane would land and come to a perfect stop, only to have the carrier move out from underneath the now stationary airplane!

In Combat Flight Simulator 2, you will see the peeling paint, the carbon stains around the exhaust and gun barrels, and the texture difference between the airframe's riveted aluminum skin and the cloth of the control surfaces. And this detail isn't only skin deep. As Figure 1-4 reveals, damage to the airplane's skin now exposes the inner structures.

When an enemy aircraft breaks apart, you will see identifiable parts; landing gear or ailerons might come flying off.

You can also see damage to your own aircraft from virtual cockpit view, rather than only from chase view, as in the original Combat Flight Simulator. The damage itself is more precise. Shooting a Zero through the wing might cause a wing fire, with the flames clearly visible on the wing rather than coming from the fuselage. There is also a higher likelihood of catastrophic failures. Airplanes felled in Combat Flight Simulator often would slowly glide to their

Figure 1-2 *This P-51 shows the maximum detail in the original Combat Flight Simulator.*

demise, while in Combat Flight Simulator 2 they are more likely to come apart in flight or explode.

Improved Artificial Intelligence Pilots

The artificial intelligence (AI) technology behind the pilots flying the other aircraft takes into account such subtleties as energy management and ideal maneuvering speeds. You can still select the level of your opponent, from Rookie to Ace, but expect the Aces to have a few more tricks up their sleeves than they did in Combat Flight Simulator. This change also applies to your wingmen, so you can expect better backup. Your wingmen will also respond to a limited set of commands, so you can order them to split up, rejoin, attack, or help you out of a tight jam. Wingmen start as rookies but learn as they gain experience. The longer you can keep your wingmen alive, the better fighters they'll become.

Combat Flight Simulator 2

Figure 1-3 *The Corsair shows the increased detail in Combat Flight Simulator 2.*

Figure 1-4 *Splash one Bandit! This Zero is done for.*

More Missions, More Information, Bigger Campaigns

Combat Flight Simulator 2 has a greater number and variety of missions than the original. Rather than having two campaigns, Combat Flight Simulator 2 has one large campaign that you can fly from either the Japanese or the American perspective. The campaign structure branches, however, so the outcome of each individual mission affects what happens in the next mission. The briefings are more complete, the reconnaissance photos more realistic, and the gossip around the ship (scuttlebutt) contains valuable tidbits of information. The missions themselves are dynamic; certain player actions

will spawn certain events in the mission. Play a mission a bit differently, and you might find a squadron of Hellcats waiting where you never noticed them before.

The Mission Builder

This built-in development tool allows you to create and design your own missions to fly or share with friends. You can also link missions together to create entire campaigns. The Combat Flight Simulator 2 development team used this tool to create the missions and campaigns that are included with the final product. Chapter 13, "Using the Mission Builder," explains how to use the Mission Builder.

Flight Model Revisions

Although less immediately noticeable than other improvements, the changes in the flight model represent changes in the whole Combat Flight Simulator philosophy. When the original Combat Flight Simulator was first developed, the team took the Microsoft Flight Simulator 98 game engine and created a version that could better handle multiple aircraft. The team also had to overcome some modeling problems that were inherent to the program. The result was some inconsistency between Combat Flight Simulator and Flight Simulator 98. With the delivery of Microsoft Flight Simulator 2000, the civilian flight simulator engine was improved and many of these problems were addressed. Combat Flight Simulator 2 has been rewritten to use the updated Flight Simulator 2000 engine. What this means for you is a better and more realistic aircraft model for

How Do They Do It?

Not only are the aircraft in Combat Flight Simulator 2 new, but they are also closer simulations of the real aircraft than ever before. In developing these aircraft, the Microsoft Combat Flight Simulator team built a database of dozens of parameters, including manufacturer's data, personal accounts, and flight data from actual WWII war birds still flying, including the last flying "George" in the world. They compared all collected data against flight test data for the game aircraft and made adjustments for any anomalies between real and virtual airplanes as best they could. Integral to this process was a computer test pilot that would fly each aircraft through a series of preset maneuvers and report the results to the game designers. In addition to the 7 player-flyable airplanes, there are 11 non-player-flyable airplanes. A few, such as the C-47, are upgraded from the versions in Combat Flight Simulator, while others are completely new.

Note: *There are two sets of keyboard commands in Combat Flight Simulator 2. One set matches the keys used in most flight combat games (Combat Standard). The other set matches the keys used in Microsoft Flight Simulator 2000 (FS Standard). You can change the set you use in the Control Assignment window. You can open this window by clicking the Controller Assignments button in the Settings window. This book uses the FS Standard configuration when describing keyboard commands.*

Combat Flight Simulator 2. It also means that you can use aircraft and scenery designed for Flight Simulator 2000 in Combat Flight Simulator 2. You always wanted to strafe Meigs field with a Zero, didn't you?

A Quick Tour of the Interface

Gamers familiar with the original Combat Flight Simulator will quickly and easily find their way around the new software, and anyone new to the software will find the layout intuitive and easy to use. Though the Main screen has a new, sleek look, it contains the same options as the original. As you can see if you compare Figures 1-5 and 1-6, the only significant difference between the two versions is that Help is

now a question mark icon in the upper right of the screen. (You'll find it there on all the Combat Flight Simulator 2 screens.) There are also a few changes and additions on the screens opened from the Main screen.

Free Flight

A new item in Free Flight is the Advanced Weather settings screen. You'll still find pull-down menus for time of day, clouds, and

Figure 1-5 *Combat Flight Simulator Main screen.*

wind available from the Time and Weather screen, but the Advanced Settings button allows greater specification of exact weather conditions. The new weather settings allow you to have different weather conditions in different places, so the sky might be clear when you take off, but the visibility over the target could drop to less than one mile in rain! Chapter 2, "Behind the Screens," offers further details about how to use the weather settings.

Figure 1-6   *Combat Flight Simulator 2 Main screen.*

Quick Combat

The big change in the Quick Combat section is a new option that lets you have up to seven wingmen accompany you into combat. Quick Combat in Combat Flight Simulator 2 also allows you to specify the mission type you want to fly. The ability to choose the mission type allows you to practice combat under a variety of conditions that will help you in flying the different campaigns.

Single Missions and Campaigns

One difference between Combat Flight Simulator 2 and its predecessor is that you select a nationality (Japanese or American) before starting a mission or campaign. After selecting your nationality, if you're flying a mission, you see the page with the mission list. If you're starting a campaign, you'll work your way through a series of screens that allow you to enter your name and select the type of campaign you want to fly. The mission structure is now dynamic, meaning the outcome on mission 1 affects the goals of mission 2. Mission success is also critical to having a successful career as a pilot. To learn more about missions and campaigns, see Chapter 12, "Missions and Campaigns."

Training Missions

Combat Flight Simulator 2 includes 10 new training missions, covering normal flight maneuvers, aerobatics, combat maneuvers, and carrier landings. In addition to the training missions, you now have the option of taking a training course. This course lets you create a character who will progress through all 10 missions and then continue as a campaign pilot. If you really want a better understanding of how your opponent's airplane handles, go through the training program once as each nationality. The 10 training missions are the same, but the aircraft are very different.

New Items in the Cockpit

Go to the Combat Flight Simulator 2 Main screen and select Free Flight. Choose an A6M2 Zero and click Fly Now. Before you start your engine, take a look around the cockpit. If you don't read Japanese, one of the first things you'll notice is that many of the instruments are hard to identify. This is part of the effort to make the cockpits as real as possible. If you move the mouse over one of the instruments or switches, you will see a pop-up ToolTip. These ToolTips are in English and will help you decode the Japanese panel. Right-click any item and select What's This to see a quick description of the instrument or switch and its function.

If you are flying on the Japanese side, the training instructions and radio communications will be in Japanese as well. Unless you speak the language, you will need to watch the subtitles to understand what is happening.

Switch from the Cockpit View to Virtual Cockpit by pressing S. Now use the numeric keypad or the hat switch on your joystick to look around. Virtual cockpit in the original Combat Flight Simulator included views of the canopy and wings of your airplane, but these views were just bitmaps that did not change. In Combat Flight Simulator 2, the virtual cockpit views are generated from the aircraft model itself. This means the view will include any damage incurred by your airplane, and the control surfaces will move in response to your control inputs. Go ahead and move your ailerons to see the effect.

Press S once again to enter Chase View. This is a good view for seeing the improved graphical detail. Use the keypad or the joystick hat switch to change

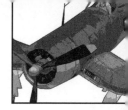

your view. Move to a position in front of the airplane, and press E to get an engine start. Once the engine is started, open the throttle so the airplane rolls forward. Notice the rolling wheels and how the landing gear struts move up and down with the uneven terrain. Press S again to switch to cockpit view and take off. Switch back to chase view and retract the gear. The new gear animations are timed to within a fraction of a second to footage of the gear on real, flying war birds.

From cockpit view, press W to see the Heads Up Display (HUD). This view has changed slightly from the original Combat Flight Simulator. There is no longer a heading display—it has been replaced by an angle of bank display. This display makes it easier to keep track of your airplane's attitude in the air during combat. In the lower right of the screen, you'll notice a controls position indicator. The top scale shows your aileron position, the center scale shows your elevator position, and the bottom scale shows your rudder position.

Importing from Combat Flight Simulator and Flight Simulator 2000

You can import aircraft, detailed terrain, and missions from Combat Flight Simulator and Flight Simulator 2000 into Combat Flight Simulator 2. You can also export the scenery and aircraft from Combat Flight Simulator 2 into Flight Simulator 2000. This compatibility allows you to create all sorts of new scenarios, such as Zeros fighting Messerschmitts in downtown New York.

To Import an Airplane into Combat Flight Simulator 2

Find the Microsoft Games folder in the Program Files folder and open it. You might see folders for Combat Flight Simulator, Flight Simulator 2000, and Combat Flight Simulator 2, depending on which products you have installed. In each folder you'll see another folder, named AIRCRAFT, which contains all the airplane

Note: *Aircraft and scenery are completely interchangeable between Combat Flight Simulator 2 and Flight Simulator 2000. Scenery is interchangeable between Combat Flight Simulator 2 and Combat Flight Simulator, but airplanes are not. The Combat Flight Simulator 2 airplanes will not work correctly in the original Combat Flight Simulator.*

models. Simply copy the entire folder for each airplane model you want from Combat Flight Simulator or Flight Simulator 2000, and paste it into the Combat Flight Simulator 2 AIRCRAFT folder. When you start Combat Flight Simulator 2, it should recognize the new airplanes. The older aircraft won't display all the new features of Combat Flight Simulator 2 aircraft. For example, the levels of detail will not improve: Virtual Cockpit in any of the older aircraft will look like the Wildcat cockpit. When you use the older planes in the mission builder, you will need to assign each one an allegiance before you can use it in missions.

To Import Missions into Combat Flight Simulator 2

You must use the Mission Builder to bring missions into Combat Flight Simulator 2. Go to the Mission Builder and click Open File. Now choose Browse and locate the Missions folder in Combat Flight Simulator. Open it and select the mission you want. If you have not already imported the mission-specific aircraft into Combat Flight Simulator 2, the mission builder will substitute a Zero. You can always change the Zero into another airplane later. If you play the mission in Europe, you will want to copy the European landscape as well.

To Import Scenery into Combat Flight Simulator 2

If you own Flight Simulator 2000 and you want to import all that great scenery into Combat Flight Simulator 2, you can. You'll need a couple of hundred MBs of hard drive space and some experience using Microsoft Windows Explorer and Notepad.

Note: *Have your Flight Simulator 2000 CD ready when you do the import. Get to the Flight Simulator 2000 scenery by clicking the Advanced Go To button. It takes a long time to start up after the import, so be patient!*

First, you need to copy the scenery and texture files from Flight Simulator 2000 to the appropriate folders in the Combat Flight Simulator 2 folder. Assuming that you've installed Combat Flight Simulator 2 and Flight Simulator 2000 to their default folders, copy the files from C:\Program Files\Microsoft Games\ FS2000\Scenery\ to the Scenery folder in C:\Program Files\Microsoft Games\Combat Flight Simulator 2. When asked whether you want to replace existing files, click No. Repeat this step for the files in C:\Program Files\Microsoft Games\FS2000\Texture, placing the files in C:\Program Files\Microsoft Games\Combat Flight Simulator 2\Texture. Finally, copy the files from C:\Program Files\Microsoft Games\FS2000\ scenedb\ world\scenery to C:\Program Files\Microsoft Games\Combat Flight Simulator 2\Scenedb\World\Scenery\. Remember to click No when you're asked whether you want to replace existing files.

Once your files are all in place, you just need to tweak the Scenery.cfg file, located in the Combat Flight Simulator 2 folder. This tweak requires copying a portion of the Scenery.cfg file from Flight Simulator 2000 into the Combat Flight Simulator 2 version of the file. After the insertion, you'll need to renumber some of the areas in the file and you'll be ready to go. Here are the steps:

1. Open the Scenery.cfg file located in the FS2000 directory with Notepad, and copy scenery areas [Area.004] through the bottom of the list, which is [Area.066] if using Flight Simulator 2000 Standard or [Area.072] if using Flight Simulator 2000 Professional.

2. Open a copy of Notepad, and paste in the text you just copied.

3. Find each occurrence of the text *Local=* and replace it with the Flight Simulator 2000 path. Typically, the path will read *Local=C:\Program Files\Microsoft Games\FS2000*. The change should have the effect shown here:

   BEFORE:

   [Area.007]
   Title=FS2000 Airport and Facilities Data
   Local=scenery
   Active=True
   Layer=7

   AFTER:

   [Area.007]
   Title=FS2000 *Airport and* Facilities Data
   Local=C:\Program Files\Microsoft Games\FS2000\scenery
   Active=True
   Layer=7

4. Copy the new text to the clipboard.

5. Make a copy of the Scenery.cfg file located in the Combat Flight Simulator 2 directory, and save it as Old Scenery.cfg to have as a backup.

6. Open the Scenery.cfg file located in the Combat Flight Simulator 2 folder with Notepad. Paste the text into the file just above the current [Area.004]. Don't replace the text; just insert the clipboard text.

7. Here's the tricky part. The text file now has two versions of the sections labeled [Area.004] through [Area.011]. The original section marked

[Area.004] will now appear after [Area.066] if using Flight Simulator 2000 Standard and [Area.072] if using Flight Simulator 2000 Professional. Renumber the original [Area.004] through [Area.011] to continue the sequence. If you have Flight Simulator 2000 Standard, [Area.004] becomes [Area.067], [Area.005] becomes [Area.068], and so on. If you have Flight Simulator 2000 Professional, [Area.004] becomes [Area.073], [Area.005] becomes [Area.074], and so on until all the areas have a unique number.

8. Save the Scenery.cfg file.

Start Combat Flight Simulator 2. You should have all the Flight Simulator 2000 scenery available. Now you can dogfight in between the buildings in New York City. The scenery from Combat Flight Simulator doesn't import very well into Combat Flight Simulator 2. You can import it if you want, but it probably isn't worth the trouble.

Game Philosophy

The slogan reads, "As real as it gets." The designers of Combat Flight Simulator 2 want the game to be as real as you want. If you want to exclusively use quick combat to dogfight over the office network during lunch hour, that's great. If you want to meet a group of war bird enthusiasts on line to re-create a famous battle in real time, that's also great. The game has something for everyone. If you do choose to create a pilot character and play out a campaign, it will be helpful to understand a few elements of the game philosophy.

You Can't Change History—Just Your Little Piece of It

The overall strategic goals for the game are history-based. The major campaigns follow the course of events of the real war and have the same overall outcome. If you create a pilot in the Imperial Japanese Navy (IJN) and play his career throughout the war, no matter how well you play, Japan will still lose the war. You can still have a successful career if you accomplish your missions, score victories against American pilots, and fight for the Emperor to the bitter end. There really were such aces even in the final days of the war. In 1945, the ace Kinsuke Muto, flying a N1K1 *Shiden* (the earlier version of the N1K2 *Shiden-kai* modeled in Combat Flight Simulator 2), shot down four of the nearly invincible F6F Hellcats in a single sortie. The reverse in also true. As an American pilot, your side is going to win overall. Your personal challenge is to complete your missions and bring your squadron back alive.

Chapter One: First Look

There's No "Me" in Team

The campaigns are designed so that your squadron of eight pilots must work as a team to do well. You lead the squadron and one of the two sections of four pilots. You decide who leads the second section. It is in your interest to keep your squadron alive. No matter how skilled you are at air combat, the rest of the squadron starts as rookies. As they gain experience, they literally become better pilots. The better your squadron's pilots, the more likely you are to succeed in your missions.

> **Combat Tip #1:** *The Japanese Zero was thought to be invincible when it debuted over the war-torn skies of China. As WW II progressed, the myth of its invulnerability was debunked and its legendary status faded as newer, more powerful Allied fighters entered the conflict. You'll find, however, that in the right hands the Zero is an extremely lethal opponent. Always remember to measure an enemy pilot not by machine but by flying skills.*

The More You Know, the Better You'll Do

The game design team made every effort to make the game as real as possible. Researchers scoured used bookstores in Japan for old photos and aircraft manuals and traveled to New Zealand to photograph the last flying N1K2 *Shiden-kai* in existence. The location of gun emplacements on small islands is based on copies of real U.S. intelligence reports from the war and personal accounts. The flight models are checked and adjusted to get all performance figures within 5 percent of the values for the actual aircraft. The object of all this detail work is not only to make sure the simulation feels real, but also to provide that real-world knowledge of the Pacific Theater of World War II that will actually help you succeed in the game.

Chapter Two

BEHIND THE SCREENS

At the heart of any good simulation game experience is the ability to suspend disbelief and, as much as possible, experience the game as if you were physically in the cockpit (or wherever the game happens to take place). Since no two people are alike, no two people will have exactly the same priorities concerning what makes a game feel real. Structurally and philosophically, Microsoft Combat Fight Simulator 2 gives you a lot of control over how you experience the game, so you can create the environment you want most. To effectively use the various settings in Combat Flight Simulator 2, you should understand how the game creates and presents its world and how the designers put the game together.

Frame Rate vs. Visual Quality

One of the most striking improvements in Combat Flight Simulator 2 over its predecessor is the level of visual detail. Combat Flight Simulator 2 offers a number of extremely compelling new visual features that simply weren't possible with the earlier generation software. However, this detail comes at a price. Your computer system might handle Combat Flight Simulator 2 with all the options turned off and produce a view from the cockpit as smooth as a Hollywood feature. With everything optimized for best graphics, that same machine might produce frame rates that make the game feel choppier than your parent's old home movies. A movie is a good analogy here because that is essentially what's happening on the screen. The quality of your gaming experience depends on the balance between the level of detail of each image drawn on the screen (visual quality) and the number of these images drawn every second (frame rate).

Frame rate and detail are in direct competition with each other for the video resources available on the PC. The more complex an image is, the longer it takes the computer to draw that image and the fewer images it can draw per second. Low frame rates result in a loss of fluidity of movement; enemy aircraft will appear to move in small hops rather than in one smooth, continuous motion. Just how low a frame rate you can tolerate is a matter of

Levels of Detail

Combat Flight Simulator 2 actually has eight models for each aircraft in the game. These eight models represent different Levels of Detail, *or LOD. The lowest level, level 1, is basically just three triangles. This LOD is used to represent an aircraft when it is still far away. As the aircraft gets closer, Combat Flight Simulator 2 draws the image larger and switches automatically to higher and higher LODs. The highest LOD is level 8, but this amount of detail will slow the frame rate. To help keep frame rate up, Combat Flight Simulator 2 will not display LOD 8 unless the frame rate is higher than 30 frames per second.*

personal preference. Keep in mind, however, that the limit of human vision is about 32 frames per second. Most people notice that the motion is no longer smooth at anything lower than 24 frames per second. Therefore, 24 frames per second is a good bottom-line value; most players find a game unplayable if the frame rate drops below 10 frames per second.

To see what your frame rate is, press Shift+Z twice while playing. As illustrated in Figure 2-1, the frame rate will appear in red in the upper left corner of the screen. Next to frame rate is the current G force experienced by the pilot. (See Chapter 6, "Combat Flight Training," for more discussion about G forces.) The next three numbers in brackets show the lowest, median, and highest frame rates so far. The first frame rate number is an average and will constantly change to reflect the different amounts of processor workload involved in the screen at the current level of complexity.

Figure 2-1 *Pressing Shift+Z twice will put the frame rate in the upper left corner of the screen in red. This number will constantly change as the frame rate changes.*

Remember that complexity of the image on screen isn't determined only by visual effects such as high-quality textures. When the on-screen image includes many aircraft and ground vehicles whose movements and position must constantly be recalculated, the rendering of each screen will slow. The calculations don't really hurt frame rate if the vehicles don't appear on screen, but with exactly the same graphics settings, your frame rate will be lower in the midst of battle than in free flight.

Your frame rate will also change depending on your current view. Cockpit view will usually give the highest frame rate, with Heads Up Display (HUD) view a close second. Virtual cockpit view and Chase view give the lowest frame rates because these views require the most processing time. Even on a fairly powerful game platform, the difference in frame rate between Cockpit view and Virtual Cockpit view can be more than 10 frames per second. Try flying different missions and quick combat scenarios with different views, and see how your frame rate changes.

> **Note:** *Higher frame rates can provide breathing room when the sky becomes filled with enemy planes. Since detail is related to frame rate, more planes will equal a lower frame rate. You might not notice the difference between your game running at 32 or 45 frames per second, but you will notice when the sky fills with planes and you're suddenly down to 15 frames per second. A friend running 45 frames per second and then dropping to 32 is still going to have a nice smooth bead on you as you struggle to figure out where you are.*

Settings to Achieve the Best Frame Rate

When you first run Combat Flight Simulator 2, the program automatically assesses your computer system and determines how much image and data processing your computer can handle. It will then set the level of complexity of the different screen effects to give you a playable frame rate that ranges between the high teens and the low twenties. This setting is only a baseline.

If you want to adjust your settings to get a better frame rate, click the Settings button on the home screen. To get a general idea of how your computer responds to different levels of complexity, move the

> **Note:** *Combat Flight Simulator 2 has an improved terrain algorithm that largely eliminates some of the slow frame rates seen occasionally in Flight Simulator 2000.*

slider to a different position on the Overall Image Quality scale and fly several different scenarios to see the result. When you're doing these comparisons, it's helpful to display the frame rate to get an arbitrary evaluation along with your qualitative evaluation game play.

Once you have a general idea of where your computer performs best, you can adjust the system specifics. From the Settings screen, check the box labeled Player Defined In Advanced Settings and then click Advanced Settings. You'll see two tabs, Hardware and Image Quality. The Hardware tab allows you to make some simple configuration changes that can have a big impact on frame rate. First make sure that you have the correct video or 3D graphics card installed and that hardware acceleration is enabled if it is an option. The Low Resolution mode is for older video cards only.

Screen Resolution and Color Depth

Screen resolution and color depth can also have a big effect on frame rate. Screen resolution is the total area that the screen draws to. Resolution is measured in pixels, or picture elements. The total resolution equals the number of pixels of width times the number of pixels of height that the program draws to. The most common ranges are 640 × 480, 800 × 600, and 1024 × 768. With newer hardware these numbers can be even higher: Combat Flight Simulator 2 will support resolutions up to 2048 × 1536. The lower the resolution, the fewer pixels need to be calculated and drawn, resulting in a faster frame rate. 640 × 480 pixels will give the fastest results and still provide decent image quality; however, the HUD is a fixed-pixel size, so it will occupy more of the screen at lower resolutions. Figure 2-2 shows the HUD at different screen resolutions.

Another problem with lower resolutions is that aircraft in the game will appear to have more ragged edges and may tend to "shimmer" as they fly on screen. If you this bothers you, a screen resolution of 800 × 600 or 1024 × 768 will help and usually still gives good results in frame rate. To change the screen resolution, go to the Display Settings screen by clicking the Advanced Settings button in the Settings screen and select a value from the Resolution list box.

Notice that you have two other choices for each resolution setting, 16 and 32. These numbers refer to color depth. This is exactly the same setting that you're probably accustomed to setting from the Settings panel in the Display Properties dialog box in Microsoft Windows.

Note: *Not all monitors support all screen sizes. It is possible that you will select a screen size that your monitor can't display. If you change screen sizes and suddenly your monitor goes blank, don't panic. Press Alt+Enter to switch out of full screen mode. This will pop Combat Flight Simulator 2 into a window so that you can switch the screen size back to something your monitor can display. Not all video cards can support 32-bit color. If you switch to 32-bit color and the screen image disappears, use this same technique to restore your previous settings.*

The number 16 or 32 refers to the amount of memory available to each pixel. The more memory devoted to each pixel, the greater the range that each pixel can display. For example, if the bit depth is 16, the number of different colors that can be displayed by a single pixel is 65,536. At a bit depth of 32, more than 4 billion colors are possible. The average human eye can easily distinguish between 3 million and 4 million colors, so a bit depth of 16 is clearly limiting. However, this limit is significant only when we deal with photo-quality images; it doesn't make much difference for most people in a gaming environment with computer-generated graphics. You can try both bit depths to see if it matters to you, but in most cases 16-bit color depth will

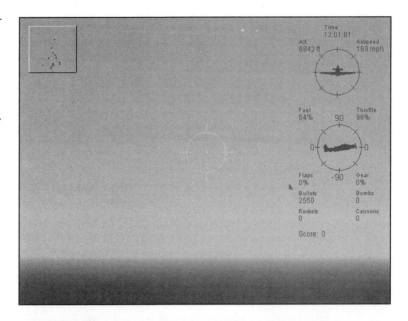

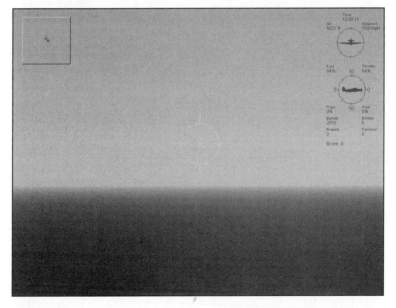

Figure 2-2   *The HUD will appear larger at different screen resolutions. The screen on the top is 640 × 480; the screen on the bottom is 1024 × 768.*

provide a fine gaming experience, and you'll gain 3 to 6 frames per second on an average system.

Image Quality

Once you've found a good screen resolution and color depth, you can turn your attention to image quality. Move the Overall Image Quality slider, and see how the sliders on the individual items move along with it. This will give you an idea of which individual effects the development team believes are the most important and which ones are the first to be cut. However, the items that are important to you might be different than what's important to the game's developers. For example, seeing aircraft shadows might make the game feel real to you, while you consider ground textures relatively unimportant. This is a trial-and-error process with no right or wrong configurations, but if you decide to fiddle with these sliders it helps to understand what they do. To do that, you need to understand how Combat Flight Simulator 2 draws the world.

Landscapes

As in Microsoft Flight Simulator 2000, Combat Flight Simulator 2 has the land data for the entire world mapped into 1-kilometer squares. The height of each crossing point on the grid is recorded, and the block in the grid is assigned a land class and filled in with that land class graphic. There are 57 land classes covering everything from oceans to deserts. One-kilometer squares might sound like a lot of detail, but 1 kilometer is almost 3300 feet, or the length of 11 football fields. This level of detail works OK if you view it from high up, but it is less impressive at close range.

To provide more realistic terrain, a higher-definition grid is added for the South Pacific. This terrain is mapped to either 300-meter squares or 75-meter squares. The 75-meter squares are 246 feet on a side (a little less than 1 football field). Figure 2-3 shows the increased detail.

The 75-meter squares come at a price. The computer now must load far more data to draw the same area. To make matters more complicated, each block can now have its own land class, which means more terrain data to further slow things down. Even if the area is uniform, you can't repeat the same image of a forest over and over again—the surface would look patchy. To prevent this tiled look, several variations of the block graphic must be used.

On top of this rendered terrain, all the lakes, streams, and shorelines are drawn in. Finally all the fixed items are added, such as airports.

Image Quality Settings

When you adjust the Image Quality settings, you are selecting when and how the computer will draw the world you see. In this section, I'll offer a brief explanation of what some of these controls do and their impact on

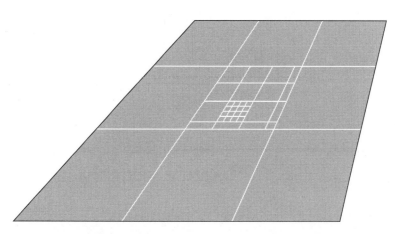

Figure 2-3   *In Combat Flight Simulator 2, the whole world is mapped to 1-kilometer blocks except for the South Pacific, which is mapped to 300-meter and 75-meter blocks.*

frame rate, marked on a scale from 1 (most impact) to 3 (least impact).

Overall Image Quality   This slider adjusts all the settings except LOD Target Frame Rate. It gives you a quick way to balance image quality against frame rate. If you adjust any of the other sliders individually, the overall quality read switches to custom. This is the same slider that appears on the main settings screen.

DEM Density Level (1)   This value determines the detail of terrain elevation data. The higher the value, the more accurate the terrain elevation will be at any given point.

Max Terrain Texture Size (1)   Textures fill the terrain grid mentioned earlier. Larger textures have greater detail and will look a lot nicer, but at the price of performance.

Terrain Complexity Level (1)   The higher the value, the more terrain elevation data is displayed on the screen at one time. If the value is too low, terrain will appear to "pop-up" into view as you approach. You may alleviate the popping by increasing this value, but will come at a high price of performance.

Max Object Texture Size (2)   Very similar to Max Terrain Texture Size, the higher the value, the better the visual quality. If the value is too low, the terrain pattern will repeat and look tiled.

Maximum Visibility Level (2)   Maximum visibility is the distance in miles at which the screen will show only haze. The haze saves the computer the effort of rendering terrain that is far away, but this limits your visual distance.

Ground Scenery Shadows (2)   This setting is analogous to aircraft shadows, but it refers to objects on the ground such as buildings and towers.

LOD Target Frame Rate (3)   This value only works when the Auto-Performance Adjustment box is checked on the Settings screen. This value is not tied to the default Overall Image Quality slider. Auto-performance will continually adjust the different image quality setting to maintain the rate set in this slider. For example, if you are currently getting 15 FPS and your LOD target is 25 FPS, the program will decrease the level of detail of textures to increase performance. If you are currently getting 35 FPS, it will increase your level of detail, but not fall below 25 FPS.

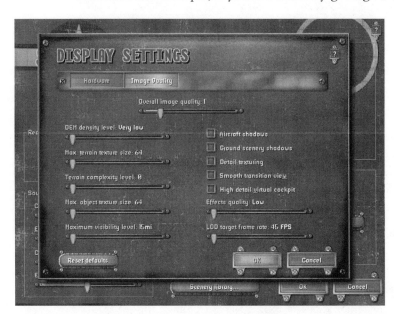

Figure 2-4   *The Image Quality page of the Display Settings screen can help you get the best frame rate while still seeing the effects that add the most realism to your gaming experience.*

Other Tweaking to Improve Performance

Besides game settings, you can improve performance in other ways. Combat Flight Simulator 2 must share processor time with all the other programs running on your computer. You can free up some resources for Combat Flight Simulator 2 by closing programs that you don't need, especially hardware dependent programs. (Playing Combat Flight Simulator 2 while copying that new CD is not a good idea.) Next you can

quit or suspend any background items that are running but don't have windows. Many background processes appear as icons in the system tray. Often you can quit these processes or just suspend them by right-clicking on the program icon and choosing the appropriate option from the pop-up menu. The advantage of suspending items is that they no longer take any processing time away from the game, but you can restart them without restarting your computer. Figure 2-5 illustrates suspending a tray application.

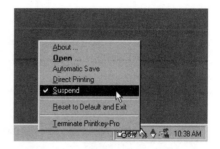

Figure 2-5 *Right-clicking a tray icon often allows you to quit or suspend a program.*

For the most part, closing background processes has only a small effect on performance, but every little bit helps. Screen size, color depth, and image quality settings are definitely the place to start.

> **Tip:** *Remember the first law of computer tweaking: if you are not comfortable messing with something, don't mess with it.*

Realism

Adjusting your system to display the best balance between graphics quality and frame rate is one way to achieve the best level of realism. In this section, I'll describe several other items you can adjust to achieve the highest possible level of realism.

Advanced Weather Settings

The Advanced Weather controls in Combat Flight Simulator 2 are very similar to those found in Flight Simulator 2000. You can open the Advanced Weather page by clicking the Advanced Weather button on the Time and Weather page. The Time and Weather page can be opened in Quick Combat and Free Flight by clicking the Time and Weather button.

The Advanced Weather options are grouped into three categories: Clouds, Temp/Pressure, and Visibility. After you select a tab, you see a window with a scale on the left showing the altitudes of each layer of weather phenomena. You can adjust this view with the Zoom In, Zoom Out, Add Layer, and Remove Layer buttons above it. You can change the properties of any layer by selecting it. To the right of the cloud scale there are drop-down list boxes and scroll boxes that let you change the properties for the selected layer. The layers cannot overlap.

Combat Tip #2: *Weather conditions, such as clouds, can help conceal you from the enemy. Keep in mind, however, that when you disappear into a layer of thick clouds, you lose sight of the enemy aircraft. You also lose your outside horizon reference, and spatial disorientation can occur rapidly. If this happens, quickly switch to a view that provides a reliable attitude reference instrument and return the aircraft to level flight until you can see again. The enemy might or might not shoot you down, but running into the ground because you got confused is always lethal.*

Clouds

Clouds can play a key role in combat, providing a place to hide and allowing you to surprise your target. Clouds can also prevent you from drawing an enemy up to high altitude, forcing you to fight a low, turning battle to which your particular airplane might not be suited.

To add or remove a layer of clouds, use the + and - cloud buttons above the window that displays the cloud layers. Next select the cloud layer you want to edit and change its properties with the two right-hand columns. Figure 2-6 gives you an idea of what to expect.

Cloud Type Cirrus clouds are typically the thin, wispy clouds that form above 25,000 feet. These clouds pose little hazard to Pacific war operations.

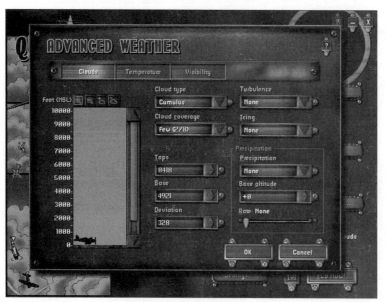

Cumulus clouds are cottony, puffy clouds, either few and far between or dense and waiting to form a thunderstorm. Stratus clouds are uniform layers of clouds with little or no turbulence. They often are associated with poor visibility and rain. Thunderstorm clouds are exactly that. Expect to see lightning as well. If you want to deal with this kind of weather like a WW II pilot, just stay out of thunderstorms.

Figure 2-6 *The Advanced Weather screen allows you to create and manipulate precise weather effects.*

Cloud Coverage   Cloud coverage is measured in octants, or eighths of the sky covered: weather observers on the ground visually divide the sky into four parts and then split each of those parts in two.

Tops, Base, and Deviation   These three settings determine the thickness of a cloud layer in feet. If you're climbing toward a cloud, base is the altitude at which you enter the cloud, tops is the altitude at which you leave the cloud, and deviation is the amount plus or minus that tops and base vary across the layer. So if you climb toward a layer with a Base setting of 2000 feet, a Tops setting of 5000 feet, and a Deviation setting of 500 feet, you would enter the clouds somewhere between 1500 feet and 2500 feet and exit somewhere between 4500 feet and 5500 feet.

> **Note:** *Cloud types often indicate certain patterns of turbulence. For increased reality, try setting moderate turbulence below these clouds and smooth skies above. When thunderstorm clouds are around, the turbulence can get extreme. To see how much of a problem this can be, try the slow flight required for a carrier landing under conditions of severe or extreme turbulence.*

Turbulence   This setting determines how much bouncing around you experience from the cockpit. Since your chair won't really be bouncing, what you will notice most are wild airspeed variations and difficulty maintaining altitude. Pressing Shift+Z twice will show you what you can't feel on the simulator. The red indicator at the top of the screen shows you how many Gs the airplane is experiencing. Under extreme turbulence conditions, this will vary from -2 to +3. If you make a high-speed turn or pull up under these conditions, the chances of over-stressing and damaging your airplane greatly increase.

> **Note:** *The Japanese were masters of using Pacific Ocean weather to their advantage. In an attack on Wake Island, 36 Betty bombers surprised the U.S. forces by attacking from behind a squall line.*

Icing   When temperatures are close to freezing and visible moisture (clouds or rain) is present, water can freeze onto the airplane. The ice changes the way air flows around the wings and makes flying much more difficult. Icing is theoretically possible in the South Pacific but is not particularly likely. Since none of the player-flyable aircraft have deicing equipment, it's probably best to leave this setting at None.

Precipitation, Base Altitude, and Rate   These options allow you to set the type of precipitation, at what altitude it starts, and how heavily it falls. Rain certainly could be an issue in the South Pacific, affecting your ability to complete a mission or see an enemy during a fight.

Combat Flight Simulator 2

Temperature

Altitude, Daytime Temperature, Day/Night Variation, and Dew Point   As the air cools, it loses some of its ability to carry water vapor. When the temperature of the air drops below its dew point, clouds or fog form because the air cannot hold the water vapor any longer. In the real world, a small difference between the temperature and the dew point would cause a pilot to worry about fog forming, which makes it very difficult to see an airport and land.

In Combat Flight Simulator 2, temperatures are set for specific altitudes rather than altitude ranges. You can set the temperature for day, how much colder it will be at night, and the dew point. Dew point is a more accurate way of describing what is often called relative humidity.

Visibility

The Visibility setting changes the distance where haze begins. This setting can have a huge impact on combat, when seeing your enemy is essential. Because adjustments to visibility do not affect labels or the tactical display, low visibility is largely negated by these features.

Flight Realism

Aircraft Modeling

Few people realize the level of accuracy of the aircraft models in the Microsoft Flight Simulator games. All the player-flyable airplanes perform within an average of 5 percent of the performance range of their real-world counterparts. That means if a real Zero loaded to 5500 lbs. takes 7 seconds to lift off the ground in a 15-knot wind, the Combat Flight Simulator 2 Zero under the same conditions will lift off in 6.6 to 7.4 seconds.

These performance figures aren't simply stored in a database. In Combat Flight Simulator 2, the computer continually calculates the performance of each aircraft based on conditions of that aircraft at a particular time. The game then renders the aircraft in a new position based on those calculations. This means that you can expect to experience the same results while flying a Combat Flight Simulator 2 airplane as you would if you were flying the real thing.

Let's look at another example. If you are cruising along in a Zero at 250 mph, the software is calculating the amount of lift produced by your wings and tail, the exact power output of your engine based on your engine settings and altitude, the amount of drag produced by the air moving across the airframe,

and the pull of gravity. Suddenly, a P-38 dives out of a cloud and strafes you with cannon fire, causing damage. Your engine is hit, and you lose two cylinders. Combat Flight Simulator 2 recalculates the reduced power output and what indications you see in the cockpit. Your right wing is also hit, tearing off the outboard tip. The software recalculates lift and drag of the broken wing and begins to roll the airplane to one side because of uneven lift. You move the stick hard to the left to compensate, but the part of the wing that was shot off had one of the two controls for roll. Your Zero is now slow to respond. The uneven lift puts you into a spiral, and you are no longer in control of the airplane.

Damage Modeling

One of the most important items modeled for combat is damage. Damage is determined in Combat Flight Simulator 2 first by dividing the airplane up into individual "hit boxes." These hit boxes, shown in Figure 2-7, are polygons that define an area in space around parts of the airplane. The bullets or cannon rounds also have a defined area. When these two areas meet, the damage is inflicted to the systems in that hit box. The type of shot determines the amount of damage. Cannon hits do more damage than bullets. Which systems are damaged depends on where you are hit, but different aircraft systems are mapped to their location on the airplane. If you are hit in the right wing, you might lose partial or complete use of the fuel, the flaps, or the weapons in that wing, but your tail and its functions are not affected.

Figure 2-7 *The hit boxes shown here are from early in program development.*

Microsoft

Combat Flight Simulator 2

The damage to each system is cumulative and not repairable. If you get hit in the elevator early in the mission, you are more vulnerable to elevator failure later in the mission. This also means that good marksmanship is rewarded. Hitting one area of the enemy repeatedly will destroy an enemy faster than the same number of hits spread out over the whole aircraft.

The damage display has also been enhanced with the use of endcaps. When a wingtip was shot away in Combat Flight Simulator, the inside of the wing appeared as a gray area. Combat Flight Simulator 2 has a graphic that covers the area inside the wing: a blown-away wing will show exposed wing ribs and torn aluminum. The effect is quite convincing.

One kind of damage that is not modeled in Combat Flight Simulator 2 is noncombat-related failures. If your landing gear system is shot up in combat, you might have to land belly up on a carrier or bail out, but the gear will never jam as a random event. Since Combat Flight Simulator 2 is built on the Flight Simulator 2000 engine, the code is in place to do this. The developers just felt it was unfair for a random failure to ruin a great mission. Failures can be linked to events from the Mission Builder. (See Chapter 13, "Using the Mission Builder," for more information on the Mission Builder.) This means that some missions might start to seem like a combat air patrol, but once you reach 4000 feet your engine will quit and the mission becomes a deadstick landing or a bailout.

Flight Realism Settings

In the upper left of the Settings page, you'll see an Overall Realism rating and a button for Realism Settings. As illustrated in Figure 2-8, the Realism page is divided into four categories: Aircraft, Stores, Visuals, and Combat.

Aircraft

The Aircraft setting allows you to set the Flight Model Realism to Easy, Medium, or Hard. These three labels are a bit misleading. What you are really adjusting is how closely the airplane you fly will perform like the carefully developed flight model for that airplane. Remember that the behavior of every airplane in Combat Flight Simulator 2 is constantly calculated based on a flight model. This model calculates the result of all the forces acting on the airplane. These forces include the four basic forces of flight—lift, thrust, weight, and drag—but they also include variables such as the twisting force of the propeller and the relative position of the center of lift versus the center of weight. (For a more complete discussion of flight theory, see Chapter 4, "Flight Theory and Practice for the Combat Cadet.")

These additional forces factored seriously into the lives of real combat pilots in World War II. For example, many pilots were killed when they applied power to the engine too rapidly at low airspeed and low altitude. The sudden increase in twisting force, or torque, at the propeller rolled the airplane upside down, sending it into the ground before the pilot could react.

High-altitude performance is another example familiar to veterans of Combat Flight Simulator. At

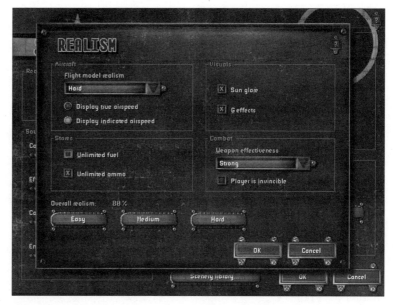

Figure 2-8   *The settings in the Flight Model Realism drop-down list box control how closely your airplane will follow the rules set in the flight model.*

25,000 feet, the flight controls feel light and unresponsive. When you select Hard in the Flight Model Realism drop-down list box, you are actually selecting the flight model exactly as programmed. In other words, Hard equals real—or as real as it gets, anyway. Selecting Medium or Easy makes the software dampen the forces and effects that were particularly troublesome or hazardous to real pilots in real airplanes. Propeller torque, P-factor, likelihood of a stall, and likelihood of a ground loop are all items affected by this setting.

The Hard flight model also determines how precisely you must perform pilot duties. For example, the Easy setting draws fuel evenly from all your fuel tanks regardless of what you set. Under Hard settings, you must manage your own fuel. Emptying the left wing while leaving the right wing full will result in an airplane that is difficult or impossible to fly straight. Another example is extension speeds. In Combat Flight Simulator, players could rapidly slow down by extending their gear at any speed. With the setting at Hard, you will incur damage if you extend the gear while moving too fast, possibly leaving you unable to maneuver away from the enemy and unable to land.

The Display True Airspeed and Display Indicated Airspeed option buttons set the indication that you will get in the aircraft cockpit and in the HUD view. The airspeed indicator in airplanes is less accurate the higher the airplane climbs. The error increases at a rate of approximately 2 percent per 1000 feet. Unless you plan to do all the flying between islands by actually flying, rather than using X to jump to the next scene, the setting here really doesn't matter. (Since it doesn't matter, you might as well set it to Display Indicated Airspeed and be that much more realistic, don't you think?)

Stores

The check boxes in the Stores group allow for unlimited supplies of fuel and ammunition. This is self-explanatory. Until you've really mastered the concept of deflection shooting (discussed in Chapter 6), Unlimited Ammo can help keep down your frustration level. Few situations are worse in the world of air combat than finally getting the window for a good shot, only to find your weapons empty.

Visuals

Sun Glare means that when you look at the sun the whole screen will whiten, simulating the glare of the sun. Attacking from the same position as the sun is a common battle technique for getting close to an opponent without being seen. The artificial intelligence (AI) pilots know this trick, so if you have sun glare on, watch out.

G Effects are simulations of the effects of experiencing too much G force. Whenever you accelerate the airplane by pulling back on the stick (in a turn or in a loop, for example), you experience a certain increase in G forces. The harder you pull, the more G force you will experience.

Combat

When you increase the selection under Weapon Effectiveness to Stronger or Strongest, two things happen. First, the amount of damage done by each round you sink into the enemy airplane increases. Second, the size of the hitbox of your shots increases, increasing the likelihood of a hit. The game considers an airplane hit when the area (hitbox) around a speeding bullet or cannon round touches the area of the airplane. By enlarging the area of your bullets, you increase the likelihood of those two areas touching. Setting your shots to Stronger or Strongest can actually help you learn skills such as deflection shooting and build your confidence early on. Chapter 6 discusses combat techniques in depth.

Other Variables

How seriously do you take your gaming? Do you have a comfortable desk or workspace? Do you have a place to rest your joystick arm? Is there music playing in the background, or are you just listening to the sound of the prop? Are you thinking about work? Bills? Wondering if someone is going to interrupt and tell you it's time for dinner?

Part of the gaming experience is the environment around the computer. Taking care of some small external details can have a big payoff in terms of how deeply into the game you can go and how real it will feel.

Cockpit Construction

The layout of your virtual cockpit is key. Even if you have both a joystick and a throttle quadrant, the keyboard and mouse should be accessible without too much fumbling around. This access is especially important if you are playing with a simple joystick, since you will need to enter some game commands from the keyboard.

Blackout and Redout

If you were really in the airplane seat when the G forces increased, you would feel pressed down into your seat. This effect is called centrifugal force. At the same time your backside is pressing into the seat, the blood is rushing from your head. No blood in the brain results in loss of consciousness, which appears on screen as a momentary blackout. This kind of blackout is a real possibility in an airplane performing extreme maneuvers. Checking the G Effects check box on the Realism page might limit how tight a turn you can perform in the game.

Redout is the opposite of blackout. This can happen when you push forward on the stick and experience negative G forces, causing all the blood to rush to your head. Your vision goes red, and you might also pass out. Most people's tolerance for negative G force is much less than their tolerance for positive G force. To see the G force you are experiencing at any time in the game, press Shift+Z twice.

Note: *Selecting the Player Is Invincible option will immediately give you a realism rating of zero.*

That rolling and swiveling desk chair that works so well for typing will make it more difficult for you to enter precise control inputs and will really show its weakness if you are using rudder pedals. Get a sturdy seat, and make it a hard seat if you want an extra dose of realism. The seat in an average WW II fighter wasn't exactly plush.

Set your monitor to a good height. Setting the top of the screen at the same height as your eyes works well. Make sure your flying arm has a good place to rest. In real cockpits, the stick sits between your legs, so your right leg makes a fine armrest. Unless you can find a good way to secure the joystick to a stand in front of your chair, this usually doesn't work too well for gamers. Take the time to create a setup that works for you.

If you are playing with friends and therefore connected by a local call while you play, you might want to all buy headsets for your phones and set up a multiline call. Nothing in combat flight simulation will get your adrenaline running like hearing the real voice of your friend with a bandit on his six calling out to you for help. Now that's realism! Multiplayer gaming is discussed in detail in Chapter 14, "Playing Well with Others."

Exercise Your Right to Game

When it's time fly, let your roommate/partner/spouse know that you don't want to be disturbed. Close the door, turn off the ringer on the phone, and give yourself permission to do nothing but play. It's your game; it's your airplane. Exercise your right to enjoy yourself to the fullest.

Chapter Three

GETTING STARTED IN THE AIRPLANE

In the early days of World War II, U.S. Navy flight training personnel faced a daunting task. They needed to take large numbers of able-bodied, intelligent cadets with a wide range of educational backgrounds and often no flight experience and turn them in to pilots capable of handling the newest, fastest, most sophisticated airplanes in the world. Upon graduation, these officers would be flying in life-threatening situations. Conditions would be extreme. There would be pressure on the pilot to protect not only his own life, but also the lives of fellow pilots. If these men failed to perform, a war could be lost. And on top of all that, the cadets needed to be trained as quickly as possible.

In response to this challenge, the navy created a ground-training program that gave the pilots the information they needed as simply and quickly as possible. This ground-training program focused on concepts the new pilots needed to understand *before* they climbed into the cockpit. This chapter imitates that navy flight training, with a more modern description of lift and a few necessary modifications. For instance, the navy cadets had to work their way up from the Stearman Kaydet biplane and the AT-6 advanced trainer. You get to hop straight into the seat of a fighter!

Note: *At the end of the war, much of this training was captured on film; the videotapes of these training films are very informative and fun to watch. The source for these videos appears in the Appendix.*

Aircraft Systems and Their Management

As a pilot, you need to understand the various systems on your airplane and how to manipulate them to get the results you want. Much of this can be ignored in quick combat and when the aircraft model is set for easy in Microsoft Combat Flight Simulator 2. To succeed on missions that contain a high degree of overall realism, you will need to monitor and adjust your airplane's systems as you go.

What, How, and Why

With any flight training, past or present, one simple way of presenting information and focusing on the key points is to ask the following questions:

- *What is it?*
- *How does it work?*
- *Why do I care?*

You must learn to answer these questions from a pilot's perspective. An understanding of how a wing works is important to both an aerodynamics engineer and a fighter pilot, but the fighter pilot doesn't need lots of detailed equations. The fighter pilot needs to know enough to figure out how to land on a carrier deck when the flaps won't go down.

Piston Engine Basics

All of the aircraft in Combat Flight Simulator 2 use gasoline piston engines. Gasoline piston engines work by drawing fuel and air into a closed chamber, compressing the mixture into a small space, and igniting the fuel. This generates a lot of heat which makes the compressed air expand, expelling the spent fuel and air out of the engine. The process can be summed up in four steps: suck, squeeze, bang, and blow.

Suck

A mixture of air and fuel vapor is drawn into the engine when the piston is pulled down, creating suction (a vacuum) inside individual engine cylinders and allowing the fuel and air mixture to enter the cylinder through an open valve. Air is sucked through the carburetor, where fuel vapor is added. The carburetor ensures that the right amount of fuel is added for the amount of air. In flight, you can adjust this ratio with the mixture control. The average ratio in a gasoline engine is about 8 parts air to 1 part fuel.

Squeeze

The fuel and air mixture is next compressed into a space usually 1/8 to 1/10 its original volume. If the fuel and air mixture is compressed into a space 1/10 its original size, the pressure goes up roughly tenfold. The piston accomplishes this by moving up the cylinder after the valve at the top closes.

Bang

As the piston approaches the top of the cylinder, two spark plugs ignite the fuel-and-air mixture, causing it to burn rapidly. This rapid burning heats up the already highly pressurized air and increases the pressure again by a factor of 4 to 6 times. This hot, pressurized air expands and pushes the piston back down. This expansion of hot gas is where the engine gets its power.

Blow

Once the hot gases have expanded and pressed the piston to the bottom of the cylinder, a valve opens at the top of the cylinder and the piston moves up, expelling the hot gases.

Controlling the Engine

The final power output of an engine is determined largely by the pressure inside the cylinder just before the cylinder starts to compress. Because of the tenfold magnification of compression and the fourfold increase during combustion, squeezing even a little more fuel and air into the cylinder has a big effect on engine power. For example, increasing the pressure of the fuel and air entering the engine by just 2 pounds per square inch can result in an increase in pressure during combustion of 80 pounds per square inch.

World War II fighter airplanes used superchargers, or turbochargers, to boost the pressure of air entering the engine. A supercharger is basically just a fan attached to the engine. When the engine turns, the fan turns, blowing extra air into the engine. The faster the engine turns, the faster the fan turns and the more pressure is available. The maximum pressure put out by the supercharger is regulated so it won't blow the engine apart.

Note: *The gasoline preferably does not explode in the engine. If it did, the resulting expansion would be too fast and could damage the engine. This is known as detonation and can destroy an engine quickly. Detonation is not modeled in Combat Flight Simulator 2.*

Radial Engines

Most airplane engines use airflow for cooling. If the cylinders were arranged in a line or V-shape as with a car, the cylinders near the front of the engine would stay cool but the cylinders in the back would overheat. The radial engine has its cylinders arranged like spokes on a wheel so that all of them are exposed to the cooling air. The engines are also cooled by small radiators, which cool the oil, and by the cool air and fuel mixture entering the engine itself. The total amount of air cooling is of critical importance and is the factor over which you as the pilot have the most control. You can adjust the cooling of an engine in Combat Flight Simulator 2 with the cowl flap control.

Combat Tip #3: *All but one of the Combat Flight Simulator 2 fighters have radial engines: the P-38. Because radial engines are air-cooled, they contain one less critical system that can malfunction. This makes radial engines slightly more resilient to combat damage when compared to liquid-cooled inline engines (as in the P-38). When trying to shoot down a radial engine opponent, try to focus your aim on other areas of vulnerability.*

You control the supercharger and the engine power output with the throttle. The throttle regulates the pressure of air and fuel sent into the cylinders. You can control the aircraft's throttle in Combat Flight Simulator 2 in three distinct ways:

- You can use the F4 key to increase the throttle and the F3 key to decrease the throttle.
- Your joystick might have a control wheel or slider that can be programmed as a throttle, or you might even have a separate throttle controller.
- You can use the throttle control in the Engine Controls window, shown in Figure 3-1. To see the Engine Controls window, go to cockpit view and press the Throttle Quadrant button. This button is marked with a white circle in Figure 3-1.

You monitor the amount of engine power on the manifold pressure gauge. The gauge shows the pressure of the air and fuel mixture before it enters the cylinder. The gauges on a U.S. aircraft (shown in Figure 3-2) measure manifold pressure in inches of mercury (Hg). To give you an idea of the role the supercharger plays, the

Figure 3-1   *The Throttle Quadrant button will show and hide all engine controls. These are the controls for the F4F-4 Wildcat.*

highest manifold pressure you could get without it is around 30 inches, while some supercharged airplanes run at nearly 60 inches. The Japanese manifold pressure gauges read in centimeters of mercury above or below standard atmospheric pressure. Straight up on the gauge equals one atmosphere or 76 cm of Hg (29.92 inches of mercury). Essentially, any time the needle is in the red area

the supercharger is boosting the manifold pressure higher than it would be at sea level. The red zone is not a warning area, though, so you can operate the engine in the red all the time if you want.

A supercharger offers another benefit. As the airplane climbs, air pressure decreases. The air pressure at 18,000' is half the air pressure at sea level. Without a supercharger, the maximum power of the engine decreases rapidly with altitude, leaving it quite anemic when flying high. The supercharger keeps the maximum pressure available at much higher altitudes.

Figure 3-2 *The U.S. manifold pressure gauges (top) read in inches of mercury. The Japanese manifold pressure gauge (bottom) read in cmHg above or below sea level pressure.*

War Emergency Power

The supercharger can only boost the incoming air pressure to a point before the combustion becomes explosive and destroys the engine. One way to prevent explosive combustion in the engine is to inject water or methanol into the cylinder with the air and fuel. The water allows the combustion pressure to go even higher and provides more power, but the super-high pressures can still damage the engine if used continuously. Three airplanes in Combat Flight Simulator 2 use water or methanol injection to provide War Emergency Power (WEP). These airplanes are the Hellcat, the Corsair, and the *Shiden-kai* (George). The sudden boost will show up on the manifold pressure gauge, and a message will appear on screen if you have Status Messages checked under the View menu. Use WEP only when full throttle still isn't enough power and your life is on the line. All WEP systems will run out of liquid after 5 to 10 minutes of use, which isn't enough time to damage the engine.

Propeller Control

The throttle controls the engine's power, but that power is turned into forward motion by the propeller. As a pilot, you will control the speed of the engine by adjusting the propeller. On the U.S. airplanes, you'll find the propeller control immediately to the right of the throttle control. On the Japanese airplanes, the propeller is the second knob to the right of the throttle.

With the propeller control, you select the highest allowable engine speed, measured on all the Combat Flight Simulator 2 airplanes in revolutions per minute (rpm). A mechanical governor adjusts the pitch of the propeller blades to take a larger or smaller "bite" out of the air and keep the engine speed exactly where you set it. Imagine that you set the engine to stay at 2500 rpm in level flight. The propeller is set to a pitch to provide just enough resistance to the engine to keep it running at 2500 rpm. Now you start climbing. Just like a car climbing a hill, the airplane engine will be under more strain in a climb and slow down. The propeller governor will sense this and flatten the propeller pitch, making the propeller easier to turn and allowing the engine to stay at a constant speed. It's similar to shifting a car to a lower gear. The opposite happens in a dive: the propeller goes to a very high pitch to keep the engine turning at the same speed, even though the pull of gravity is helping to propel the airplane. This is a huge benefit in full-power dives because it prevents the engine from exceeding its maximum (redline) rpm.

The propeller control affects both engine power and engine efficiency. The propeller is much more efficient at lower rpm settings, but lower rpm means lower power output. Using the same manifold pressure setting, your airplane will fly slower at 2200 rpm than at 2800 rpm. However, you can increase the manifold pressure setting to add the power back in and still take advantage of the better propeller efficiency. If a setting of 2200 rpm and 35" of manifold pressure results in the same airspeed as a setting of 2800 rpm and 28" of manifold pressure, the 2200 rpm setting will burn fuel more slowly. You can save a little fuel if you set the propeller to a lower (cruise) rpm setting before you warp to the next waypoint in your mission, but this level of efficiency isn't necessary for any of the missions that come with Combat Flight Simulator 2. The most important thing to remember about the propeller control is that it should be full forward for all takeoffs, landings, and combat to allow for maximum rpm and maximum power when you need it.

Engine speed is measured on the tachometer. All the airplane tachometers show the engine speed in rpm, but they use several different formats. The P-38 and the George use tachometers similar to what you would find in a car. The Wildcat and Corsair use a two-needle tachometer where a large needle displays hundreds of rpm on an outer scale and a small needle displays thousands of rpm on an inner scale. The Hellcat tachometer is very similar except that a single number appears on the inner scale to show thousands of rpm. Both Zeros in Combat Flight Simulator 2 use a tachometer where one needle goes around twice, reading 0 to 2000 rpm on an outer scale and 2000 to 3500 rpm the second time around on an inner scale. Figure 3-3 shows the tachometer from a Zero and a Wildcat.

Figure 3-3 *The tachometers from the Zero (left) and the Wildcat (right) are slightly harder to read than conventional automotive tachometers.*

Mixture Control

Mixture control is the third lever on the engine controls. This lever determines how much fuel is added to the engine intake air. The engine can operate within a range of fuel-to-air ratios. This range is fairly narrow at full power but widens at lower power, allowing a pilot to reduce the amount of fuel per unit of air, increasing fuel efficiency.

To make things easier for you as the pilot, the fighters have an auto mixture feature. You can enable or disable this feature on the settings page. If you want to set the mixture manually, set your airplane for the cruise rpm and manifold pressure you want, and lean the mixture listening to the engine. When the engine starts to run rough or quits, you have gone too far. Push the mixture knob rich enough to keep the engine running, and leave it there.

Note: *Both Japanese and U.S. aircraft often flew missions at the maximum range of their airplanes by pulling the propeller control to a low rpm, choosing a moderate manifold pressure, and leaning the engine (decreasing the amount of fuel in the fuel/air mix) as much as possible. The difference was significant. An A6M2 Zero at combat power burns close to 40 gallons of fuel in an hour. In a high-power cruise, this figure was reduced to about 28 gallons an hour. Operating at peak efficiency a pilot could get fuel burns as low as 18 gallons an hour. Each increase in efficiency came with a reduction in speed.*

Note: *Instead of simply using the auto mixture control, some radial engine pilots would adjust their fuel mixture based on the color of the flames coming out of the aircraft exhaust.*

Cowl Flaps

The engine cowl is the metal housing that surrounds the engine. The cowl not only keeps the engine protected and aerodynamically clean, but it also controls how much air flows over the engine. All the U.S. fighters have air-cooled engines except for the P-38. The P-38 has a liquid-cooled engine and has no pilot-controlled cowl flaps. Figure 3-4 shows the cowl flaps of the Wildcat.

With the air-cooled engines, adjustable flaps on the cowl control how much air flows over the engine and keeps it from getting too hot or too cold. Generally, the cowl flaps should be open when the engine is working hard, such as when climbing or in combat, and closed when the engine is not working hard, as when cruising or landing. Monitor engine temperature with the oil temperature gauge and the cylinder head temperature gauge. Red lines indicate never-exceed temperatures. The U.S. fighters do not require careful management of temperature, so while the temperature will vary with the use of cowl flaps, ignoring them will not lead to overheating. (If engine temperature were accurately modeled, four out of five Combat Flight Simulator 2 players would experience engine failure in the first five minutes of combat.)

Engine Gauges

Several engine gauges allow you to monitor the health of the engine. The most critical one for you to check is the Cylinder Head Temperature (CHT) gauge that shows the temperature of the metal of the engine. All the airplane CHTs in Combat Flight Simulator 2 read in degrees Celsius. As mentioned earlier, engine damage because of overheating is not likely, but if you want to operate your engine in a realistic manner, open the cowl flaps as necessary to keep the CHT below 215 degrees in normal operation and below 250 degrees at all times. Oil temperature also gives an indication of how hot the engine is running, although it isn't your primary indicator. The oil temperature gauge is often combined with the oil pressure gauge and the fuel pressure gauge. Oil pressure must stay high enough to provide

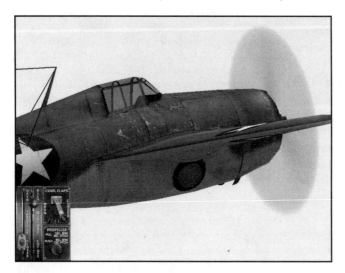

Figure 3-4   *Cowl flaps (closed on the top, open on the bottom) control the airflow over the engine, thereby controlling engine temperature.*

adequate lubrication for the engine, and fuel pressure must stay high enough for adequate fuel flow. All the airplanes show oil temperature in degrees Celsius. The American airplanes show pressures in pounds per square inch (psi), and the Japanese airplanes show pressure in kilograms per square centimeter (kg/cm^2). Three kg/cm^2 is equal to about 43 psi. The engine gauges will almost always show normal readings while you play Combat Flight Simulator 2. Figure 3-5 shows an example of the CHT gauge from the George and the combination gauge from the P-38.

Figure 3-5 *The single gauge (left) is the cylinder head temperature gauge from the George. The combination gauge (right) is from the P-38 and shows oil temperature on the top, oil pressure on the left, and fuel pressure on the right.*

Magnetos

Even in most present-day airplanes, aircraft ignition uses a system that is totally separate from the aircraft electrical system. The fuel and air mixture must be ignited by a spark. This spark is generated and delivered by the magnetos. All of the U.S. airplanes have two magnetos per engine. For safety reasons, the magnetos are wired so that each cylinder receives a spark from both magnetos. Even if one magneto fails, the other will still supply enough of a spark to keep the engine running, but at slightly poorer efficiency. You can use the four-position magneto switch to check the operation of each magneto before flight. This switch allows you to short-circuit one magneto to check the operation of the remaining one. The magneto switch also has a setting used for normal operation and an off setting to keep the engine from starting accidentally. Since the magnetos will never fail in Combat Flight Simulator 2, you can use this switch for a manual engine start and then leave it alone.

Fuel System

The fuel systems on combat fighters were more complicated than the average single-engine airplane. Most fighters have three or four fuel tanks built into the airplane, plus one or more external tanks called drop tanks. These drop tanks look like bombs hanging from the bottom of the fighter and were dropped into the ocean when empty or before combat. You must select which tank you want to use at any given time. The fuel selector in each airplane was a little bit different, but the fighters in Combat Flight Simulator 2 have been somewhat standardized to help avoid confusion, as shown in Figure 3-6. Roll the mouse over a selector position to verify that it's the fuel tank you wanted. The fuel quantity gauge in each airplane

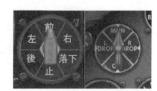

Figure 3-6 *The fuel selectors in Combat Flight Simulator 2 airplanes have been somewhat standardized to help avoid confusion.*

will show you the fuel remaining in the tank selected on the fuel selector. All the airplane fuel quantity gauges look the same, except that the Japanese gauges have the Kanji for full and empty replacing the American letters F and E.

Flight Exercise: Engine Control

Now it's time to try out using some of these new controls. Go to the main screen, and select Free Flight. Set your airplane to a P-38, because its engine gauges are easiest to read. Next click Settings and uncheck Enable Auto-Mixture so that you can experiment with the mixture control. Close the Settings window, and click Fly Now! to get seated in the airplane.

You are now in the airplane with both engines off. You could start them by just pressing E, but don't. We'll use your new knowledge for a manual start. Begin by calling up the throttle quadrant and moving it to the upper left part of the screen so that none of your instrument panel is blocked.

Start the left engine first. Right now, the mixture control (red knob) for the left engine is all the way at the bottom of the slider. This is the no-fuel position called idle cut-off. In this position, the engine will not start. Move the left-hand red knob all the way up to the top. This position is full rich, or maximum fuel. The blue knob is for the propeller. It should be all the way up for maximum rpm. The black knob is for the throttle. Move the left-hand throttle down to the letter E in throttle, or about 25 percent throttle. Switch the master electrical switch to ON. Now go down to the magneto switches on the bottom left of the panel, and click the left-hand switch until the switch is set to Both. Figure 3-7 shows what all these settings looks like.

Above the magneto control is a switch that says Off/On. Use the mouse to hold it in the On position, and listen for the engine to start. Once it starts, you can let go of the switch. Repeat the sequence for the right engine.

Now press the period key to hold the brakes, and bring up both throttles together by dragging in the area just between the two black knobs. Go to full power, and watch what happens to the manifold pressure (MP) gauges and the tachometers directly above them. Notice how the rpm and the MP go together to 3000 rpm and then only the MP changes. Now pull the blue propeller control down, and watch the rpm. The rpm will decrease, but the MP will stay roughly the same. Try bringing the mixture controls down and listen to the engine to see how lean you can go.

Bring both throttles back to idle, and try different settings on the fuel selector. Since you don't have a drop tank installed, choosing drop will make the

fuel gauge read empty and cause the engines to start to quit. A quick switch to a tank that has fuel will get them running again. Pull the right engine mixture all the way to the bottom at idle cut-off. The engine will shut down. This is how pilots normally shut down their engines to ensure there is no fuel left in the motor. Switch the left engine's magneto switch to off. The will also cause the engine to quit since there is no spark to ignite the fuel.

Figure 3-7   The P-38 panel just before starting the left engine.

Try starting some of the other airplanes by selecting Change/Modify Aircraft… from the Aircraft menu. (You can view the menu by pressing the Alt key.) When you are done, exit from free flight.

The next step is learning the basics of flying the airplane, but before you take the controls in flight, you must learn the theory behind flying an airplane.

Chapter Four

FLIGHT THEORY AND PRACTICE FOR THE COMBAT CADET

What is the purpose of a fighter airplane? It's a way to carry weapons and a person through the air, under control, for a fixed period of time and use these weapons to shoot down other airplanes. That's what it boils down to. Early flight tests showed that simply strapping a machine gun to a soldier and having him jump off the end of a carrier resulted in a short, uncontrolled flight that had a sudden and unpleasantly wet ending. (See Figure 4-1.) Something else was needed. That something was the wing.

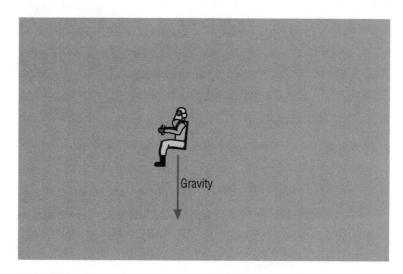

Figure 4-1   *Every time we try leave the ground, gravity continually pulls us back.*

The Role of the Wing: Lift

The wing's first and foremost role is to allow the pilot and his stuff to stay aloft. Since gravity is constantly pulling objects back to earth, the wing must somehow apply a force to keep the airplane up. The more the airplane weighs, the more force the wing needs to apply to keep everything airborne. Instinctively we know in which direction to apply this force. To tread water, you continually push water down or away from you to stay on the surface. To remain airborne, the wing redirects air down toward the earth in order to keep the aircraft up. The downward flow of the air results in a net upward force on the wing called *lift,* as shown in Figure 4-2.

The reason a wing can redirect air downward is that as the air passes over the wing, it follows the surface of the wing, over both the top and the bottom surface. Figure 4-3 shows the path of the air flowing over and under the wing. Now, if you were studying to be an aeronautical engineer, we'd talk about how airflow accelerates over the top of the wing and results in a

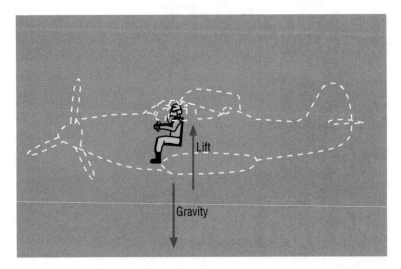

Figure 4-2   *To counteract the force of gravity, we create a force of lift.*

low-pressure area above the wing and how calculating the pressure differences above and below the wing can tell us how much lift the wing produces...but hey, we're pilots. We need to know how to control the lift the wing produces so that the airplane will go where we want it to go. There are two fundamental components to your control of lift: *angle of attack* and *airspeed.*

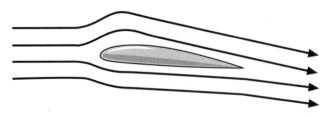

Figure 4-3   *Air passing over the wing will follow the upper and lower surfaces of the wing.*

Angle of Attack

Imagine sticking your hand out the window of a moving car. When your hand is open flat and parallel to the ground, you

feel the air rushing over the top and bottom of your hand. If you tilt the windward side of your hand up slightly, you can feel it being forced upward and slightly backward. You are experiencing the force of lift. The more you tilt your hand into the airflow, the more air you direct downward, and the more upward force you experience. The greater the angle between the plane of your hand and the oncoming air, the greater the upward force of lift. The angle between the oncoming air and the wing is called *angle of attack*. The steeper the angle of attack, the more steeply you force air down and the more force is applied to lift the wing up. As a pilot, you use angle of attack as one of the two fundamental components that control the amount of lift your wings produce.

Airspeed

If the driver of the car speeds up or slows down, you'll notice a change in the amount of lift your hand is producing. The speed of the air rushing around a wing (or your hand) is critical in determining the amount of lift it produces. The speed of the air meeting the wing is called, simply enough, *airspeed*. The more airspeed you have, the more air is sent downward each second and the more total upward force is applied to your hand. Your control of airspeed is the second fundamental component of how you control lift.

In general, to control the wing's angle of attack, you will use the joystick. The exceptions and limitations to this rule are discussed later, but in most flight situations, when you pull back on the stick, the airplane will pitch upward and you will increase the angle of attack and increase the total lift. Likewise, pushing forward on the stick will decrease the angle of attack and decrease lift. The control of airspeed has some exceptions and limitations as well, but as with angle of attack there's a general rule. In most flight situations, to increase airspeed, you can open the throttle so that the engine is generating more power. To decrease airspeed, you'll close the throttle.

Thrust

All fighters use one or two propellers to convert engine power into airspeed. The propeller is a wing that moves through the air and redirects it, just like the airplane wings. The difference between the airplane wing and the propeller is that the propeller is perpendicular to the ground. Instead of forcing air down toward the ground (as a wing does), a propeller forces air behind the propeller.

This results in the plane being pushed forward, as shown in Figure 4-4. The net forward force of the engine is called *thrust*.

You control thrust by using the throttle and the propeller control. Simply put, the higher the reading on the MP gauge and the higher the engine rpm, the higher the thrust.

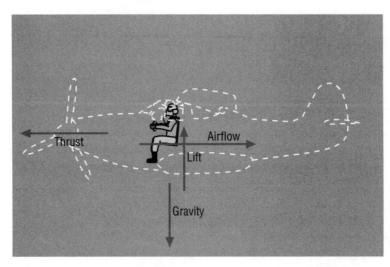

Figure 4-4   *Thrust is the third force acting on the pilot and airplane.*

Drag

The generation of lift comes at a price, and that price is drag. Drag falls into two main categories: *parasitic drag* and *induced drag*. The faster the airplane moves through the air (airspeed), the more resistance it will meet. This resistance has many sources: the friction of the airplane's skin, the energy needed to split the flow of air as it travels over and under the airplane, and eddies of wind that move around different parts of the airplane. This drag is parasitic drag. Whenever you increase your airspeed, you increase lift but you also increase parasitic drag.

As the wing moves through the air and generates lift, there is a slight rearward component of that lift. Remember that the more you increased the angle of your hand, the more your hand was forced both upward and rearward. This rearward force that accompanies generation of lift is induced drag. Whenever you increase your angle of attack, you increase both lift (upward) and induced drag (rearward). Figure 4-5 shows all four forces involved in flight.

No matter how you try to increase lift, you increase drag. By selecting how to increase lift, you choose what form that drag will take, like so:

- The greater the angle of attack, the more lift and the more induced drag.
- The greater the airspeed, the more lift and the more parasitic drag.

In flight, one of your primary tasks as a pilot is to adjust the balance of angle of attack and airspeed to get exactly the amount of lift you need to overcome the resulting drag. This is best seen in flight, but before you can conduct this flight you must understand how to read three key flight instruments.

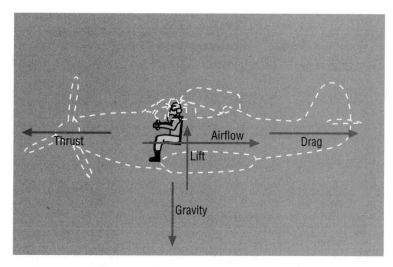

Figure 4-5 *Drag is the remaining force needed to complete a basic picture of the four forces of flight.*

Key Flight Instruments

Your familiarity with the following instruments is crucial to successful flying.

Altimeter

The altimeter is really just an air-pressure gauge. It measures the decrease in air pressure as you climb and converts that information into a distance above sea level. U.S. altimeters have three hands. The smaller, fatter hand shows your altitude in thousands of feet; the longer, skinnier hand shows altitude in hundreds of feet. If you climb above 10,000 feet, the hands continue to go around as before, and a third very small hand will move from the 0 to the 1 position to show tens of thousands of feet. (Of course, if you can't tell the difference between being 13,500' in the air and being 3500' in the air you're probably going to wash out of flight school.) Figure 4-6 shows Japanese and American altimeters.

The Japanese altimeter displays altitude in meters. Like the U.S. instrument, the fat needle indicates thousands of meters and the skinny needle indicates hundreds of meters. What's tricky about the Japanese altimeter is that 0

Figure 4-6 *Japanese altimeters read in meters (left); American altimeters read in feet (right).*

is at the bottom and that the hand goes around twice for each thousand meters. Each position on the face has two numbers, such as the 1 and the 6. The first time the needle comes around you read the 1; the second time you read the 6. The Japanese altimeter in Figure 4-6 reads 4115 m (equal to 13,500'). Notice that the short needle is just past the 4, indicating over 4000 meters. The long needle is either just past the 1 or just past the 6. You can tell by looking at the short needle. Since the short needle is so close to the 4, the long needle must be going around for the first time, so the altitude is 4115 m. If the fat needle were past the halfway tick between 4 and 5, the thin needle would be on its second pass around the face and the altitude would be 4615 m.

Note: *Before each flight and several times during a long flight, a pilot must readjust the altimeter to account for changes in air pressure due to weather. This is not modeled in Combat Flight Simulator 2, so you do not need to set your altimeter.*

Vertical Speed Indicator

The vertical speed indicator (VSI) also measures the air pressure, but it senses how fast the air pressure is changing and converts that information into a rate of climb or a rate of descent. If the VSI shows a climb of 1000 ft/min, the hundreds hand on the American altimeter will go around once in a minute and the thousands hand will move one number. The VSI will read a maximum rate up or down (6000 ft/min on most U.S. fighters) and will stay at that rate for any faster speed. The Japanese VSI reads up to 1000 m/min, which is 3280 ft/min, or about half the maximum rate that the U.S. gauges read. Figure 4-7 shows the U.S. and Japanese vertical speed indicators.

Figure 4-7   *The Japanese gauge reads in hundreds of meters per minute (left); the U.S. vertical speed indicator reads in thousands of feet per minute (right).*

Airspeed Indicator

The airspeed indicator shows the speed of the airplane moving through the air. All the airspeed indicators, except for that of the P-38, are dual scale, meaning the needle can go around twice. On the Japanese airspeed indicators, which read in knots, airspeeds under 160 knots are read on the outer scale and speeds over 160 knots are read on the inner scale. You must also append a 0 to the display number on all the Japanese airspeed indicators—for example, 12 on the face equals 120 knots. The U.S.

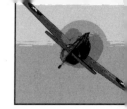

airspeed indicators all read in knots except for the P-38. You switch from reading the inner scale to the outer scale when you reach 200 knots. The P-38 airspeed indicator displays speed in a single scale (just once around the dial), but the numbers get closer together as the speed gets higher. Figure 4-8 shows the U.S. and Japanese airspeed indicators.

Flight Exercise: Pitch and Power

Go to the Settings screen and select Enable Auto Mixture and Enable Auto Rudder. Next chose the Realism Settings screen and set the flight model to Hard. (Remember that hard just means real.) Close the Realism settings screen, and close the Settings screen. On the home screen, click the Quick Combat button and do the following:

1. Set the Player Aircraft to an A6M2 Zero.

2. Set the Player Flight to 0 Wingmen.

Figure 4-8 *Most of the airspeed indicators display dual scales, with the outer scale used for slower speeds and the inner scale for faster ones.*

3. Click the Enemies button to open the Enemies screen, and then select the No Enemies checkbox. (Learning to fly is always harder with someone shooting at you.)

4. Close the Enemies screen by clicking OK, and then click Fly Now.

These settings make Quick Combat just like Free Flight, but you get to start out already flying. You start in cockpit view. While you're in the cockpit, you can use a joystick control or F3 and F4 to adjust your throttle. Look at the gauge in the lower right part of the panel with the red-and-black face. Adjust the throttle to put the needle on 0. This is about 71 percent power. Now press W to switch to Heads Up Display (HUD) view. Using the joystick, gently adjust the pitch of the airplane until it stabilizes at a constant altitude. The exact altitude is unimportant; just adjust your pitch so your altitude is not increasing or decreasing.

You should stabilize at a speed of about 136 mph. Once you have it steady, press P to pause the game. Notice that the gun sight is about two-thirds its own diameter above the horizon. This is the pitch

Note: *You can change the color of the HUD information on the right of the screen by pressing Shift+W. This might be useful if you find the color of the sky makes this display difficult to read.*

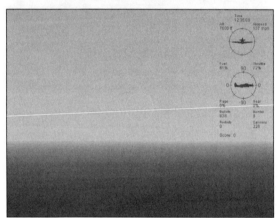

Figure 4-9   *Cockpit, HUD, and chase views for the Zero in level flight at 71 percent power.*

needed to produce just the right amount of lift at 136 mph to maintain level flight. Press W twice to return to cockpit view. It's harder to see, but the gunsight is the same height above the horizon as in HUD view. Press S twice to get to chase plane view, and use the hat switch to adjust your perspective to the side of the Zero. Now you can see the angle of attack. Since your airplane is flying level and not climbing or descending, the angle of attack is the angle made between the wing and the horizon. It's not a very big angle, but it's definitely there. Figure 4-9 shows these views for an A6M2 Zero. As you adjusted stick to try and get a constant altitude, you might have noticed how your airspeed kept changing. Whenever you pitched too low, the total lift was too small to keep the airplane flying at a constant altitude, and it began to descend. Once the airplane began to descend, it gained airspeed. The opposite happens when you pitch too high, start to climb, and lose airspeed.

Now go back to HUD view by pressing W, and press P to release the pause. Bring the throttle up to 100 percent. This will initially result in an increasing airspeed. Increasing airspeed will lead to an increase in lift, and if left unattended, the airplane will begin to rise. To decrease the total lift back to the right amount for level flight, you must decrease the angle of attack. Apply forward pressure on the controls to keep altitude constant. Again, the exact altitude doesn't matter, as long as you

push forward enough to keep altitude constant. Once the aircraft stabilizes, the airspeed should be near 212 mph. Pause the game again, and look at both the position of the gun sight on the horizon and the angle the wing makes with the horizon in chase view. The airplane weighs the same as before, so the same amount of lift must be produced, but now you are generating that lift by using a greater airspeed and a smaller angle of attack.

Try the exercise a third time, but with only 57 percent power. You will require a much greater angle of attack to generate enough lift, as the airspeed will be only 95 mph. Once you've stabilized your altitude, pause the game and look at the new flight attitude again. Figures 4-10 and 4-11 show the high and low power examples for the Zero.

Now you can see the relationship between pitch, power, airspeed, and altitude. These relationships are summed up in Figure 4-12. These relationships apply for most operations you will conduct in the airplane.

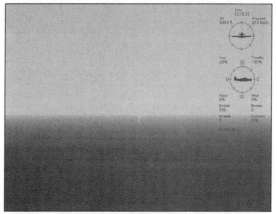

Flight Exercise: Trim

In the previous flight exercise, once you got the pitch in the proper position by using the stick, you had to hold the stick in that position to keep the pitch from changing. This might be trivial if you don't have a force-feedback joystick pushing against your hand or plan to press X to skip all the long flying parts

Figure 4-10   *Cockpit, HUD, and chase views for the Zero in level flight at 100 percent power.*

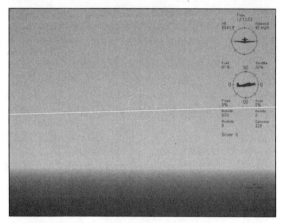

Figure 4-11 *Cockpit, HUD, and chase views for the Zero in level flight at 57 percent power.*

of a mission. If you want the airplane to do the work, however, you need to use trim. Trim will hold the pitch where you want without you having to hold the stick. The keyboard controls for trim are keypad 7 (Num Lock off) for more nose-down pressure on the stick (known as *nose-down trim*) and keypad 1 for more nose-up pressure on the stick (known as *nose-up trim*).

Go to Quick Combat with no enemies, and select the F4F-4 Wildcat. The F4F-4 Wildcat is a good airplane to use in this exercise because it trims well and the elevators are painted different colors on the top and bottom.

Start with the throttle at 30" MP and the propeller set for 2200 rpm. Trim the airplane so it flies level with your hands off the controls. Hold the nose where you want it, and adjust the trim with keypad 1 and keypad 7 until you can let go of the stick and have the airplane stay at basically the same attitude. This should settle the plane down to a speed of about 200 mph.

If you have trouble getting the trim just right, hold the stick, press keypad7 or keypad1 many times, and then let go of the stick. The Wildcat should make a rather wild pitch change. Now re-trim the airplane. Often it's easier to make a large trim adjustment than to make a small one. While you're in the Wildcat, go to chase view and position yourself behind the airplane. As you move the stick forward and back, you will see a hinged surface moving on the tail of the Wildcat. This surface is

the elevator, and as you move it you change the forces on the tail, which changes the pitch of the entire airplane. Without the elevator, you have virtually no pitch control. Your elevator or its control cable can be destroyed in combat. If the elevator is missing from your airplane or it won't respond to your stick inputs, bail out.

Flight Exercise: Climbs, Glides, and Power-On Dives

In the previous exercise, you adjusted pitch and power to fly a constant altitude at different airspeeds. Now you will adjust pitch and power to climb and descend at different airspeeds.

Go to quick combat with no enemies again, and select the F4F-4 Wildcat. Open the throttle to full. The airplane will begin to speed up and climb. Since the throttle is at full power, the only primary control over your airspeed is pitch. Pitch your airplane for 140 mph and you will see a climb speed of around 4000 feet per minute. Use your pitch to keep 140 mph, and reduce your power to get a slower rate of climb. Reduce your power even further to about 25", and you'll fly level at 140 mph. If you reduce the power to idle, you can still maintain 140 mph with sufficient pitch down. Notice that now you are using pitch to control airspeed and power to control altitude. This system will work in any flight regime, but it will be of utmost importance when coming in to land.

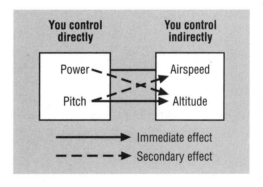

Experiment with climbs, glides, and power-on dives in the Wildcat, A6M2 Zero, and the P-38 Lightning. You will see a big difference in how they handle the up and down at speed. Try each of the following scenarios:

- Make full-power climbs at different airspeeds and notice how fast you climb. Look for the speed where you climb the fastest. Watch your VSI for the rate.
- Try no-power descending glides at different airspeeds, noticing how fast you descend. Look for the speed where you descend the slowest. This is approximately your best speed for gliding to a landing spot if your engine fails.

- Try full-power dives at different airspeeds. Notice how at shallow angles the speed will stabilize and remain steady. Try noting your airspeed and altitude before some very steep, high-speed dives. Pull out of the dive if you can, and note your altitude when your airspeed returns to its starting value. Find out if steep pull-ups are more or less energy-efficient than shallow climb-outs.

Up and Down Is All About Energy

In the first Zero flight exercise, the nose of the airplane was pointed at various angles to the horizon but the airplane itself was traveling level. What makes the airplane climb or descend, if not where the nose is pointed? The big mathematical answer to this question includes terms such as excess thrust and excess horsepower. To you, the combat pilot, what really matters is how much energy (E) you have available. When it comes to up and down, energy management is the name of the game.

There are two categories of energy that matter to the pilot. One is all the energy available in the speed and mass of the airplane. This is the airplane's kinetic energy. The faster you fly, the more kinetic energy you have. More power from your engine will mean more kinetic energy for the airplane. The second kind of energy is potential energy. This energy is mostly a function of your altitude. You have already seen how pitching down will increase your airspeed. When you descend from altitude, you are taking the potential energy stored up as altitude and converting to kinetic energy in the motion of the airplane. So the total amount of E that you have available depends on three things: airspeed, altitude, and engine power.

When your airplane is sitting on the ground, its E is basically zero. Once the engine is running and the airplane is building up airspeed as it rolls down the runway, it's also building up E. As you take off and climb out, you continue to build up E, in the form of both altitude and airspeed. There is no free lunch here. You are also constantly losing E to the forces of lift and drag. Energy can't be destroyed, but the forces of drag are converting your E into heat, sound, and disturbances in the air. Since you can't reclaim E that is lost to drag, this E is lost to you.

Acceleration and Climbs

The balance between E that is used by the pilot and E lost to lift and drag determines how the airplane will behave. Whenever the engine is producing more power than is needed to replace the E lost to lift and drag, the airplane begins to both accelerate and climb. If you push the nose over just enough to prevent any climbing, the airplane will continue to gain speed. As speed increases, so does parasitic drag; therefore, E is draining off faster than before. At a certain point, even at full power the engine produces just enough E to balance the losses to lift and drag, and the airplane won't go any faster in level flight. For the Zero, this speed is about 212 mph. If you add power and pitch up, your speed will not increase and neither will parasitic drag. Your E will be drained at exactly the same rate as in level flight at that speed. This means excess E is available from the engine, and as a result you will climb. The climb converts the extra E into gain in altitude.

Deceleration and Glides

If you decrease the engine power while cruising level, you will not have enough power to make up for the E lost to lift and drag. You now have a choice between slowing down and pitching up to keep the same altitude but at a slower airspeed so not as much E is required, and keeping your airspeed and descending. In the second scenario, you are getting some of the E you need from the engine and getting the rest from the potential energy stored as altitude. Even if you stop your engine entirely, the airplane will continue to fly in a gliding descent. It still needs energy to create lift and overcome drag, but the energy is available as stored E in the form of altitude.

How fast you descend is determined by how much engine power you use and how fast you want to burn your E reserve. Suppose you have an enemy closing in on your Zero. You need some serious speed, and you need it now. If, in level flight, full throttle gives you only 175 mph, you can dip into your E reserve and trade some of that altitude you saved up for additional airspeed. In this way, you can dive at over 300 mph.

The only limit to how much extra E you can use is the airplane itself. You may have noticed that in the high-speed dives, the airplane can be difficult to control. Turning a Zero while diving at over 300 mph required almost super-human strength. At very high speeds (over 400 mph), the tail of early P-38s would vibrate and could be ripped completely off the airplane. (This doesn't happen in Combat Flight Simulator 2.)

You can put the kinetic energy of high airspeed back into the E reserve by pulling up out of the dive and gaining altitude. Remember that at high speed, E is lost very quickly to drag, however. This penalty occurs in dives every bit as much as in level flight or climbs, so when you pull up out of the dive you will not get all your E back. Speed always costs E, and the faster you go, the more E it costs. Experiment with the power of E thoroughly. As a fighter pilot, your life depends on your management of E.

Carving a Turn

The last piece of flight theory you need to master is the turn. The physics of the turn have confounded many pilots. Luckily, you don't need to know the physics to fly the airplane well. Here is a simple example that should give you the big picture. Imagine making a turn on a bicycle. To make a smooth turn at speed, you must do two things: you must turn the handlebars slightly, and you must lean in the direction of the turn. To get a clean, crisp turn, you must coordinate these two actions. If you tried to turn by simply turning the handlebars hard to one side, you would be flung over the handlebars and onto the street. If you tried just to lean in the direction of the turn and kept the handlebars perfectly straight, you might turn slowly, but you would be leaning over excessively far. More likely, you'd just fall over.

Turning an airplane requires the same kind of coordination. Instead of handlebars, you have the rudder pedals or the twist grip on your joystick. This control swings the nose of the airplane left and right. Instead of leaning the airplane, you bank the wings to one side or the other. You control the banking by moving the stick right or left. Movable surfaces on the wings, called ailerons, accomplish the banking.

Note: *To see the effects of using the rudder, make sure that on the Settings page, Enable Auto-Rudder is unchecked.*

What Happens in a Turn: Rudder

The rudder is part of the vertical section of the tail and moves the tail to the right or to the left. If you step on the right rudder pedal, press the Enter key on the numeric keypad, or twist the joystick grip to the right, the nose of the airplane will swing right. As in our bicycle analogy, the result is not the desired turn. As shown in Figure 4-13, the nose points right, but the airplane skids sideways for a bit before heading off in the new direction.

Seeing this skid on screen in Combat Flight Simulator 2 is difficult, but you can try looking at it from chase plane view to see it best. If you actually try a right-hand rudder-only turn, you will notice that first the nose swings to the right, or *yaws* right in proper airplane lingo, and soon after the airplane begins to roll to the right. The reason the airplane rolls is that when the nose swings right, the twist makes the left wing move forward. This actually speeds the

Figure 4-13 *A rudder-only turn will skid the airplane before it finally moves in the correct direction.*

wing up and increases its angle to the wind and its angle of attack, producing more lift. The opposite happens to the right wing: it loses speed and angle of attack and, subsequently, lift. The result is that the left wing lifts more than the right and the airplane banks to the right. This right bank happens too late, though. The turning and banking must work together for maximum efficiency.

What Happens in a Turn: Ailerons

Creating uneven lift on the left and right wings is the best way to bank the airplane. Ailerons are moving surfaces on the airplane's wings that you can use to change the camber, or curve, of each wing separately. Since airflow follows the curved surface of the wing, increasing the curve will direct air down more steeply and result in increased lift. Ailerons angle up or down in opposite directions on each wing, so the increase in lift

> **Combat Tip #4:** *Your rudder is also an effective targeting tool, so don't forget about it. The typical bullet spray pattern from a fighter aircraft's machine gun or cannon is narrow. Sweeping your gunsight from side to side across a target by gently using rudders while firing can increase your chances of a hit.*

happens only on one wing. The opposite wing experiences a decrease in lift. Uneven lift on the two wings will cause the airplane to bank. The bank redirects the lift of the wings slightly to the side so that the lifting action of the wings not only keeps the airplane aloft against gravity but also pulls the airplane around in the turn.

To enter a right turn, you will apply right stick and right rudder. Once in the turn, you must re-center the stick and the rudder. If you keep holding the stick to the right, the airplane will continue to roll into a steeper and steeper bank. If you keep going, the airplane will roll completely upside down. (You'll practice rolls in Chapter 5.) To roll out of the right turn, apply both left stick and left rudder until you are level. Figure 4-14 shows the view

Figure 4-14   *The Wildcat rolls into the turn with stick and rudder, maintains the turn with the controls neutral, and rolls out of the turn with opposite aileron and rudder. The controls are exaggerated in this example.*

from behind a Wildcat rolling into the turn, established in the turn, and rolling out of the turn.

How Much Stick and How Much Rudder?

In a real airplane, you can feel when the balance between stick and rudder is not right. In Combat Flight Simulator 2, you must use both your view out the window and your slip/skid indicator. The slip/skid indicator in the Wildcat cockpit is at the bottom center on the instrument labeled Turn Bank. It's the black ball in the glass tube. When the ball is in the center, between the two lines, you're using rudder and roll in the correct balance and the turn is coordinated.

Figures 4-15, 4-16, and 4-17 show three views from the Wildcat cockpit: correct rudder, too much rudder, and too little rudder. It's important to remember that these snapshots were taken during the roll into a right turn. Once the airplane is turning, the controls are mostly neutral, with only small corrections as needed to keep the turn coordinated.

Figure 4-15 shows the view for rolling into a coordinated turn. The bay was centered in the gunsight before the roll began, and it is still centered. The ball is centered between the lines. In Figure 4-16, there is too much rudder, the bay is already to the left of the gunsight, and the ball has moved left. Figure 4-17 shows the roll begun with no rudder. Now the ball has swung left and the bay has moved left of center. The airplane's nose has actually moved in the wrong direction (right) while rolling into a turn to the left.

The turn is caused by banking and redirecting some of the lift generated by the wings, with the rudder providing just enough assistance to make the process coordinated. Redirecting the lift to one side, however, reduces the amount of lift available to hold up the airplane, and the airplane begins to sink.

As illustrated in Figure 4-18 on page 65, the solution to the sinking airplane and falling nose is to pull back some more on the stick. This increases the angle of attack of the wing, increases the lift of the wing to keep the airplane up, and increases the forces of the tail, pulling the airplane around the turn faster.

Note: *If you have trouble remembering how to interpret the slip/skid indicator, remember that with rudder pedals you step down on the same side as the ball to get it centered, or "step on the ball." With a twist grip, you twist toward the ball to get it recentered; on the keyboard, you use the 0 and Enter keys on the numeric keypad. Coordinated turns are best for most flying, but there are plenty of times in combat when you will want uncoordinated turns. In fact, one weakness in Japanese flight training was that it insisted on coordinated turns. This limited the options for some Japanese pilots in combat.*

Why Understanding Turns Matters

There are two important reasons to understand turns. You may lose some of the controls that allow you to turn when they get hit by enemy fire. In a pinch, you can use just your rudder and some back stick to force the airplane to turn, even with missing ailerons. If the rudder and the right wing are damaged, you may need full left stick and left rudder just to fly straight. You can still turn by relaxing some of the left aileron or rudder or both, but you will only be able to turn right.

The other important concept in turns is that the increased lift required for the turn must be paid for with some E. In other words, turns cost E. Remember, E pays for lift as well as drag. If you turn without adding back

Figure 4-15   *Correct rudder.*

Figure 4-16   *With too much rudder.*

stick, you lose E by sinking. If you turn and hold the stick back to maintain altitude, you lose E by losing airspeed.

The steeper you bank, the faster you will turn, but the more back stick you will need to maintain altitude. High-speed turns are exactly what you need in combat, but these turns will cost you lots of E. How much E you lose in the turn depends on how fast you want to turn around. In the turn, the pilot experiences the seat pressing against him harder and harder. This sensation is called centrifugal force. You can't feel centrifugal force in Combat Flight Simulator 2, but you can see it on the screen. Press Shift+Z twice to see the frame rate and G-force. Just to the right of the frame rate is the total G force on the wings. In straight and level flight, the G force of the lifting wings is 1.0 G, just enough to counter the pull of gravity. As you bank and pull the stick back, the G force will increase. At 30° of bank in a level turn (a level turn being one where your altitude doesn't change), the G force is +1.15, or 115% the normal pull of gravity. From there, the G force exerted goes up exponentially. At 60° of bank in a level turn, the G force is +2.0, twice the force of gravity. At 70° of bank in a level turn, the G force is +3.0, three times the force of gravity. See Figure 4-19 on page 66 for an example.

At shallow bank angles, you can make up for the extra E loss by adding power. In combat, you are likely to already be at full power, so this won't be an option. I'll cover how to make the most efficient turns in Chapter 5, when I talk about cornering speed, but it's important that you understand this point early on. *One sure way to lose E in a hurry is to get into a dogfight that forces you to make constant steep turns.*

Figure 4-17 *With too little rudder.*

Here are the key points about turns:

- Turns require both rudder and aileron to be conducted smoothly.
- Turns can be made in slips or skids by using rudder and aileron independently.
- Turns cost E, and the harder the turn the more E it costs.

Flight Exercise: Turns, Coordinated Turns, and High-G Turns

Go back to the settings screen and make sure Enable Auto Rudder is unchecked. Return to quick combat with no enemies and experiment with turns. Here are some things to try:

In chase plane view (press S twice):

- Adjust your view to behind the airplane, and move the stick and rudder pedals to see how they move the control surfaces on the airplane.

In cockpit view:

- Practice rolling in and out of turns, both coordinated and uncoordinated. Use the skid/slip indicator as a reference.
- Roll into a turn, and then apply back stick. Notice how the turn rate increases.
- Press Shift+Z twice to see how turns affect your G loads. Try level turns, climbing turns, and descending turns.
- Combine full-power climbs and dives with turns. Full power turning climbs and dives are the heart of fighter pilot maneuvering.

Stalling the Wing

There's a limit to how large the angle of attack can be and still allow air to smoothly follow the top surface of the wing. When the angle gets too large, the air no longer follows the top surface and instead creates turbulent eddies behind the wing. These eddies don't redirect air downward, resulting in a rapid loss of lift on the wing. This loss of lift is called a stall.

The only way to recover from a stall is to reduce the angle of attack, which you do by reducing the amount of back stick. It doesn't matter which way the airplane is facing when you stall. You can stall even while diving straight down

if you pull the stick back too far or too fast and exceed the maximum angle of attack.

The most common stalls you will encounter in combat flight simulator are when flying slowly for landing, when pulling out of steep dives, and while making steep turns. In all three cases, your first action in recovery will be to reduce the angle of attack with some forward stick. The stall in a high-speed turn will have a second component in that the airplane can both stall and spin. When the airplane spins, it is stalled, but it also rotates around in a circle. The result is disorienting, but the cure is straightforward. Since you're in a stall, reduce the back stick, but to stop the spinning, use rudder in the opposite direction of the spin and pull the throttle to idle. If you don't know which way you are spinning, try the rudder one way and then the other. The airplane will recover in a dive, so you then simply need to pull out of the dive (without stalling, of course).

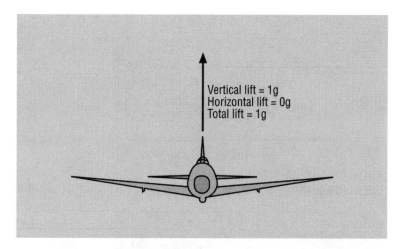

Vertical lift = 1g
Horizontal lift = 0g
Total lift = 1g

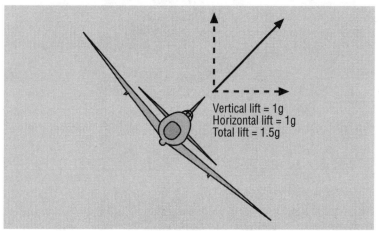

Vertical lift = 1g
Horizontal lift = 1g
Total lift = 1.5g

Figure 4-18 *The pilot must pull back on the stick to generate more lift to prevent the airplane from sinking. This action will also cause the airplane to turn faster.*

Flight Exercise: Stalls

Go to quick combat with no enemies and choose the F4F-4 Wildcat, using the hard flight model and with auto-rudder unchecked. Reduce the throttle to idle, and fly level until the speed reaches 120 mph. Then smoothly pull up with full stick aft (back). As speed decreases, hold full back stick, and the nose will fall. The airspeed may reach 0. Recover to flight by letting off the pressure and using a shallow dive to get your airspeed back up to a flyable number. This type of stall is good for flight training, but it is unlikely to happen in combat. If you fly in a straight line at 120 mph, you will be shot down long before you stall.

Next put the Wildcat into a full-power dive at about 45 degrees nose down. When you reach 190 mph, pull up with full back stick. The airplane will stall as the nose points back up, even though the airspeed is over 140 mph.

For the spin, start in level flight and bank the Wildcat 70°; then pull back with full back stick, just as if you were making a hard turn to get on an American pilot's tail. After an initial turn, the airplane will snap into a spin, as shown in Figure 4-20. Now not only are you not in position to shoot down the enemy, but you are completely out of control and plum-

Figure 4-19   *As bank angle increases, the G force exerted by the wings increases exponentially.*

meting to earth. The Wildcat is very forgiving and will recover from the spin on its own if you just let go of the stick for a few seconds. The Zero can also get into a nasty spin, so try spinning that airplane as well. The Zero will require a manual recovery. Practice spins until you can recover quickly unless you want to help some enemy pilot become an ace.

Figure 4-20   The views from a Zero (1) before the spin, (2) banking and turning but not yet spinning, (3) in the spin—notice how the airplane is upside down and the stall warning is lit on the right on the

Chapter Five

TAKEOFFS, LANDINGS, AND ADVANCED FLYING

You can stumble your way through takeoffs in Microsoft Combat Flight Simulator 2 and use X to skip the landings, but to seriously say you completed the mission you should master them. Landing successfully after a grueling mission adds that sense of satisfaction to the whole event, especially if you're landing on a carrier. Taking off and landing also involve some more advanced areas in flying. Let's look at the hardware you'll use to get the airplane into the air and back down again.

Landing Gear

Landing gear actually serves two purposes for the pilot. The more obvious function is to give the airplane wheels to roll on during takeoffs and landings. The second function of landing gear is to help slow down the airplane. In flight, the gear retracts out of the air stream to reduce drag and allow the airplane to fly faster. On approach to landing, the pilot needs to slow down the airplane, and extending the gear is part of this process. The gear indicators, which vary from aircraft to aircraft, will tell you whether your gear is up or down. To drop or retract your landing gear, press G.

Aircraft that land on carriers also have a tail hook. (For example, see Figure 5-1.) This hook catches a cable on the deck of the ship, rapidly slowing the

> **Note:** *Most of the fighters use hydraulic pressure to raise and lower their gear. If your hydraulic system is not working, you can sometimes put the gear down manually by pressing Control+G repeatedly. If that doesn't work, your best bet in a fighter is probably to bail out.*

Figure 5-1 *A Hellcat with its tail hook and gear down.*

Note: *In the first version of Combat Flight Simulator, many people used the technique of extending landing gear in combat to slow down from high speed without fear of damage. In Combat Flight Simulator 2, trying this technique will either cause gear damage or have no result because of a safety mechanism that prevents gear extension at high speed.*

airplane. It's possible—but much more difficult—to land on the carrier deck without the hook. To drop the hook, press Shift+H. Note that the hook is down when it looks like it's lower than the tailwheel.

Flaps

Flaps increase wing camber and affect both lift and drag. Flaps allow the airplane to remain airborne at a slower speed, although the airplane usually requires more power to fly with the flaps down than with flaps up. In general, flaps up is for cruising flight, flaps partially down is for takeoff, and flaps full down is for landing. Some airplanes use full flaps for takeoff from carriers, and some can use flaps in combat to improve turning ability. You'll find specific flap recommendations for each airplane in Chapter 10, "Player-Flyable Aircraft."

Different fighter designs use different types of flaps, but what matters to you is that the airplane will fly somewhat differently with the flaps extended. Flight with flaps is part of the following flight exercises. You control flaps with four buttons: F5 will fully retract flaps, F6 will retract flaps in steps, F7 will extend flaps in steps, and F8 will fully extend the flaps.

Operating Speeds

Your flaps and gear can be damaged if you use them while flying too fast. If you try to put the gear down in a George at 300 knots, the gear will jam partway down and parts may be ripped off. The Wildcat actually uses a system where the gear simply won't come down until you're doing less than 110 knots (127 mph) and the flaps won't come down if you're flying over 130 knots (150 mph). The operating speeds for gear and flaps for each airplane are listed in Chapter 10.

Getting Around on the Ground

Early aircraft generally used the conventional tailwheel-type landing gear, with two main wheels under the wings and a third small wheel under the tail. All but one of your fighters use this arrangement. As shown in Figure 5-2, that exception is the P-38, which uses the more modern tricycle gear arrangement, with the main gear further back under the wings and a third wheel under the nose. The conventional tailwheel gear arrangement has the advantage of keeping the propeller high off the ground or carrier deck. More clearance means bigger propellers that take advantage of high horsepower engines. The disadvantages of tailwheel gear are

Figure 5-2   The P-38 (top) has the newer tricycle gear, giving a pilot better visibility on takeoff. The Wildcat (bottom) uses conventional tailwheel-type gear.

that it's virtually impossible to see the runway directly in front of you and that tailwheel airplanes are trickier to handle on the ground. Tricycle gear means shorter propellers, but visibility is excellent and ground handling is much improved.

Regardless of whether the third wheel is under the nose or the tail, that wheel does the steering and you control it with your rudder. Once you get the hang of steering with your feet or the twist grip of your joystick, taxiing around is pretty easy. Getting around in the P-38 requires opening the throttle to about 75 percent to get going and then bringing it back to about 20 percent to keep rolling. Steer where you want to go. To stop, bring the power to idle and step on the brakes using the period key.

Note: *The period key will apply the brakes on your left and right wheels simultaneously. Airplane brakes can also be applied individually to the left or the right wheel to help the airplane turn or aid in directional control. To apply the left or the right brake, use the F11 or F12 key, respectively.*

Taxiing a tailwheel airplane requires a little more care because the third wheel is behind you and the airplane will have a tendency to spin 180° if you're not careful. By analogy, taxiing a tailwheel airplane is like trying to push a shopping cart backwards. It's easy so long as the steering wheels stay in line behind the fixed wheels. As soon as you start to turn, though, the whole thing will have a tendency to keep turning and roll over onto a wing. This unfortunate occurrence is called a ground loop.

Flight Exercise: Ground Loop

Go to Free Flight, and choose Henderson Field as a location with a P-38 as your airplane. Start the engines, and go to HUD view by pressing the W key so that you can see a little better. Bring the throttle to full, and accelerate to 40 mph. Now cut the throttle to idle, and apply full left rudder. As shown in Figure 5-3, the P-38 will bounce a bit as it turns to the left and the left wing will dip, but you should turn around and come to a stop without too much trouble.

Now change the aircraft to a Wildcat. Before you open the throttle, turn the rudder slightly to the right, which will help keep you straight. Unlike the twin-engine P-38, the powerful single-engine fighters will try to turn to the left as you add power. This is primarily because the propeller is pointed slightly upward while the airplane is moving forward and the descending blade on the

Chapter Five: Takeoffs, Landings, and Advanced Flying

right has a higher angle of attack than the ascending blade on the left. The result is more thrust on the right and a tendency to turn left. If you start with a bit of right rudder and anticipate the left-turning tendency, you should be able to keep rolling reasonably straight.

Open the throttle and accelerate to 35 knots, keeping the airplane rolling as straight as you can. Cut the throttle, and add full right rudder. The result should be dramatic. Figure 5-4 shows what this looks like from Chase view.

Figure 5-3   *The P-38 can make a high-speed turn and only lean over slightly. Notice how the left gear strut is more compressed and the right wheel is almost off the ground.*

Improved ground control will come with practice, but here are a few tips:

- Anticipate the left-turning tendency before you add the throttle, and be prepared to counteract it.
- Use prompt rudder inputs to keep the nose going where you want, but beware of overcontrolling. You might stop a ground loop to the left only to create a worse one to the right.
- Cut the power if things get bad. Better to start the takeoff a second time than break the airplane.
- Differential braking can save the day. When the right wheel is off the ground and you're turning faster than the rudder can stop, pressing the left brake will sometimes swing the airplane back to the right. Be careful, though. Too much braking will just create a worse ground loop to the right.

Figure 5-4 *The Wildcat will not handle the sudden turn quite as well as the P-38. The tail tends to swing around, and the airplane rolls into its wing. This is a classic ground loop. The Wildcat is especially prone to rolling over because of its narrow main gear.*

- Hold full back stick as you taxi. This will help keep the tailwheel on the ground and help you maintain control.

Takeoffs

Now that you have the basics of taxiing the airplane on the ground and the basics of flying the airplane in the air, you just need the transition between the two. The objective of the takeoff is to build up enough speed in the taxi to generate the lift needed to get the airplane off the ground and not hit anything in the process. If you can taxi, you can take off. In the tailwheel airplanes, you have three variations of takeoff to choose from, as described in the following flight exercises.

Flight Exercise: Three-Point Takeoff

Go to Free Flight at Henderson Field in a Wildcat. The Wildcat is tough to control on the ground, so once you can handle this airplane you can handle any of them. Start your engine, and go to HUD view so that you can see ahead better. Instead of bringing the stick full back, pull it about halfway back so that the triangle on the indicator is at the first long line, as shown in Figure 5-5. With the controls in position, open the throttle to full and keep the airplane rolling straight down the runway. The Wildcat should fly off the ground on its own at about 87 mph.

Once climbing, you'll need to keep holding right rudder and adjust the pitch of the nose to climb straight ahead and at a steady rate. For the Wildcat, 125 mph will give the best rate of climb, but it'll be difficult to see ahead of you in Cockpit view. A speed of 140 mph will give you a good rate of climb and allow for some forward visibility in Cockpit view. After you have the airplane climbing at a constant speed, retract your landing gear. Once you have the gear up, press Esc to stop the flight and start over. Try some takeoffs with Cockpit view instead of HUD view, and try some of the other airplanes.

Figure 5-5   *For the three-point takeoff, hold the stick partially back as shown on the center scale. Note the slight right rudder (bottom scale) to correct for the left-turning tendency.*

Flight Exercise: Wheeled Takeoff

A second option for takeoff is to get enough speed to lift the tail of the airplane and build up the rest of the speed in a level attitude where it's easier to see, as shown in Figure 5-6. It's also usually easier to control the airplane in the wheeled position.

For the wheeled takeoff, go back to Henderson field and choose a Wildcat again. Stay in Cockpit view this time. Start the engine, and begin the takeoff run with the stick full back. When your speed hits 30 knots, push the stick smoothly to full forward. At about 60 knots, the tail will come off the ground. The difference in the view out the front window of the plane is shown in Figure 5-7. As the airplane continues to accelerate,

Figure 5-6   *The wheeled position affords better forward visibility and slightly better directional control. On a rough field, however, the propeller might be damaged by the ground.*

you'll need less and less forward stick to keep the tail up. When you reach flying speed of 80 knots or so, gently bring the stick back and the airplane will lift off. This is known as *rotation*. In the wheeled position, the wings have a lower angle of attack than in the three-point position. Less angle of attack means less lift, so the airplane will remain on the ground at a far higher speed when wheeled. Rotation increases the angle of attack, which increases lift and causes the airplane to fly off the runway. The wheeled takeoff will usually use more runway than the three-point takeoff, but you'll lift off the ground at a higher speed and the airplane will be easier to control.

Figure 5-7   *The top image is the Wildcat in a three-point position, and the bottom image shows it in the wheeled position.*

Flight Exercise: Carrier or Short-Field Takeoff

When the runway is very short, such as on an aircraft carrier, flaps are used to get the airplane up and flying in a shorter distance. Go back to Henderson in the Wildcat, and get the engine going. Now extend the flaps to 100 percent by pressing F8. Since the point of this takeoff is to get airborne as soon as possible, use the three-point takeoff attitude, but this time position the stick about three-quarters back. For a better view and an easier time keeping the nose straight, go to HUD view.

Smoothly open the throttle to full, and keep moving straight ahead. At about 75 mph, the airplane will begin to lift off. At this low speed, the airplane is unresponsive to control inputs and you'll have some difficulty keeping the wings level. Don't try climbing right away. Keep the airplane close to the ground until you build up a little speed. Get the gear up right away to reduce drag, and bring the flaps up in steps once your speed is over 85 mph and increasing. This is basically the takeoff you'll use from an aircraft carrier, although the exact flap setting will differ from airplane to airplane.

Once you feel you have takeoffs pretty well down, try the takeoff training mission and see how well you do.

Landings

Landing is really the process of taking an airplane with E in the form of speed and altitude and bringing it to a place where it has no E because it has no speed and no altitude. The approach to landing, then, is to reduce E as much as possible up to the moment the airplane touches the ground. In the Wildcat, your target speed as you reach the runway is 85 mph. The airplane is in basically a three-point attitude when flying at 85 mph, so it should be in the correct position for a three-point landing.

Flight Exercise: Three-Point Landings in HUD View

Go back to Henderson in the Wildcat, and take off over the water. Climb up to 2000' while flying straight out. Turn around and bring the throttle back to 50 percent in Full view so that the picture looks something like Figure 5-8. Alternatively, press Y to use the slew command to move the airplane to the desired position.

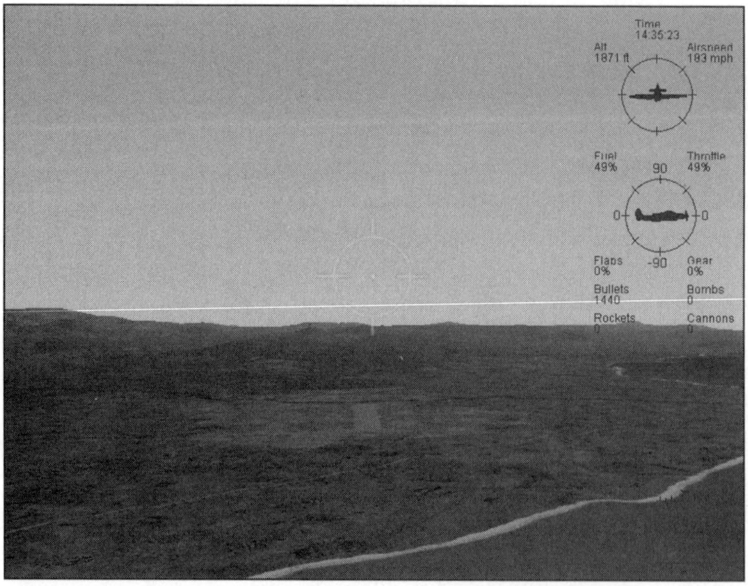

Figure 5-8 *Get your Wildcat into this position, where you can see Henderson airfield and the coastline from an altitude of 2000'.*

Bring the throttle back to 40 percent, and adjust the pitch of the airplane so that the end of the runway is halfway between the gunsight and the bottom of the screen. When your speed gets below 150 mph, deploy full flaps by pressing F8. When your speed gets under 120 mph, drop your gear. Keep adjusting your pitch so that the end of the runway stays halfway between the gunsight and the bottom of the screen, and add power to slow your rate of descent if the end of the runway appears to move up toward the gunsight. About thirty percent throttle will give you the right speed and right descent.

Once speed reaches 100 mph, use your pitch to keep that speed the same and your throttle to control your rate of descent. As shown in Figure 5-9, if you get too slow, pitch down to gain speed and add throttle to prevent losing too much altitude. If you're too fast, pitch up to lose airspeed and reduce the throttle to keep from climbing. You're using pitch and power differently than you normally do in cruising flight, but you'll find the airplane responds more quickly to commands and your control is more precise. Keep your speed at 100, and keep the runway end in the halfway position.

At 100 mph, you're close to the target airspeed. All that needs to happen

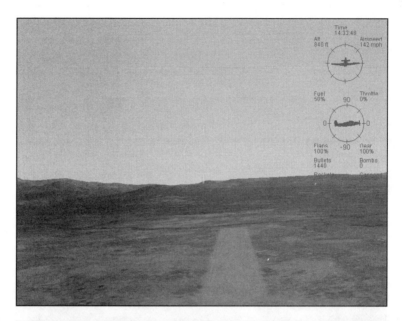

Figure 5-9 *If you're too going too fast, pitch up and reduce throttle. If you're going too slow, pitch down and add throttle. Either way, keep the end of the runway in sight at all times.*

now is to bleed off the remaining 15 mph before you reach the runway. As the runway gets closer, you're on *final approach* and can slow to 95 mph, as shown in Figure 5-10. When the end of the runway stretches all the way across the screen, bring the throttle to idle and slowly but continuously pull up the nose, as shown in Figures 5-11 and 5-12. With the throttle at idle, you're not adding any more E, so all that has to happen now is bleeding off the remaining E by raising the nose and slowing down. You actually will use this last bit of E to slow your rate of descent as well so that the airplane touches down gently. This part of the landing is called the *flare*. At about the same time the airplane reaches its three-point attitude with the

Figure 5-10   *Slow to 95 mph as the runway nears.*

gunsight high off the horizon, the wheels will touch down and you'll have full back stick. Apply the brakes to come to a stop.

Flight Exercise: Three-Point Landings in Cockpit View

The three-point Full view landing procedure will actually work for all the landings you ever need to do in Combat Flight Simulator 2, including carrier landings. Some of your friends might challenge you to do the landing again in

Cockpit view or Virtual Cockpit view. This landing is doable but more difficult. The problem is that you can't see the end of the runway unless you put the nose down, but if you put the nose down you'll gain airspeed. That airspeed is extra E you must bleed off when you flare the airplane, and as a result the airplane will "float" in the air just off the runway for a good distance. Once the extra E is bled off, the airplane will land on three wheels just as before.

Go to Free Flight, and get yourself in a position to land from about 2000' just as you did earlier. Once you're there, go to Cockpit view and adjust your pitch to put the far end of the runway in the middle of

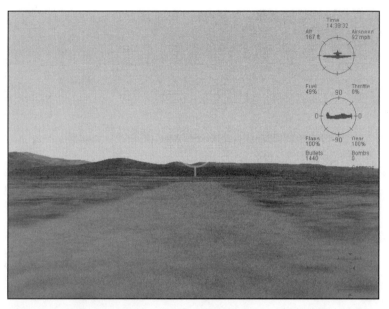

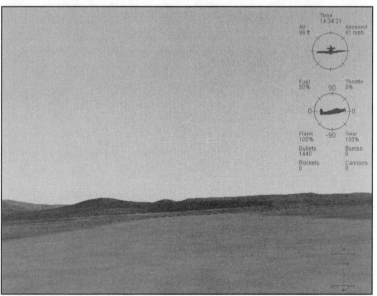

Figure 5-11 *When the end of the runway is as wide as the screen, reduce the power to idle and raise the nose.*

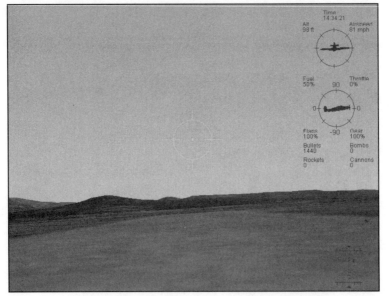

Figure 5-12 *Once down on all three wheels, apply the brakes.*

your gunsight. Put out full flaps and gear. If you can't slow down enough to get your gear down, pitch up to slow down, drop your gear, and pitch down to put the far end of the runway in the middle of your gunsight. Keep adjusting your pitch to keep the runway in place, and adjust your power as needed to keep about 100 knots. One hundred knots is about as slow as you can fly at this pitch attitude. When the runway reaches both sides of the screen, cut the power to idle and slowly pitch up into the three-point landing attitude. You won't be able to see the runway, so you must have faith that it's there. You can look briefly with a left or right forward view to see a bit better, but this is often

distracting at such a critical moment. It's better to just look to the sides of the screen to keep yourself landing straight. Figure 5-13 shows the cockpit picture for this type of landing.

There are two common mistakes in this type of landing. The first is thinking you're closer to the ground than you really are. The third image in Figure 5-13 looks pretty close to the ground, but a Chase view of that same moment shows that the airplane is still about 70 feet in

Figure 5-13 *These are the views for a three-point landing as they appear from the cockpit of the Wildcat.*

the air. The other problem is not getting the nose up to a three-point attitude before the main wheels touch. If this happens, the tail will pivot down and the angle of attack of the wings will suddenly increase. The airplane will then fly back into the air and come down hard the second time. This is usually referred to as a bounce and is generally considered bad form. (See Figure 5-14.) If you do bounce, hold the airplane in the 3-point attitude at the top of the bounce and add power to touch down gently.

Note: *Pressing pause on a landing and then using Chase view allows you to see where you are in relationship to the runway and helps you critique your own landings.*

There is a type of landing where you do touch down on the main wheels first. This wheeled landing is essentially the opposite of the wheeled takeoff. It takes good timing and an excellent ability to judge height, but it can be done. Make the approach at 100 knots using Cockpit view. When you'd normally

Figure 5-14 *Anatomy of a bounce. The airplane touches down with the main wheels first. The tail then swings down rapidly, and the airplane lifts back off the runway.*

cut the throttle and flare, slowly reduce the throttle and just bring your nose up to a level attitude as during the wheeled takeoff. Just as the main wheels touch the ground, apply forward stick to keep the tail from swinging down. As the plane decelerates, use more and more forward stick to keep the airplane in a level attitude until you can no longer keep the tail up. You can see the result in Figure 5-15. You may use brakes to slow down in a wheeled landing, but you'll need to apply some back stick to keep the airplane from nosing over and slamming the propeller into the ground.

Once you have a good feel for the landings, go to the landing training mission and see how you do.

Carrier Landings

The carrier landing can be successfully accomplished using the exact same techniques you used on dry land in Full view. As shown in Figure 5-16, you'll also need to lower your *tailhook* by pressing Shift+G. The tailhook is designed to catch one of five cables stretched across the landing side of the deck. The cable will extend as the airplane drags it down the deck, but there's enough resistance to the extension that the airplane will stop quickly. The other difference between carrier and dry land landings is that the carrier deck is both moving forward and mov-

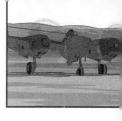

ing up and down. The forward motion is a help to you because it means you have a 35-mph headwind. This means that if you land with an airspeed of 95 mph, your actual speed over the carrier deck is only 60 mph. The up and down motion makes things a bit tougher, however, since an approach that looks like a perfect descent to the cables can turn into a wreck when the end of the carrier deck suddenly moves up into your way.

The Landing Signal Officer

You probably noticed the little guy in the upper left of Figure 5-16. This is your Landing Signal Officer (LSO), and it's his responsibility to guide you in for a safe landing. The LSO was essential to real

Figure 5-15 *Both pictures show the moment after the wheels touch down. In the three-point landing, the stick is full back. With the wheeled landing, the stick is slightly forward.*

naval aviators, who relied on his commands to bring their airplanes down safely; the aviators often couldn't see the carrier deck over the large aircraft nose. The LSO in Combat Flight Simulator 2 can be used for landing, but he isn't required if you use Full or HUD view to get a better picture.

Figure 5-16 *This Wildcat is just about to touch down on the carrier deck. Note the five black cables running across the carrier deck.*

Flight Exercise: Carrier Landings in HUD View

Go to Single Missions, and select Carrier Approach And Landing from the list of available missions. This mission will put you in a Wildcat at 600' about three miles out from the carrier. Switch to HUD view, and reduce your power to 40 percent. Put the end of the runway between the gunsight center and the bottom of the screen, and let the airplane slow down. When you reach 150 mph, add full flaps by pressing F8. When you reach 125 mph, extend your landing gear and tailhook by pressing Shift+G. Keep adjusting your pitch to keep the landing end of the carrier deck halfway between the gunsight and the bottom of the screen, and adjust your power to reduce your speed to about 95 mph. The throttle will be near 47 percent. Your LSO will not like this approach technique and will try to wave you

off. Ignore him. When the deck almost stretches across the screen, cut the throttle and pitch up very slightly to avoid crashing into the end of the deck. You should be able to hook a cable and stop without having to touch the brakes. Figure 5-17 shows the whole process.

Flight Exercise: Landing in Cockpit View with the LSO

Fly the training mission again, but this time stay in Cockpit view. Reduce your power to 17"MP, and pitch to center the aircraft carrier in the middle of the lower half of your gunsight. You're pitched much lower than during the Full view landing, and airspeed will be higher. Once the speed drops

Combat Tip #5: *Carrier landings during WW II were done with the canopy open to help facilitate a pilot's speedy escape in the event of a mishap. Although you can't open the canopy in Combat Flight Simulator 2 during your carrier approach, be sure that you know where the X key is. Time is the commodity you don't have at your disposal when your carrier approach goes sour at the "round down" (a naval aviator term for the stern or back end of the aircraft carrier's flight deck).*

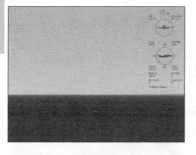

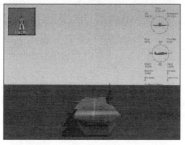
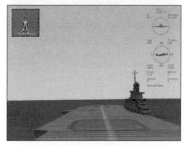

Figure 5-17   *The carrier landing can be done in Full view just like during a normal landing. Remember to lower your tailhook and keep your speed exactly at 95 mph.*

Figure 5-18 *If you're too high, pitch down slightly to correct and reduce power momentarily. If you're low, pitch up slightly and add power momentarily.*

below 130 knots, extend half flaps by pressing F7 twice. The Wildcat should stabilize at about 122 knots. Extend your tailhook now as well so that you don't forget it. As shown in Figure 5-18, if you find yourself too low on the approach, pitch up slightly to put the carrier deck in the bottom of the gunsight. If you're too high, pitch down slightly to keep the carrier deck in the center of your gunsight. Whatever you do, try to keep the carrier deck in sight at all times and adjust your power to keep airspeed constant.

When the LSO appears, pitch up slightly to allow you to lower full flaps, lower landing gear, and slow to 95 knots; then pitch back down. Now follow the LSO's instructions, but try to keep the end of the deck in the same position in the bottom half of your gunsight. When you get the command to cut and land, cut the throttle to idle and very slowly pitch back to the three-point landing attitude. You're still traveling at 95 knots, so if you pull back sharply, the airplane will climb right over the arresting cables before coming down on the deck. This is not a nice controlled landing. You basically level off in the airplane and drag your tailhook across the deck to get a cable. Once hooked, your airplane flies right into the deck. Figure 5-19 shows the landing using an LSO.

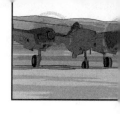

Flight Exercise: Landing from the Carrier Pattern

Figure 5-19   *The LSO will allow you to land in Cockpit view even though you can't see the carrier deck.*

In the real Pacific Theater, straight-in landings like the ones just described were not possible because the pilots couldn't see the LSO on the approach. Instead the pilots had to fly a landing pattern that took them over the carrier and then around in a racetrack pattern next to the carrier at the height of the carrier deck (about 100' off the water). The pilots waited until they were abeam the end of the carrier and began a turn toward the landing end of the deck. Throughout the turn they could see the LSO, and when they got the cut-and-land signal they stopped turning, rolled level, and landed in to the arresting cables. Or so they hoped. You can make these landings too, but they're not easy. Figure 5-20 shows you

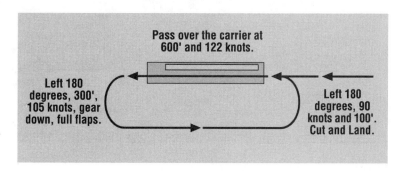

Pass over the carrier at 600' and 122 knots.

Left 180 degrees, 300', 105 knots, gear down, full flaps.

Left 180 degrees, 90 knots and 100'. Cut and Land.

Figure 5-20   *The real carrier approach.*

how a carrier approach should look. Figure 5-21 is a photo of an aircraft on approach to a carrier landing.

Go to the carrier landing training mission and fly it, but this time slow your Wildcat so that you pass over the carrier at 600' and 140 knots with half flaps, as shown in Figure 5-22. Next begin a shallow right descending 180° turn, slow to 120 knots with full flaps, and gear down at an altitude of 350', as shown in Figure 5-22.

You now need to look right or use the Tactical Display to keep track of the position of the carrier as you move parallel to it. As you move past the landing end of the carrier, begin a turn toward the carrier deck. Watch the carrier move from right to right forward to forward view. When the carrier reaches forward view, you should be at 100' and 95–100 mph and the LSO should give the cut-and-land signal. Roll out of the turn as the carrier deck lines up with your forward view, cut your throttle, and land. This maneuver can be quite a challenge, but it can be done.

Another tough maneuver to try is landing on the carrier without using the tailhook. It requires very precise airspeed control, but it can also be done.

> **Note:** *Taxiing on a carrier poses a new challenge because there is now a 35 mph wind blowing. To keep control of the airplane, hold full back stick when taxiing into the wind and full forward stick when the wind is at your back.*

Figure 5-21   *This TBD Devastator is on approach for a real carrier landing.*

Taking Off and Landing in the P-38

With two engines and tricycle gear, the P-38 is handled a little differently during takeoffs and landings. If you can handle the other fighters, however,

you should have no trouble taming the Lightning.

The P-38 takeoff had two distinct differences from the other fighters. First, the airplane will accelerate in a level attitude. If you just wait for the airplane to fly itself off the ground, you might be on the ground a long time. You'll need to build up speed on all three wheels, and then you'll rotate the nose upward, just as you did for a wheeled takeoff. Raising the P-38's nose will increase the angle of attack, and the P-38 will lift off the runway. The second difference is that because there are two engines whose propellers turn in opposite directions, there's no left-turning tendency for you to counteract—that is, as long as both engines are running. If one engine was to quit, the airplane would turn and roll quickly toward the dead engine, since the thrust from the good engine is unbalanced. As the pilot, you would probably add rudder and aileron to stop the turn, but as it turns out, the force needed to prevent the one-engine P-38 from rolling into its dead engine isn't possible below 120 mph. That means that if the engine fails on takeoff below 120 mph, the only way to control the airplane is to reduce power on the good engine, which means the P-38 will descend and probably crash. In

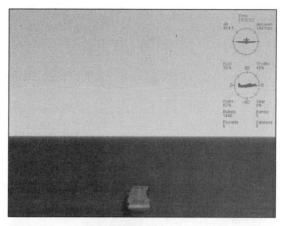

Figure 5-22 *Pass over the carrier at 600' and 140 mph.*

Combat Flight Simulator 2, the engine won't fail, but to be true to the flight of the P-38, you should stay on the ground until 150 mph and then rotate.

For landing, you'll approach the field just like during a tailwheel landing and land in a pitched-up attitude similar to a three-point landing. Hold back stick and keep weight off the nosewheel until you have full back stick and the nose settles on its own. You can safely use hard braking in the P-38 because the airplane cannot nose over onto its prop.

Flight Exercise: Taking Off and Landing in the P-38

Go back to Henderson Field in Free Flight, choose the P-38, and make sure that Auto-rudder is off in settings. Start the engines, and add full throttle for takeoff. If you hold the stick about 50 percent back as you did for the three-point takeoff, you'll lift off at around 125 mph. Climb at about 150 mph. Just to see what happens, turn off the magnetos on the right engine. The P-38 will begin turning left. You can override the turning tendency with rudder and stick at 150 mph. Now start pitching up toward 120 mph. Soon you'll be unable to override the turn, and trying to do so will put the airplane into a stall and a subsequent spin. The P-38 can take off with 1/2 flaps for short fields, but it will become airborne below 120 mph.

Landing the P-38 requires the same approach as with the other fighters except that its approach speed is the fastest at 110 mph. Use the three-point landing technique, and keep adding back stick in the flare until the stick is all the way aft. Figure 5-23 shows what the landing looks like from Chase view.

Gear-Up and No-Flap Landings

There will be times when you nurse a damaged plane back to your home field and find out that either the flaps or the gear, or both, will not lower. Now you must choose between trying to land and bailing out. No-flap landings on dry land are pretty easy. Just add about 15 mph to your approach speed, and the landing will be fine but will require more runway. No-flap landings on a carrier are tricky. Try a few of these for practice before you attempt it with a pilot character whose life you value. Gear-up landings are more difficult but can be done on dry land. Gear-up landings on a carrier are "right out." If you have any doubts and don't want to risk the pilot, just bail out by pressing O three times.

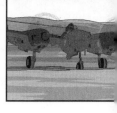

Instrument Flying

When you're navigating or flying through clouds, you'll need to use some of the other instruments on board the airplane. Following is a brief overview of their names and functions.

Flight Instruments

Compass/Remote Compass

A compass of some sort was an essential instrument for all the pilots in the Pacific Theater, who had to fly over a lot of water with few landmarks. As you can see in Figure 5-24, the Japanese and U.S. airplanes display their compasses differently. On all the Japanese airplanes, the compass is a rectangular box with the directional numbers appearing vertically, like marks on a tape measure. On the Zeros, the compass is low and in the center. On the George, the instrument is low and just to the right of center. For all the Japanese airplanes, you'll need to add a 0 to the number—so, for example, 6 on the instrument indicates a heading of 60°, or roughly NE.

On all the U.S. airplanes, the compass is actually remotely located in the fuselage or wing and is connected to the cockpit instrument electronically. The instrument displaying compass information is a round instrument with a

Figure 5-23   *The P-38 will land in a tail-low attitude. The nose will settle on its nosewheel on its own.*

Figure 5-24   *On the Japanese airplanes (left), the compass is in the cockpit and is marked like a tape measure. On the U.S. airplanes (right), the compass is remotely mounted and the information shows in the cockpit on a round display with a needle.*

needle on its face. The needle shows the heading of the airplane. There was a second needle on the face of these instruments for radio navigation, but it's not used in Combat Flight Simulator 2.

Directional Gyroscope

There's another instrument in the U.S. cockpits that looks just like the Japanese compass, but it isn't a compass—it's a directional gyro. One of the problems with a compass is that it's often inaccurate while the airplane is turning, accelerating, or decelerating or when the airplane is in turbulence. An instrument called a directional gyroscope (DG) helps alleviate this problem. A spinning gyroscope will stay still in space, resisting any forces trying to move it. When the airplane starts up, its DG starts spinning. Attached to this spinning gyro is an indicator that displays compass directions. The pilot manually turns the DG indicator to point in the desired compass direction. As the plane flies, the spinning gyro remains pointed in the same direction and the DG shows the correct heading even while the airplane is turning, changing speed, or bouncing about in turbulence. As you can see in Figure 5-25, the DG in a U.S. airplane looks just like the compass in the Japanese airplane. Conversely, the DG in the Japanese airplane looks like the remote compass in the U.S. airplane. Magnetic compass errors are modeled in Combat Flight Simulator 2, so keep your eye on the DG when flying.

> **Note:** *In real airplanes, the DG does slowly drift off course and must be realigned with the compass every 15 minutes or so. This drift is not modeled in Combat Flight Simulator 2, so it's not a concern. If you're flying the George, you must use the compass because the George has no DG.*

Figure 5-25 *The U.S. DG (right) looks like the Japanese compass, and the Japanese DG (left) looks like the U.S. remote compass.*

Artificial Horizon

When flying in clouds or at night with few light sources, the pilot cannot see a horizon and determining which way is up becomes quite difficult. As you can see in Figure 5-26, the artificial horizon shows this information in the cockpit, using a gyroscope to determine orientation. The artificial horizons in the Japanese Zeros are painted so that the sky is blue and the ground is black, making the instrument easy to interpret. (The Japanese were ahead of the Americans in this area.) The U.S. instrument shows a white line for the

horizon, with black above and below. The side representing the sky has a white tick mark pointing straight up. This instrument can be far more confusing than its Japanese counterpart. Interestingly, the Japanese George has a black-over-black artificial horizon just like the U.S. airplanes. The reason for this is still unclear.

Figure 5-26 *The artificial horizon provides the pilot with a way to keep the airplane upright when the real horizon is obscured.*

Turn and Bank Indicator and Inclinometer

As you can see in Figure 5-27, the turn and bank indicator is actually two instruments in one. The needle shows the direction of a turn and the rate of a turn. The faster the turn, the farther the needle will deflect. The rate of turn really isn't a concern to you in combat—your turns will often be at a rate off the scale for the turn and bank indicator. The second instrument on the same face is the inclinometer, or slip/skid indicator. This instrument tells you if you're using your flight controls in the proper coordination. You read this instrument as you would read a carpenter's level. If the black ball is in the center, the controls are coordinated. If the ball is off to one side, they're not.

Figure 5-27 *The turn and bank indicator and the inclinometer appear on the same face.*

Vertical Speed Indicator

The vertical speed indicator (VSI) shows your rate of climb or descent. The American gauges read in thousands of feet per minute, and the Japanese gauges read in hundreds of meters per minute. (One thousand meters per minute is about 3280 feet per minute.) This instrument is useful in instrument flying, but it's also useful in verifying your rate of descent as you come in to land. A normal rate of descent for landing is 400–600 feet per minute (121–183 meters per minute). As shown in Figure 5-28, the needle can show rates of climb or descent. If the needle is on zero, the airplane is in level flight.

Figure 5-28 *The vertical speed indicator shows rates of climb or descent.*

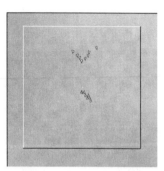

Figure 5-29 *The Tactical Display window shows you both friendly and enemy aircraft, vessels, and ground equipment in an approximately 6000-yard radius.*

Combat Flight Simulator 2 Special Items

Tactical Display

The Tactical Display takes most of the guesswork out of determining the enemy's location. The Tactical Display is helpful in maintaining awareness of the locations of other airplanes in combat, and it can also locate an aircraft carrier awaiting your landing. F9 toggles the Tactical Display on and off. As you can see in Figure 5-29, the Tactical Display window appears as a transparent square in the upper left of the screen, showing the area in an approximately 6000-yard radius around your airplane. You're always the yellow dot in the center. Enemies will appear in red and friendlies in green. Surface targets can also appear on the Tactical Display. There are four modes for the display, denoted by a letter in the upper left corner:

- **G** All ground targets
- **V** Vehicles only
- **S** Ships only
- **None** Air targets only

To cycle through the different Tactical Display modes, press M. When there are no enemies in the area, the Tactical Display will also display the course to fly for your next waypoint as a blue or green line.

Labels

Aircraft labels show the type, distance, and allegiance of any aircraft in your field of view. Press N to toggle labels on and off. As in the Tactical Display, enemy targets are red, and friendlies are green by default. To change the color of enemy labels, press Shift+V; to change the color of friendly labels, press Ctrl+V. The label text shows the distance in yards and what the target is. Labels, as you can see in Figure 5-30, are useful for locating targets, since the label will appear full size even if the target is too far away to see. You'll find the distance label extremely helpful in combat.

Note: *An airplane will always be just beneath the center of the text in the label. At a distance the airplane is often difficult to see.*

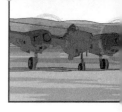

Position Display

Pressing Shift+Z once calls up the position display, showing position in latitude and longitude, altitude above sea level, heading, and speed. This information is superimposed on your screen near the top of the window. You can use this information for navigation or to record the location of a specific place. Figure 5-31 shows the position display.

Flying on Instruments

You'll rely on your instruments alone to fly your fighter at times when you can't see the horizon. You'll rarely need to fly on instruments for long while playing Combat Flight Simulator 2, but sometimes it will be necessary. A mission starting before dawn would require an instrument takeoff. The clouds are great hiding

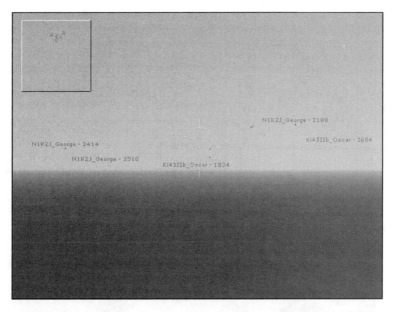

Figure 5-30 *Labels are an excellent way both to identify aircraft and vessels and to see their distances from you.*

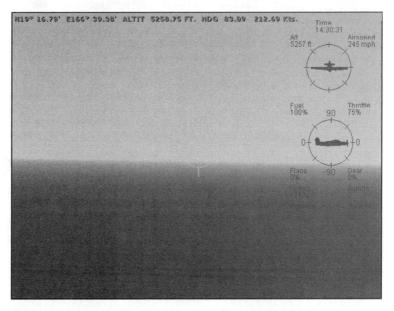

Figure 5-31 *Pressing Shift+Z shows your position, altitude, heading, and air speed.*

Figure 5-32 *The top view shows the horizon obscured by cloud. The bottom view is exactly the same position but with the horizon visible.*

places in combat, but staying upright within clouds requires flying on instruments.

During the short times you're flying on instruments, your focus should be on the attitude indicator. This instrument replaces the horizon that you cannot see for some reason or another. Flying by the attitude indicator takes some practice, especially with the black-over-black types that are in the U.S. fighters. Remember to look for the small tick mark at the top of the instrument that always points up. Figure 5-32 shows the view of the same situation with the horizon visible and the horizon obscured. A little practice popping in and out of the clouds is all you really need.

Chapter Six

COMBAT FLIGHT TRAINING

Success in combat—in both real and virtual aircraft—relies on a mixture of tactics, skill, aggression, ingenuity, and luck. Of these five items, all but luck will improve with training and experience. However, only one item, tactics, can actually be taught. The next two chapters present the what, how, and why of aerial combat tactics and maneuvers. I've included several example maneuvers to illustrate certain points, but many more possibilities are out there. Over time, you'll develop a set of maneuvers that works for you, your airplane, and your wingmen. This set of maneuvers will become the tactics that you carry into combat. A Japanese combat training document captured on Saipan in 1943 summed up this idea well:

> In close combat, achieve mastery of the tactics which are your own strong points. After gradually reaching proficiency, you will discover your own characteristics in battle. When you fight with your favorite tactics, victory will be easy. When you become aware of these tactics, study and master them at once. When in battle, it is important to entice the enemy into your favorite battle tactics.

It's also important to keep in mind the goal of fighter airplanes: fighter aircraft exist to provide use of the sky to friendly forces and to deny use of the sky to the enemy. Although many fighter airplanes can carry bombs and torpedoes, there are better airplanes for those tasks, so those roles are secondary. Your job is aerial control, and the primary method you have for maintaining this control is putting your guns on enemy targets and promptly removing them from your personal piece of the sky.

Weapons

Since weight is a critical factor in airplane performance, the necessary compromise in weaponry is usually a balance between number of shots delivered and the lethality of each shot. Machine guns deliver many shots, or rounds, per second, but each bullet does little damage unless it happens to hit a critical area.

Enough bullet strikes will down an airplane. Cannon fire much larger, heavier shells that explode on contact. Only a few cannon hits are needed to destroy an airplane, but the shots do not travel as far, and making a hit is more difficult. Since cannon rounds weigh more than bullets, the airplane cannot carry as many. When firing a cannon with a limited ammo supply, you need to make as many rounds count as possible. Projectiles can be described by diameter in millimeters or in inches. Caliber actually refers to hundredths of inches; so .50 caliber rounds are .5 inches in diameter. All the American player-flyable airplanes, except the P-38, carry only .50 caliber machine guns. The two Zeros and the P-38 carry a combination of machine guns and cannon; however, the Zeros' machine guns are a lighter .303 caliber compared to the P-38's .50 caliber guns. The George carries cannon only. In Microsoft Combat Flight Simulator 2, all the player-flyable aircraft have fixed, forward-firing guns. The guns are all set to converge at approximately 300 yards. Details of each type of gun are found in Chapter 11, "Machines of War," of the Combat Flight Simulator 2 documentation.

Note: *To help poorer shots make a hit, some U.S. aircraft had their guns aligned to create a spread of bullets, similar to a shotgun. This configuration increased the likelihood of a hit but decreased the hit's damage potential.*

Bombs, Rockets, and Drop-Tanks

All of the player-flyable airplanes can carry some combination of ordinance and extra fuel under their wings. Weight is always a limiting factor in aviation however, so if you need to carry extra fuel in drop-tanks, you may not be able to carry heavy bombs or rockets. Not every airplane can carry every weapon either. Rockets are only available on the Wildcat, the Hellcat, and the Corsair. The drop-down menu marked Loadout will show you the available options for your selected airplane.

Using Views

One of the most important aspects of combat flying is situational awareness. Approaching airports and carriers requires use of lateral views. These views are important, but the key views will be the 45-degree-up view (shown in Figure 6-1) and the straight-up view. As seen in Figure 6-2, your enemy will often end up in this part of your field of vision during maneuvering; you'll need to slowly work the enemy into your forward field of view to gain an advantage. Once you have an enemy in the forward view, you can get him into your sights. It takes practice to successfully switch from one view to another and remain oriented.

Figure 6-1 *The 45-degree-up views are key to keeping sight of your enemy while maneuvering for position.*

Padlock View

You can use Padlock view (shown in Figure 6-3) to have the computer automatically choose the correct view to keep sight of the enemy. To use Padlock view, first press Tab. This will engage the Padlock function, and a set of yellow bars will appear around the target. If more than one target is available, you can cycle forward through the targets using Tab or cycle backward through the targets with Shift+Tab. Once you have the chosen target padlocked, press ` (the key above Tab on your keyboard) and your view will switch to Virtual Cockpit and

Note: *Your views to the right, left, forward, and back are assigned to a hat switch on your joystick by default. It can help a great deal to program all the 45-degree-up views to either a hat switch or to the keypad without a modifier key so that you can easily access these views in combat. (By default, the 45-degree-up views require holding down the Control key while pressing a key on the numeric keypad with Num Lock engaged.) To customize these assignments, go to the settings screen, click Controller Assignments, and select View Commands from the Event Category drop-down list box. Now you can change the assignment of any view command to whatever keyboard or joystick button that you want.*

will automatically follow the target. The disadvantage of this view is that it can be hard to figure out where you're looking and therefore distracting. Padlock view also tends to make you fixate on your target, rather than remain vigilant for enemies targeting you and for other shots of opportunity.

Enemy Indicator

Another option you can use with the padlock function is the enemy indicator, illustrated in Figure 6-4. To use this function, engage the padlock on the selected target and then press U. A yellow cone will point in the direction of the selected enemy. This function can be helpful in showing you where to look, allowing you to manually choose a view for that direction. Using the enemy indicator allows you to split your attention between following the enemy and watching where you're going. Pressing U a second time will toggle off the enemy indicator.

Virtual Cockpit View

Virtual Cockpit can be helpful in the initial stages of combat, when you're searching for the enemy. Virtual Cockpit view allows you to scan the sky in a natural manner; you can pan smoothly from inside the cockpit in a manner that's similar to turning your head. Once you're engaged with enemy air-

Figure 6-2   *Use your 45-degree-up views to keep your enemy in sight until they are brought in line with your gunsights. Keep checking ahead so that you don't forget in which direction you're flying.*

craft, however, it usually responds too slowly to meet the demands of combat. You can get to Virtual Cockpit view by pressing S once. To look around, use your joystick's hat button or the keyboard commands listed in Table 6-1.

View	Keystroke Combination
Pan left	Ctrl+Shift+Backspace
Pan right	Ctrl+Shift+Enter
Pan up	Shift+Backspace
Pan down	Shift+Enter
Snap to front view	Ctrl+Spacebar
Snap to rear view	Ctrl+Shift+Spacebar
Zoom in	Equal Sign (=)
Zoom out	Hyphen (-)
Zoom normal (1x)	Backspace

Table 6-1   *The keyboard shortcuts used to control the view from the Virtual Cockpit.*

Combat Scan vs. Normal Scan

In a noncombat situation, you must divide your attention between tasks inside the cockpit—such as checking the operation of the engine, switching fuel tanks, and calculating courses for navigation—and scanning outside the cockpit to maintain awareness and avoid collision. In combat, you still have all these tasks, but you also must remain aware of the dangers around you. Your awareness of the world outside the aircraft now must include looking for the

Figure 6-3   *Padlock view enables you to follow a selected aircraft automatically.*

enemy's hiding places. Attacking from the direction of the sun and from be-hind clouds are two common ploys to close in on a target without being seen. Another part of your scan might be a bomber or torpedo group you're escort-ing. When flying alongside slower aircraft, you must keep your speed high for potential combat. This actually provides an excellent opportunity to keep checking the area behind you. Imagine you're flying high cover above a bomber group. You keep your speed up by weaving back and forth. Each time you pass over the escorted airplanes, look over your right wing, look ahead, and look over your left wing. You have just checked three out of four quad-rants of the sky. When you reverse direc-tion over the escorted airplanes, make the same check to cover the rest of the sky. When you're centered over the bombers it's a good time to check above, and while you're banking in the turns it's a good time to look below.

Combat Tip #6: *Even while flying only in a formation of fighters, keep checking the six o'clock position. You can calculate how often to weave and check behind you if you know how far out you can see the enemy and how close they can come before they start shooting. If you can see enemy aircraft at 1000 yards and you assume that they won't fire until they are within 300 yards, you have 700 yards to detect their presence. Assume that since they're attacking they have already built up a speed advantage by attacking from above or in faster aircraft. If they have the speed advantage of 60 knots, they're moving 100 feet per second. Seven hundred yards is 2100 feet, so with the enemy gaining on you at 100 feet per second, they'll move from visual detection range into firing range in 21 seconds. If you check behind and above you every 15 to 20 seconds, you should see any enemy airplane before it's close enough to take a shot.*

Tactical Display and Labels

The Tactical Display and labels available in Combat Flight Simulator 2 take most of the guesswork out of locating the enemy. As I mentioned in Chapter 5, "Takeoffs, Landings, and Advanced Flying," enemies appear in red and friendlies in green. You are always the yellow dot in the cen-ter. On the Tactical Display, a padlocked target also appears in yellow, and a dead enemy that is still falling to earth appears in black. Remember that the Tactical Dis-play shows only information on a single plane, so it says nothing about whether an enemy is above you or below you.

The distance measurement on the label is also helpful when you judge closure rate between you and the target. Controlling the rate of closure is important in the early stages of combat. On missions, labels will show the name of the squadron, rather than the type of airplane, so you'll need to identify the airplane by its appearance. Recognition tips for all the Combat Flight Simulator 2 airplanes appear in Chapter 10, "Player-Flyable Aircraft," and Chapter 11, "Non-Player-Flyable Aircraft."

Judging Distance

Combat pilots 60 years ago did not have labels to help them judge their distances from other aircraft. They used experience and the size of objects relative to their gunsights. Most of the fighters in Combat Flight Simulator 2 are similar in size, so gunsight ranges work pretty well for all the airplanes. (See Figure 6-5.) At 500 yards, a fighter takes up about 1/4 of the sight; at 250 yards, the fighter takes up about half the

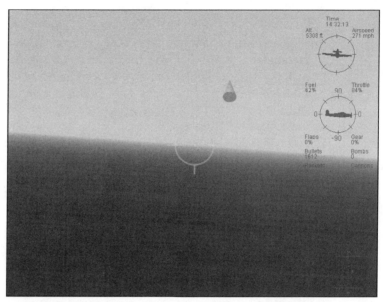

Figure 6-4   The enemy indicator will point to a selected aircraft–in this case, it's above and in front of you. Using the enemy indicator, you can momentarily choose the view you need without losing track of what's in front of your own airplane.

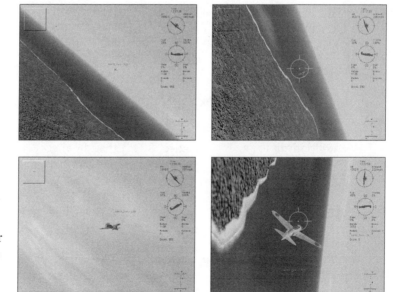

Figure 6-5   You can use the gunsight to judge the distance to a target, even without the help of labels.

sight and is now in range. Depending on your relative position to the fighter, you might want to hold your fire and continue to maneuver for a better shot. At 100 yards, the fighter will fill the sight and its wingtips will reach the extensions off the sides of the sight. This is usually a good time for a shot. At 50 yards, the shot is a sure thing. At such close range, you should try for a kill on the cockpit or to shoot off the tail. On a Zero, you can also go for a wing tank and watch the explosion. When you're less than 100 yards from the target, be careful not to fly into a broken piece of your enemy as you disassemble his airplane with your gunfire. Flying debris will cause collateral damage to your airplane. Also be ready for an aircraft to maneuver suddenly when its pilot realizes the airplane is taking damage.

Flight Exercise: Targeting Distance

Go to Quick Combat, and choose any airplane to fly. Make your enemy a C-47. The C-47 is a twin-engine, unarmed transport that can't maneuver very well. Set the tactical situation as Advantaged. Press N to toggle labels on if they are off. Fly the scenario. Watch the size of the C-47 in your sights, and double-check against the label. The C-47 is much larger than a fighter, so it will appear to fill more of the sight at a particular distance than the fighters will. Since it's unarmed and poorly maneuverable, it's good for practice. Close on the C-47 from several angles, and try to estimate the distance with the labels turned off. Turn on the label to verify your guess. Once you have the knack, try this exercise with fighter airplanes.

Combat Theory

Combat theory is one of those things that sounds great on paper but can be difficult to put into practice. It isn't that the theory doesn't apply. You can find many texts that accurately describe the techniques that separate the aces from the rookies. The problem is that the best pilots have a feel for what they need to do in combat rather than a formula. The following list best sums up their principles of battle:

- Be aggressive.
- Maintain high airspeed.
- Turn to face your adversary whenever possible.
- Keep your lift vector—that is, the top of your wings—pointed at the enemy.

- Surprise the enemy if at all possible. Attack from the sun or from behind clouds.
- Be patient.
- Fight your battle, not theirs.
- If you find yourself in a dogfight, you've already messed up.
- If you don't win early on, escape and live to fight another day.

These are all excellent words to live by (and in combat we do mean live), but none of these words of wisdom help you actually put your guns on the target. Guns on target is the fundamental goal of any type of combat flying that doesn't involve air-to-air missiles. Guns on target means that the ultimate goal of your offensive maneuvers is to create a shot opportunity. To achieve guns on target, you go through a process that can be broken down into four steps: detection, pursuit, engagement, and disengagement.

Detection

In this stage, you're still searching for the enemy or you've found the enemy but haven't yet chosen to attack. Since you don't yet have a target for your guns, your main objective is to keep your guns' potential motion as free as possible. This includes flying in formation with enough space to maneuver, searching all quadrants to prevent surprises and give you more time to maneuver, and acquiring more E whenever practical to give you more energy with which to maneuver.

Prioritization and Threat Assessment

Once you have your targets, you must decide how high a priority their destruction is and the level of danger they pose. The first decision comes back to your mission goals. Both in the real Pacific theater and in the Combat Flight Simulator 2 campaigns, achieving the mission goals is your first priority; anything that compromises your mission should be questioned. The more complicated mission environment in Combat Flight Simulator 2 allows a mission designer to put enticing traps into the mission. For example, if your mission is to torpedo an enemy ship, the mission design might include two or three opportunities to engage a small band of enemy fighters that your squadron easily outnumbers. However, if you attack these enemy fighters, the ship you were to torpedo might spawn a large band of fighters and move to a new location. When you approach your target, the fighters will be airborne and ready rather than caught off guard. If your mission goals are best served by engaging the enemy, you can move on to threat assessment.

When assessing a threat, you must again consider mission goals. The greatest threats are the enemy targets that jeopardize the completion of your mission. The next greatest threats are targets that could destroy large resources, such as your ships or airbases. A dive-bomber, about to drop down on one of your ships, is more of a threat than a single fighter, even though that fighter poses a greater threat to you personally. Your personal safety is still part of the threat assessment. Aircraft that have a better chance of shooting you down pose a greater threat. If you're a Hellcat squadron, the three Georges on the horizon are a bigger threat than the four Zeros. This threat is tempered, however, by the ease of making a quick kill. If you can dispatch three of the Zeros before the Georges get in range, you've reduced the number of people shooting at you and bettered your odds of survival. Even a rookie in an inferior airplane gets in a lucky shot once in a while.

Pursuit

Once you've chosen your target and begun to close the distance, you're in pursuit. (Pursuit is what the P stands for in P-38.) The purpose of the pursuit phase is to achieve guns on target from the most favorable position possible given the circumstances. Success in the pursuit phase sets the stage for a successful attack. Your method of pursuit will, in part, determine how rapidly you close on your target, the angle at which you close on your target, and the E you have available as you close on your target. You have three kinds of pursuit to choose from: pure pursuit, lead pursuit, and lag pursuit.

Combat Position Terminology

When describing relative position, it's helpful to have a few agreed-upon terms to ensure everyone gets the same picture in their minds. Here are a few common terms:

- **Head-to-head** This refers to two airplanes with their noses pointed at each other, although they might be at different altitudes.
- **Nose-to-tail** This is when one airplane has its nose pointed at the other airplane's tail, though again, they might not be at the same altitude.
- **Angle Off Nose (AON)/ Angle Off Tail (AOT)** This describes in greater detail the relative position of two airplanes. For example, if you were directly behind another airplane flying in the same direction, you would be Head-to-tail with an AOT of 0 degrees. If you were diving at

a 45-degree angle on another airplane but flying in the same direction, you would be head-to-tail with an AOT of 45 degrees. If you were lined up directly with an opponent's wing, you wouldn't be head-to-head or nose-to-tail, but you would have an AOT (or AON) of 90 degrees.

- **Angular advantage**   This is the measure of AOT for the airplane in the stronger position. If you are 45 degrees off your opponent's tail, you have a 45-degree angular advantage. If they were 45 degrees off your tail, they would have the 45-degree angular advantage. Angular advantage is always measured off the tail, so if you had your guns on your opponent and were 45 degrees off his nose, you would have a 135-degree angular advantage because your AOT was 135 degrees.

- **Rate of closure**   This is the rate at which the distance between two airplanes decreases. Two airplanes converging head-to-head will have a high rate of closure, while one airplane slowly gaining on another from behind will have a low rate of closure.

- **Twelve o'clock high**   When you describe the position of another airplane, you use the clock positions to give the direction around you horizontally and then add high, low, or true (at your altitude) to add the vertical direction. One of the hardest parts of combat to the new pilot is to think in three dimensions.

- **Crossing**   As two airplanes converge, pass each other, and separate, there's a point at which they are closest to each other. That is the point of crossing. What is important here is that crossing does not mean the airplanes met at the same spot at the same time. Suppose you're flying north and closing with another airplane flying west. The westbound airplane now moves from your two-o'clock position to your twelve o'clock position to your ten o'clock position. The brief moment when the other airplane was in your twelve-o'clock position was the crossing. Whenever two airplanes cross, at least one of the airplanes can maneuver for a shot opportunity.

- **Horizontal and vertical separation**   When two airplanes cross, there's always some distance between them horizontally, vertically, or both. If there were no horizontal or vertical separation at a cross then the airplanes would collide. In combat, as you close on an opponent with the intention of crossing, you'll maneuver to either increase or decrease separation, depending on the combat tactics you want to use.

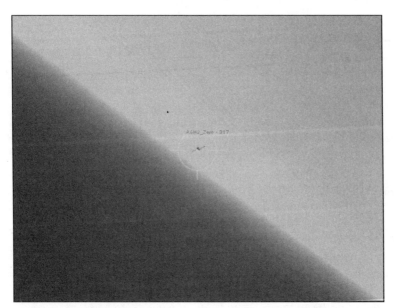

Figure 6-6   *Pure pursuit is the simplest pursuit: just put your sight on the target and close the distance.*

Figure 6-7   *Pure pursuit also includes head-to-head approaches.*

Pure Pursuit

Pure pursuit is simply pointing your nose directly at your target and moving in, as shown in Figures 6-6 and 6-7. Pure pursuit works well when the target has little lateral motion, meaning it is not rapidly climbing, descending, or turning. Two examples of this are closing from directly behind the enemy and closing head-to-head. If your airplane and the enemy airplane have comparable performance, pure pursuit also puts you in the best position to follow any evasive maneuvers the enemy tries to perform.

With a head-to-head approach or a nose-to-tail approach from the enemy's 6 o'clock, pure pursuit will ultimately end in a collision. When you make a pure pursuit approach from the side, you need to continually

adjust your course in the direction the target is moving to keep it in your sights. In the last dozen yards, the rate at which you must turn to keep up with the target will exceed your airplane's capabilities and you will overshoot. Pure pursuit to very close range is only practical from directly behind a target.

Lead Pursuit

In lead pursuit, you point your nose ahead of the target. Lead pursuits are usually used while turning—see Figure 6-8—but also apply to closing on an aircraft from the side. Lead pursuit has two advantages: it has the most rapid closure time, and it allows you to maintain a shot opportunity by training your guns on a point directly ahead of your target. When performing a lead pursuit in a turn, you must have a smaller turning radius than

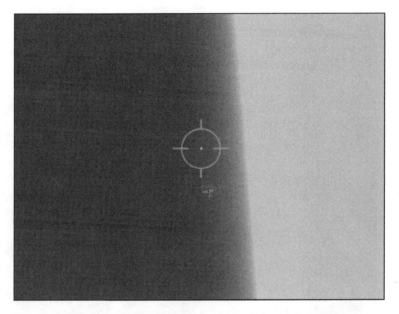

Figure 6-8   *Lead pursuit provides the fastest closure but requires a smaller turn radius. Lead pursuit also keeps your guns in position to make a shot if you lose the lead.*

your target, but you don't need to be moving as quickly to still converge. Picture yourself in a Zero on the 6 o'clock position of a Wildcat but still out of shooting range. The Wildcat turns left and you follow, but you aim for a position ahead of the Wildcat. As you both turn, your Zero is actually traveling in a smaller diameter circle and the distance between the two airplanes will close even if they are traveling the same speed. Essentially, you're "heading him off at the pass." As you close in lead pursuit, you're increasing your AOT in relation to the Wildcat. If that doesn't make sense, remember that you're constantly aiming for a spot in front of the other airplane. Eventually you would move into that spot so long as both airplanes kept turning. You wouldn't take the lead pursuit that far. Once you got within range, you would relax the lead angle a bit and let your guns move into position for a shot. High lead pursuits can result in very rapid closure. One danger in a lead pursuit is that closure on the target can be so rapid it results in an overshoot, putting you in the role of target.

Lag Pursuit

Lag pursuit involves putting your nose behind the enemy airplane, as shown in Figures 6-9 and 6-10. This approach sounds ineffective, but it has several advantages: It is the slowest method for closing on the target, and with aircraft of comparable speed the rate of closure will slow as the two aircraft converge. Even though rate of closure slows down, continued lag pursuit decreases your AOT (improving your position at the target aircraft's six o'clock), thereby reducing the danger of an overshoot. Lag pursuit is most useful when you're faster than your target. If you're in a P-38 diving on a Zero that is slightly ahead of you, initially making a lag pursuit is a good choice. Lag pursuit can be skillfully used even by a slower aircraft, because the distance traveled by the pursuing airplane is slightly shorter. Lag pursuit also keeps the enemy slightly above your airplane rather than below it. This positions helps keep the enemy

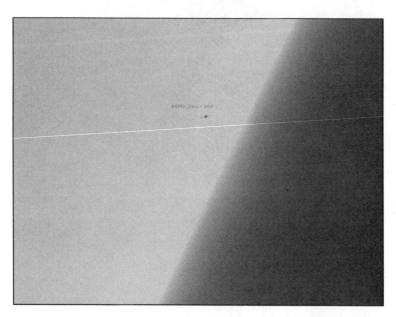

Figure 6-9   *Lag pursuit offers slower closure rates and steadily works you behind your target.*

in the viewing area you want and makes escape maneuvering more difficult. There's a danger in a lag pursuit of an airplane with a tight turning radius, such as in the Zero and P-38 match up. If the enemy turns inside your turn, he can gain an advantage. You'll know this is happening when the distance your sight lags behind the target steadily increases. This is a warning that you need to change your tactics. Lag pursuit never provides a shot opportunity by itself. The goal of lag pursuit is to get into a position where the AOT is low and a pure or lead pursuit can be taken for a shot.

Lag and lead pursuits work for closing on the target from any angle and will have roughly the same effect. These same principles apply even when converging nearly head-on.

In practice, all the pursuit techniques are used in conjunction. For example, you might first pursue an enemy Hellcat in pure pursuit to judge its distance and then in lead pursuit to close quickly so you can make a shot with the cannon of your George. As you close, you decide the Hellcat hasn't seen

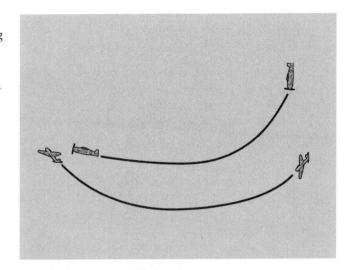

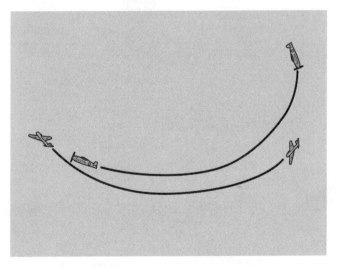

Figure 6-10   *Both lead (top) and lag (bottom) pursuits result in closure because of shorter distances traveled by the pursuer.*

Combat Tip #7: *One of the biggest mistakes a pilot can make in lead and lag pursuits is following with too much angle of bank. Often the lead or lag position can be maintained with less bank and more speed. When in pursuit, use the smallest amount of bank necessary to get the job done.*

you yet, so you switch to lag pursuit to slowly move into a better position and extend the time available to put your guns on target. From the close six o'clock position you pull into a pure pursuit and with your guns on target blast the tail of the Hellcat clean off the airplane. Table 6-2 gives the key points of each pursuit.

Type of Pursuit	Advantages	Disadvantages
Pure pursuit	• Easiest.	• Poor shot opportunity from sides.
	• Good closing time.	• At high AOT, requires rapid increase in rate of turn at close distance.
	• Best for head-on or tail-on attacks.	
Lead pursuit	• Fastest closure.	• Highest risk of overshoot.
	• Best shot opportunity.	
Lag pursuit	• Moves you toward opponent's tail.	• Slowest closure.
	• Least likely to overshoot.	• Vulnerable to a tighter-turning opponent.
	• Hardest to escape.	• No shot opportunity without switching to another form of pursuit.
	• Can be used to slow closure when needed.	

Table 6-2   *The three types of pursuit.*

Flight Exercise: Lead Pursuit and Lag Pursuit

Go to Quick Combat, and fly a Zero against a Wildcat. Set the enemy to Rookie and the tactical situation to Advantaged so that you're above and behind the enemy. Now set up straight, lead, and lag pursuits to see the effect of each. Figure 6-11 illustrates establishing a position with lag pursuit, switching to lead pursuit, and letting the enemy fly into the line of fire.

Engagement

As you close within firing range, you're ready to engage. It is possible, but quite difficult, to consistently score a hit at a distance of 1000 yards. As you close in pursuit you must decide when to fire. Remember that your target might be unaware of your presence, and once alerted will cease to allow you to pursue so easily. Use this pursuit time to get properly lined up with your opponent to make a good tracking shot.

Tracking Shots

A tracking shot is any shot that affords you the ability to establish aim before your shot and the ability to readjust your aim while shooting. The best angles for tracking with the fixed sights in the player-flyable aircraft are between 0 and 30 degrees AOT. To get a good tracking shot you need to be "in plane" with the target. (In plane means that the lift vectors of your wings point in the same direction as those of your target.) If the bars off the sides of your gunsight are parallel to the other airplane's wings, you are in plane. To position yourself for a good tracking shot, get into the rear hemisphere of your target. Next establish sight parallel to the other airplane's wings and pull your gunsight to a pure pursuit or a lead pursuit. Readjust your airplane's attitude to stop all relative motion. Now relax the lead angle as you fire, allowing the enemy to fly into the line of fire.

Pulling Lead

A bullet moves at a rate of 2500 to 3000 feet per second. That means that if you fire on a target 900 yards away, the bullet takes only 1 second to reach its target. During this second, the bullet is being pulled down by gravity, and in 1 second the bullet drops 16 feet. Thus if your guns are right on target when you

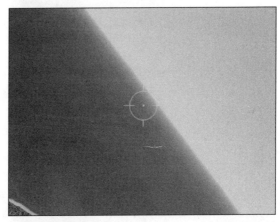

Figure 6-11   *An example of both lead and lag pursuit in a combat maneuver.*

fire, the bullets actually falls 16 feet below your intended target. The effect of gravity causes fewer problems as you close on the target. At 300 yards, the drop is less than 3 feet. Even at close range, the effect is worse with turns. A shot fired directly at a target only 300 yards away but in a 3-G turn will miss by 8 feet. The answer to this problem is to "pull lead." This means putting your crosshairs ahead of your target. How much lead to give a target depends on distance, rate of turn, size of target, and type of weapon used. Figure 6-12 shows the tracers striking the tail of the Corsair even with a large lead, while the B-25 required only enough lead above the target to account for the drop of the bullets over the distance. The following are the biggest factors in estimating lead:

- The farther you are from a target, the farther above and in front of the target you must fire.
- A target crossing your path at 90 degrees requires much more lead than a target only 10 to 20 degrees off your nose.
- The harder you turn (more Gs), the farther in front of the target you must fire.
- The larger the target, the more it will fill your gunsight and the less lead you'll need.
- Japanese cannon require slightly more lead in front of and above a target because of their slower projectiles. The cannon on the Japanese fighters can require 50 percent more lead than machine guns on the same airplane.

Note: *Tracers are bullets with a coating that burns brightly while in flight, showing you the actual path of your shots. Tracers help with your aim but also give away your position.*

Distance and crossing angle are the greatest factors in calculating how much to lead a target. For both of these, you'll use your gunsight to judge how much lead is needed.

There are no lead computing sights on any of the Combat Flight Simulator 2 airplanes, so judging lead is one skill you must master.

Flight Exercise: Deflection Shooting

As in the previous exercise, go to Quick Combat and choose a Zero vs. Wildcat with an advantaged position. Once you close in to guns range, pull lead on the enemy and shoot. Adjust your lead as necessary to get hits. Fire short bursts instead of continuous fire to better see the effects of using different amounts of

lead. If the enemy is not turning, a short burst of machine gun fire to the tail will usually get him to turn. Try this exercise against other airplanes.

Snapshots

In many situations, maneuvering for a tracking shot is impossible. In these instances, you get only a brief chance for a shot before you need to maneuver again for a second chance. These are *snapshot shots*, or *snapshots*. Because snapshots almost always occur at high AOT and rapid rates of closure, they will almost always need some amount of lead and require excellent timing. Picture the scenario where the enemy airplane starts in your two o'clock position, passes in front of your nose, and ends up in your ten o'clock position. As the enemy passes in front of your nose you have a snapshot opportunity, but you must actually begin firing before the enemy reaches the twelve o'clock position. The best thing to do is to start your burst of fire early and allow the target to fly into your line of fire. Take note of when your shots actually strike home to learn how to better estimate the lead requirement for a snapshot. Figure 6-13 shows two examples of snapshots. One firing advantage you have with a snapshot opportunity is that the high relative motion between you and your target makes it more difficult for the target to maneuver to avoid your fire.

Deflection Shooting and the Grumman Wildcat

In the years before the outbreak of war in the Pacific, the U.S. Navy began to educate its fighter pilots in the art of pulling lead, otherwise know as deflection shooting. Although deflection shooting was something the best combat pilots learned instinctively, only the U.S. Navy trained in this technique explicitly. Part of what made this possible was the Wildcat cockpit configuration, which allowed the pilot to see 8 degrees down over the nose. This downward view allowed the Wildcat pilot to get his guns pointed ahead of the enemy flight path while still keeping the enemy aircraft in sight.

Combat Tip #8: *Large dogfights can be very exciting and also very lethal. The best way to survive one of these dynamic air battles and add to your kill score is to master deflection shooting and snapshots. Although outmaneuvering an enemy aircraft one on one is an important skill, the key to survival in a multiplane engagement is getting quick kills. As a general rule in large fights, try not to turn with any potential target for more than 180 degrees. Instead, keep checking your tactical display for other enemy planes that will be crossing your nose from another part of the fight. When you detect another enemy plane entering into this zone, switch off of your previous target and try to get a quick kill on the new target.*

The kind of a shot opportunity you'll have depends largely on your position relative to the enemy airplane and on your relative amounts of E. Figure 6-14 shows the relative positions for tracking shots and snapshots. When you have a large E advantage compared to your target, you're unlikely to be able to make a good tracking shot. Tracking requires a few seconds during which the two airplanes move in the same plane and at roughly the same speed. Extreme differences in E make every angle a snapshot. The outer circle in Figure 6-14 represents the maximum range at which you can make a hit; the inner circle represents the minimum range at which you can avoid debris after making a hit. The area between these circles is divided by whether a snapshot

Figure 6-12 *The amount you must lead your target is best decided through feel and experience. Tracers help show the actual path of your shots.*

or a tracking shot is most feasible. The type of shot you think you can make largely determines the tactics you use to maneuver into position.

Angles and Energy

Air combat has two core tactics: the angles fight and the energy fight. You must consider both tactics in any combat scenario, but one or the other will predominate. In general, the angle fighter relies on turning ability to gain a position for a tracking shot, while the energy fighter uses an energy advantage to establish a position for one or more snapshots.

The Angles Fight

The goal of the angles fight is to gain angular advantage. As two airplanes converge head-to-head, neither has an angular advantage. As the airplanes cross, there are two

Figure 6-13 *Snapshot firing opportunities require a well-timed burst of fire and some lead.*

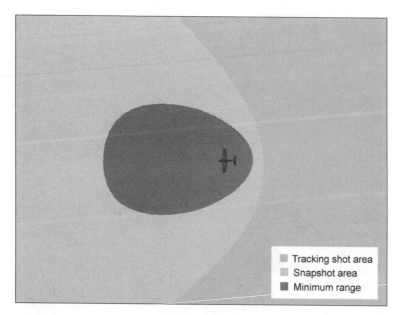

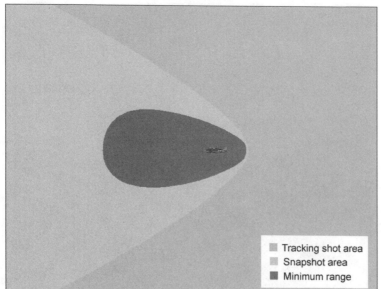

Figure 6-14 *Relative position and firing range determines whether your shot is a snapshot or a tracking shot.*

possible ways they can turn, relative to each other. They can turn in toward each other (nose to nose) or they can turn opposite each other (nose to tail). Either way, the airplanes will converge again, with the tighter-turning airplane, or the faster-turning airplane, at some angular advantage, as Figures 6-15 and 6-16 illustrate.

The angles fighter continues to cross paths with the enemy, slowly working toward an angular advantage of 90 degrees or more. The angles fighter also has an opportunity for a snapshot at some of these crosses. Once the target airplane crosses in front of the angles fighter at 90 degrees or more, the angles fighter can turn to follow the target airplane and establish a tracking shot from behind.

The angles fight is what we tend to think of when we imagine a dogfight and is the kind of fight that makes the most intuitive sense. Success in the angles fight requires you to have a quick-turning airplane and the ability to anticipate your opponent's moves, allowing you to turn early and gain an angular advantage. The danger in the angles fight is that all those turns drain your E. It's easy to get so preoccupied with out-turning your opponent that you find yourself stalling in the turn. Recovering from the stall requires you to abandon your turn and give up your hard-earned angular advantage. In the recovery, you are slow and not maneuverable. This kind of vulnerability can prove fatal in combat. Figures 6-17 through 6-20 illustrate the maneuvers of angles fighting.

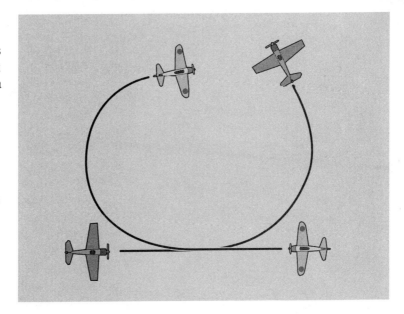

Figure 6-15   *The Zero and the Wildcat pass and turn head to head. The Zero turns in a smaller radius and gains angular advantage.*

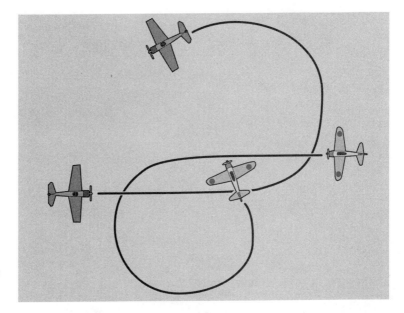

Figure 6-16   *The Zero and the Wildcat again pass head to head but this time turn nose to tail. The Zero turns at a faster rate and gains angular advantage.*

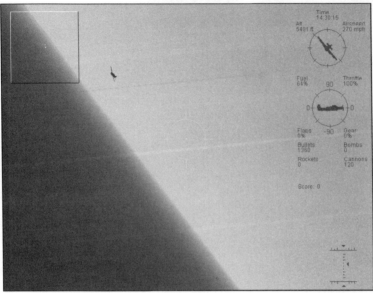

Figure 6-17 *Cross with separation and break left or right at the pass—or even slightly before the pass.*

Flight Exercise: Angles Fighting

To fly the scenario shown in Figures 6-17 through 6-20, go to Quick Combat and fly an A6M5 Zero against a Wildcat. In this match up, the Zero's excellent turning abilities should allow it to easily get behind the Wildcat and make a kill. Set the Enemy Position to Neutral (on the Enemies page) so that you pass head to head, and set the Enemy AI Level to Rookie so that the moves will be easier to execute. Make each cross with as much separation as possible, and use lead turns to gain angular advantage. Judge your angular advantage on your opponent, noting his position on the canopy. Try reversing

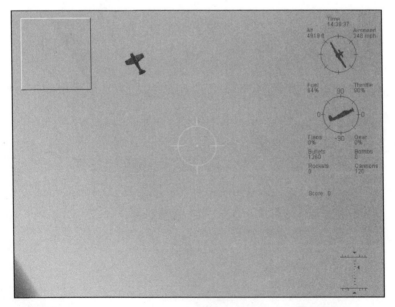

Figure 6-18 *Continue to turn steeply to work your way to greater angular advantage.*

roles and forcing an angles fight flying the Wildcat against the Zero. Try other matchups, and see which ones lend themselves to angles fighting.

The Energy Fight

The energy fight is a more difficult tactic and requires greater patience to make it pay off. The goal of the energy fighter is to continuously increase his E advantage over his opponent, which he does by getting the opponent to lose E faster. As the two airplanes cross, the angles fighter slowly gains angular advantage. This is acceptable to the energy fighter because gaining that advantage costs the angle fighter E. The energy fighter will continue to let the other airplane slowly gain angular advantage, as long as it also keeps losing E in the tight turns. At each cross, the energy fighter must maneuver

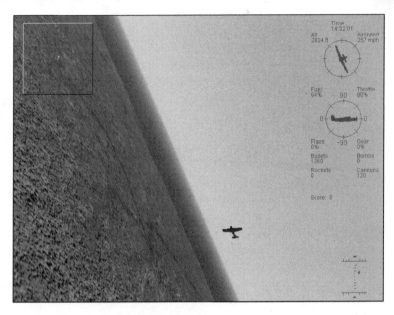

Figure 6-19   *When possible, turn hard to establish a tracking position. Use lead or lag pursuit as appropriate to close in.*

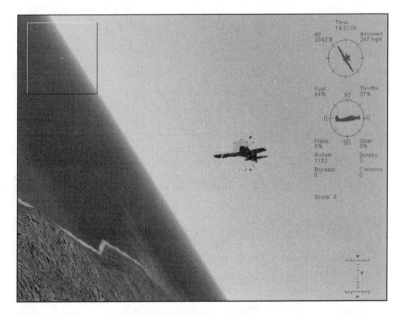

Figure 6-20   *Fire when in position and range.*

to prevent the angles fighter from getting a good snapshot. An energy fighter does this by varying the descent rate during the cross erratically and then climbing slightly after the cross while momentarily safe from the opponent's guns. After several crosses, there's a greater difference between the E levels of the two airplanes.

The only way to kill with nothing but an E advantage is by a midair collision. That might kill the enemy, but you don't live to brag about it. The energy fighter now has two options. One option is to use the energy difference to make a sudden reversal in angular advantage and then take a shot. If after one of the crosses the energy fighter pulls into a steep climb, the angles fighter now is in a bind. If he follows the energy fighter up, he will run out of E quickly and be a sitting duck when the energy fighter comes back down. If he doesn't follow the energy fighter up, the energy fighter will turn around and have a high attack from directly above. Either way, the energy fighter gets an excellent shot opportunity. Figures 6-21 through 6-25 illustrate gaining advantage in an energy fighter.

If you miss the target in the dive, you can pull out of the dive into another overhead attack or slip in behind the fighter for a brief tracking shot. You'll have a large speed advantage, so the shot opportunity will be short. Moving from a position of being tracked to a position of doing the tracking is known as a *reversal*. Essentially, the energy fighter built up a speed advantage so as to use that speed to create a reversal.

If the reversal is too difficult, the other option for the energy fighter is to use the E advantage to keep taking head-to-head snapshots and speeding out of

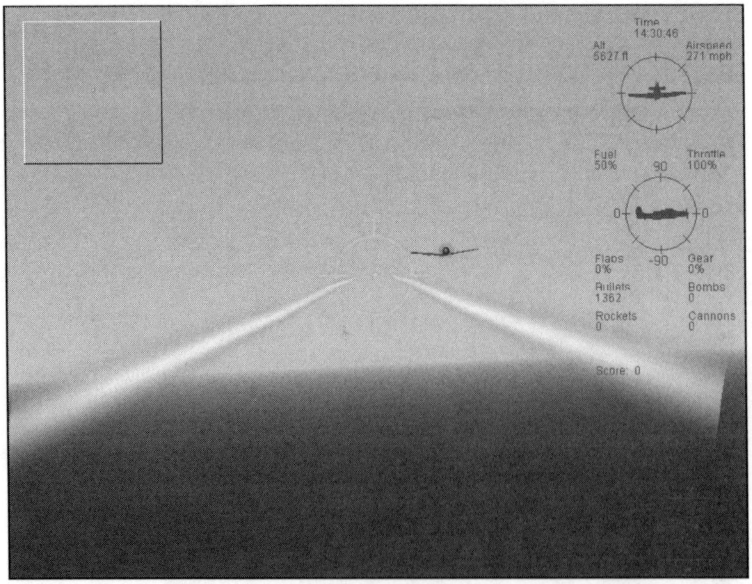

Figure 6-21   *Pass with little separation and always try for an early shot.*

range before the opponent can turn around. This strategy has the disadvantage of never providing anything but a snapshot, but it's much less complicated than executing a reversal.

Flight Exercise: Energy Fighting

To fly the scenario in Figures 6-21 through 6-25, go to Quick Combat and fly the Wildcat against an A6M5 Zero. The odds are definitely in the Zero's favor, but patience and practice will reward the energy fighter. Set the Tactical Situation to Neutral so that you pass head to head; set the Enemy AI Level to Rookie so that the moves will be easier to execute. Cross and re-cross with as little separation as possible, and

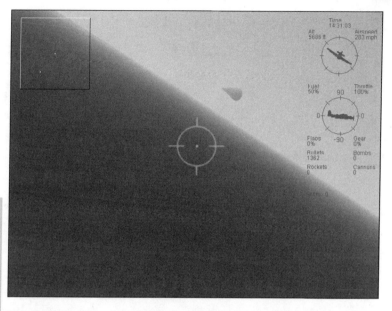

Figure 6-22 *Turn to face the enemy with a descending medium turn, preferably a nose-to-nose turn.*

Figure 6-23 *Cross and recross, allowing the Zero to reach an angular advantage by tight turns. Control your climbs, dives, and medium turns to maintain speed. The Zero in this picture is crossing behind at about 90 degrees AOT. The Wildcat has enough E advantage to pull up.*

Figure 6-24 *Before you lose too much speed, pull through inverted flight with your nose pointed in the direction of the enemy and find the enemy by looking through the top of the canopy.*

use shallow turns to maintain your E. When the Zero has 90 degrees or less angular advantage, fly upward and drop back down on your adversary from above. Try other matchups and other methods for making the energy fight pay off. Also try building up a large E difference and then using it to disengage. Finally, try starting the situation at a disadvantage and working your way back to a neutral situation and then to an advantage.

Choosing Your Tactics

Your tactics in battle will be determined largely by the matchup of the two fighters in the fight. In Combat Flight Simulator 2, the Zeros are the best angle fighters but they are poor energy fighters. The P-38 is an excellent energy fighter

Figure 6-25 *Roll into a diving attack on the side of the Zero. Use whatever controls needed to keep guns on target. Fire when in range.*

but a terrible angles fighter. The Wildcat is not particularly good at either tactic but isn't particularly bad at them either. (This is why Wildcat pilots need to use teamwork to have a chance against better Japanese pilots.) The Corsair is primarily an energy fighter—and a formidable one at that—but it can be flown either way. The most versatile fighters of the seven are the George and the Hellcat, which can be flown to a victory by using either core tactic. As you might imagine, the George and Hellcat matchup is one of the most interesting in Combat Flight Simulator 2.

> **Combat Tip #9:** *Often referred to as "slash and dash," the hit-and-run tactics used by Wildcat pilots early in the war worked well on the superior-turning Japanese Zero. To perform a slash and dash, start by climbing well above your adversary. Then dive down through the enemy formation, targeting only one aircraft. Take your high-speed deflection shot, break off, and continue diving away. Separate from the fight, and then climb back up and repeat the procedure. Getting the kill on the first pass will require some practice, but keep working on your deflection shooting and your slash-and-dash capability will soon become deadly.*

Of the two tactics, angle tactics are quicker and easier. Angle tactics usually work better for the low-skill attacker as well. With a particularly aggressive opponent, energy tactics might work better, since energy fighting is more likely to bleed off the opponent's E while he makes aggressive, tight turns. The best pilots can select aspects of both angles and energy fighting and use them as needed; as you play, you'll gain this skill. Here are the core tactics in a nutshell:

- Angle fighters use turns to gain position for a tracking shot.
- Energy fighters build an E difference (altitude, airspeed, and engine powr) to gain a position for a snapshot or brief tracking shot.

Turn Performance

No matter what tactics you use in combat, your success will be tied to how well you turn. In Chapter 4, "Flight Theory and Practice for the Combat Cadet," you saw how turning worked in an airplane. You also saw that all turns cost some E and the more radical the turn, the more E it costs. What I left out of this picture was the effectiveness of different turns—turn performance varies widely with pilot technique. Two identical airplanes can deliver radically different levels of performance if flown only slightly differently. To measure the effectiveness of a turn, we need to consider three items: load factor, turn rate, and turn radius.

Load Factor (n)

Load factor is how many Gs the wing is experiencing in a turn. As you saw in Chapter 4, to make a level turn (neither climbing nor descending), the load factor goes up with angle of bank. In a level turn with 30 degrees of bank, the wing supports 15 percent more weight than when not turning, so the load factor is 1.15. At 60 degrees, the wing supports twice the weight of the airplane, so the load factor is 2. Any increase in bank causes load factor to rise rapidly. A level turn at 70 degrees of bank has a load factor of 3.

Turn Radius (R_T)

Turn radius, which is the measure of the radius of the circle an airplane draws in the sky as it turns, is measured in yards or meters. The smaller the circle, the better the turn radius. When two airplanes pass and turn nose to nose, the one with the smaller turn radius will gain angular advantage. (See Figure 6-15.)

The Mathematics of Turning

The best turning fighters will have a high turn rate and a small turn radius. Because velocity is variable, however, these two measurements are not constants. The following equations sum up turn rate and turn radius for any fighter (or for any airplane, for that matter), where n is load factor and V is velocity:

$$TR = n/V$$
$$R_T = V^2/n$$

What these equations mean in plain English is that a given airplane will achieve its best turn performance when its load factor is as high as possible and, simultaneously, its speed is as low as possible. Achieving this state, however, poses a problem. As you slow down to increase your turn performance, your maximum load factor also goes down, thereby decreasing your turn performance. The solution to the turning problem is to find the speed at which turn performance is maximized by the best balance between speed and load factor. This speed is known as cornering speed.

Turn Rate (TR)

Turn rate, which describes how quickly the airplane can change direction, is measured in degrees per second. An airplane with a turn rate of 20 degrees per second could turn 360 degrees, or a complete circle, in 18 seconds. When two airplanes pass and turn nose to tail, the airplane with the better turn rate will gain angular advantage. (See Figure 6-16.)

Cornering Speed

For any given fighter, the best combination of high turn rate and low turn radius is achieved at that fighter's cornering speed (V_c). You should memorize V_c for whichever airplane you're flying. When you maneuver in combat, try to manipulate your

E so that you stay as close to V_c as possible. A pilot in a Wildcat maneuvering at cornering speed can out-turn a Zero if the Zero pilot neglects his V_c. Table 6-3 lists the various cornering speeds of the Combat Flight Simulator 2 airplanes. In truth, a cornering speed is only good for one weight, altitude, power setting, and configuration of flaps and gear, but the variations are usually insignificant in combat when expressed as the indicated airspeed that the pilot sees in the cockpit.

Plane	V_c
A6M2 Zero	164 knots
A6M5 Zero	186 knots
N1K2 George	175 knots
Wildcat	178 knots
Hellcat	151 knots
Corsair	219 knots
P-38	192 mph

Table 6-3 *Cornering speed is the best balance of load factor and speed to get the smallest radius of turn at the best rate.*

Maximum performance turns at V_c can be tricky. If you pull the maximum number of Gs but fly a little bit too slowly, the airplane will stall in the turn and enter a spin. If you go a little too fast, you'll pull too many Gs and could damage the airplane. Traveling at V_c doesn't mean you must make all your turns at maximum performance. Even at cornering speed, maximum-performance turns still cost a great deal of E. Suppose you're in a Hellcat, with a cornering speed of 151 knots, flying against a Zero and you want to make an energy fight. Keeping your speed at 151 knots will allow the best turns, but it won't allow you to zoom away from danger the way 251 knots would, so maintaining V_c is not the best option. For the Zeros, which are trying to gain angular advantage, the higher the performance of the turn, the greater the angular advantage gained on each cross, so they would want to maintain V_c. Maintaining cornering speed might allow the Zero to line up a tracking shot in two passes instead of three, which could mean the difference between your Wildcat getting away and getting shot out of the sky.

For the energy fighter, maximum performance turns aren't necessary until the reversal, but at that point maximum performance is key. The energy fighter should engage at a speed higher than his V_c, since he will lose some speed as he maneuvers to gain the energy advantage. Ideally, the energy fighter will reach V_c at exactly the moment he attempts the reversal. This gives the energy fighter maximum performance turning when he needs it most. After the reversal, the energy fighter wants to keep his speed as close to V_c as possible. The closer the energy fighter's speed is to V_c, the faster and farther he can move his guns from a lag position to a lead position and make a shot.

Flight Exercise: Turn Performance

Steep turns are the most fundamental move in combat. If you're flying with Flight Model Realism set to Hard, a poorly executed turn will put you in a spin you might never get out of. Go to Quick Combat, and take any fighter. Check No Enemies so that you won't have any unwanted company. Accelerate to cornering speed for the airplane you chose, and time a 180-degree turn. Try different angles of bank to learn the maximum angle of bank for the turn without losing altitude. Try the same turn two more times—once going 100 knots slower, and again going 100 knots faster.

Working in Three Dimensions

Gravity affects load factor and turn performance. Consider the turning performance of an airplane in a loop, shown in Figure 6-26. Before the loop, the airplane flies along with a load factor of 1 G (the force of gravity). At the bottom of the loop, the pilot pulls up to a load factor of 3 Gs. At point A in the loop, the pilot is still applying the same pressure but the effect is now 4 Gs because there's no gravity resisting the turn. At point B, the airplane is upside down and has a turning rate equal to 5 Gs because gravity now adds to the load factor and assists in the turn. At point C, the force is back to 4 Gs; at the bottom, it returns to 3 Gs. What this means to you is that any downward component to your turn will increase the turn rate and decrease the turn radius, while any upward component to your turn will have the opposite effect.

Load factor affects roll rate as well. The airplane's roll rate increases with a decrease in load factor. If you push forward enough on the stick to reach 0 G just before you move the stick sideways for a roll, the rate will increase. Roll rate also increases almost linearly with speed, to the point of limiting the pilot's physical ability to move the controls. The Zero had poor roll performance at high speeds because of high air loads on the ailerons. No pilot was strong enough to move the control surfaces. This factor is simulated in Combat Flight Simulator 2.

Disengagement

Disengagement occurs when the fight ends, whether with a victory, a draw, or an escape. Whatever the reason, your task as a pilot is to assess your current status and act accordingly. The fight has probably controlled your attention, so now you need to reestablish a global situational awareness and look for any other potential threats. The fight has also cost you at least some amount of E. You need to regain that E so that you're ready for another fight. Finally, you should check your remaining fuel and ammunition and decide if you can continue on your current mission or if you must change your plan.

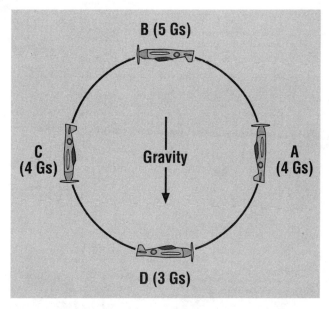

Figure 6-26   *The force of gravity decreases load factor when upright but adds to turn rate while moving through inverted flight.*

Combat Maneuvers and Aerobatics

Successfully using sound tactics in combat means confidently making the move that gets the desired result. This takes practice. Practice in Quick Combat will help, but the following guided exercises will allow you to focus on particular points and practice them without getting shot down. Try these flying these exercises in a variety of airplanes from both the Japanese and American sides. You might never want to fly airplanes from "the other side" in combat, but a better understanding of your enemy better will help you in the air. I show these maneuvers from Cockpit View; see the game's manual for diagrams.

Basic Combat Practice

These basic maneuvers are practiced without any enemy aircraft. Their purpose is to get you familiar with maneuvering the airplane in unusual attitudes while still maintaining situational awareness. These moves will also provide the basis for the maneuvers you fly in combat.

Rolls

A plain roll isn't anything you'd do in combat, but it's fundamental to many combat maneuvers. Go to Quick Combat with no enemies. Establish level flight. Apply full control stick to the left or right and hold it there, rolling completely around until you're upright again. You probably noticed how the nose of the airplane dropped during the roll. Try the roll again but start with the nose pointed up about 30 degrees. Just before you begin the roll, push forward on the stick very slightly to unload the wings and tail.

Try the roll again, but this time start with the nose on the horizon and use both stick and rudder to keep it there. As you move through the first quarter of the roll, apply some opposite rudder to keep the nose in place, as shown in Figure 7-1. This is called top rudder, because as the airplane rolls 90 degrees,

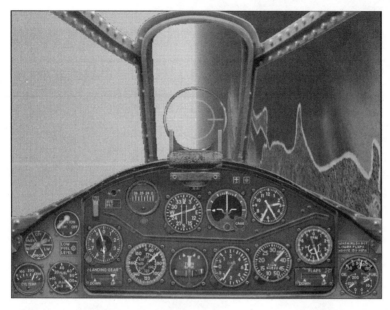

Figure 7-1 *As you pass the first quarter, use a bit of left rudder to keep the nose up.*

the rudder now controls the motion of the nose up and down on the horizon. As the airplane rolls through the second quarter of the turn, push forward on the stick to keep the nose up on the horizon. At this point the rudder is back to center. (See Figure 7-2.) As you roll through the third quarter of the turn, ease off the forward stick and add top rudder. (This time that's the rudder on the same side as the turn.) Finish the roll with no rudder and just enough stick back to keep the nose on the horizon. (See Figure 7-3.) This kind of roll, called a *slow roll,* really helps you understand the independent functions of stick and rudder.

Loops

A loop is probably the best-known aerobatic maneuver. In

Figure 7-2 *As you pass through inverted flight, press forward on the stick. The rudder should be centered by now.*

Chapter Seven: Combat Maneuvers and Aerobatics

Microsoft Combat Flight Simulator 2, loops are best used by the angles fighters as a way to get into position behind an adversary. To perform a loop, start with an entry speed of at least 200 mph. Pull straight back on the stick with the wings level. As you proceed upward, if you hold constant back stick, the result is an e-shaped loop. You can also ease up on the back stick a bit as you become inverted and then add more back stick as you pull out. The

Figure 7-3   *In the last quarter, add right rudder to keep the nose up. There should be no forward stick at this point and only enough back stick to keep the nose up as you return to level.*

practice loop in the training missions is a true loop that goes straight up and comes straight down. In combat, a *slanting loop* is more common. The maneuver is basically the same, but you first roll 30 to 45 degrees to the left or right before performing the loop.

The slanting loop costs a bit less E and is less predictable for your enemy. The slanting loop can be a good evasive maneuver if at some random point in the loop you add another 30-to-45-degree roll and then complete the loop. The result is radical relocation that's difficult for the enemy to follow.

The training missions have a lesson for performing the loop. An AI instructor will guide you through the maneuver.

Immelman

An Immelman is half loop and half roll. The result is a 180-degree turn with a loss of airspeed and a gain in altitude. It's a useful combat maneuver that allows you to turn around quickly and make an attack from above. Its danger is the loss of airspeed at the top of the half loop. Perform this maneuver only when you're in no immediate danger of attack by your enemy and you have plenty of airspeed

The training missions have a lesson for performing the Immelman.

Split-S

The split-S is the opposite of the Immelman. It's a half roll to inverted flight, followed by a half loop. The result is a 180-degree turn with a gain of air-speed and a loss of altitude. This is an excellent escape maneuver.

The training missions have a lesson for performing the split-S.

Note: *"The most common maneuver of the [Japanese] fighter at present is the split-S, which happens usually when he is approached from ahead or astern. In normal combat, if he cannot be hit before he has started down, he is usually gone."*
—Major G. "Pappy" Boyington

Inverted Flight Practice

Sustained inverted flight isn't something you'll do in combat, but it's a useful technique for gaining spatial awareness and a better understanding of the flight characteristics of an airplane while upside down. Some combat situations will require you to remain inverted for several seconds while you locate an enemy target.

Go to Quick Combat, with no enemies, and set yourself up as if you were going to do a slow roll. Roll only to the inverted position, and then stop the roll. You need to hold forward stick to maintain level flight. Once you're stable flying upside down, try a few shallow turns. To make the turns, you'll need op-posite rudder. Remember that since you're upside down, the rudder pedals are essentially backward. Inverted flight is a bit like balancing on a beach ball, but it's fun.

Barrel Roll

A barrel roll is an excellent training maneuver for maintaining situational awareness while maneuvering aerobatically. For a barrel roll, you'll pick a point ahead of you and 45 degrees to your left or right. (See Figure 7-4.) If the point is on the left, pull the stick to the lower left. This will start a simultaneous roll and loop. The airplane will seem to roll around the 45-degree point on the

horizon, as shown in Figure 7-5. The goal of the roll is to adjust rate of roll and bank so that the 45-degree point seems to stay put throughout the maneuver. (See Figure 7-6.) For practice, try the roll while holding the 45-degree forward view. One of the biggest challenges in flying a simulator in combat is looking at a true 45-degree or 90-degree angle to the direction you're actually flying. If you can master this ability, you'll gain a real edge in combat. Go to Quick Combat with no enemies, and try a few barrel rolls.

Angles Tactics

These moves are the basics for the angles fighter. They will improve your angular advantage and get you in position for a shot, preferably a tracking shot.

Figure 7-4   *Start the barrel roll looking left or right at a point on the horizon.*

Figure 7-5   *Roll and loop while looking out the forward 45-degree view.*

Figure 7-6   *Continue the barrel roll back to level.*

Break

The break is a standard move to evade pursuit and give the pursuer only a brief, high-deflection snapshot. If you're being pursued, you're already at an angular disadvantage. Your first goal is to get to neutral ground. The break is a sudden, unexpected turn in any direction that you hope your pursuer can't follow. A break of 90 degrees followed by a partial roll and a second break is more effective than a single break. For example, a right turn of 90 degrees followed by a split-S would create some distance between you and your opponent, possibly allowing you enough time to turn and face him.

To perform a break, select Quick Combat, flying a Zero against a fast, poorly turning foe, such as a P-38. Set the tactical situation to Disadvantaged so that you're being pursued. Let the enemy get close on your tail, but keep making random, shallow turns to prevent a tracking shot. Keep your speed at cornering speed (V_c). When the enemy is close, roll 30 degrees, pull a hard 90-degree turn, roll 30 degrees further, and pull another 90-degree turn. Roll level, and look at the distance to your enemy and the direction he's moving. He should no longer be on your tail, and there should be enough room for you to begin maneuvering to get on his tail. If your pursuer follows you into the turn in the break, you might actually end up behind him as he overshoots your position. Take advantage of this opportunity to make a shot. Practice this escape method with other fighter combinations.

Lead Turn

The lead turn, or *early turn,* is a way of gaining some extra time to turn around and get behind your opponent. The key is to cross with separation so that you can begin your turn before the cross but not give a shot opportunity.

To perform a lead turn, use the same Quick Combat scenario that you used with the break but set the tactical situation to Neutral. As the two airplanes approach, increase the horizontal separation between you and the other airplane. Before you cross, start your turn. This early start combined with your better turning ability should put you in position for a tracking shot. Figures 7-7, 7-8, and 7-9 give you a Heads Up Display (HUD) view of the lead turn in action.

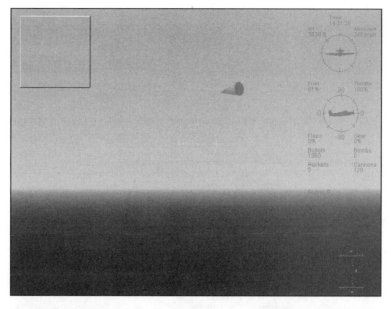

Figure 7-7   *Make an early turn with enough separation so that you're not vulnerable to a shot.*

Figure 7-8   *Continue in a maximum performance turn to get behind your opponent.*

Yo-Yo

This odd-sounding maneuver actually gets its name from its Chinese creator, Yo-Yo Noritaki. The Yo-Yo comes in two versions: the high Yo-Yo and the low Yo-Yo. The difference between the two is in how you use your E. The Yo-Yo is often thought of as a way to reverse positions, and, although such a reversal is possible, the Yo-Yo is best employed as a way to get better angular advantage by turning behind your opponent.

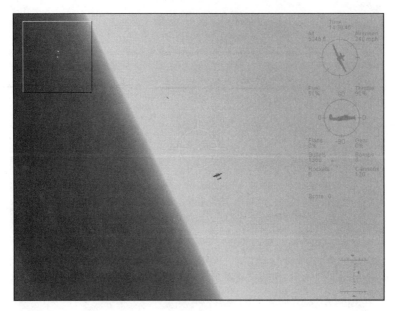

Figure 7-9   *Assume the best pursuit—usually a lead pursuit—and move in for a kill.*

To perform a Yo-Yo, you'll have to be in a situation in which you're crossing an enemy's path at nearly 90 degrees—you'll have to maneuver a bit to practice in Quick Combat. As you cross at 90 degrees, watch which way your enemy is turning. If you're at or above V_c, pull up and bank in the direction of the enemy's turn. After turning 90 degrees in heading, roll level and nose down. This is a high Yo-Yo. It should put you closer to your opponent's six o'clock in a lead or pure pursuit. If your speed at the cross was below V_c, dive and turn toward your opponent, pulling up as you roll out. This is a low Yo-Yo, which should put you closer to your opponent's six o'clock in a pure or lag pursuit. A common error in the Yo-Yo is applying too much pitch up or pitch down. Don't be greedy: you can do more than one Yo-Yo to get into a better position. Figure 7-10 through 7-13 show the Yo-Yo in HUD view.

Scissors

The scissors is a series of nose-to-nose turns in which the better-turning fighter continuously gains angular advantage. Each turn is a three-part maneuver: a nose-to-nose turn, a lead turn as your opponent appears in your 45-degree up-forward view, and a reversal of direction by your opponent. The scissors works only with an adversary who keeps turning nose to nose and falls into your trap. When turning nose to nose, a faster airplane appears to move forward on the horizon at each change of direction. If you see this in your opponent, you're gaining advantage. Be careful, however: repeated tight turns cost a lot of E. A savvy opponent with a large E advantage

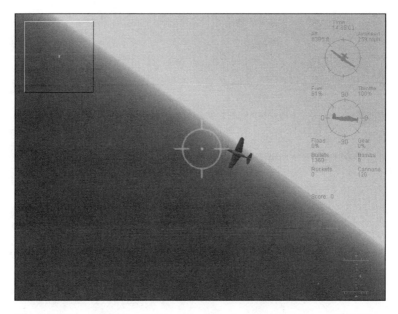

Figure 7-10 *Cross the P-39 with approximately 80 degrees AOT. Try the snapshot as you cross—you might get lucky.*

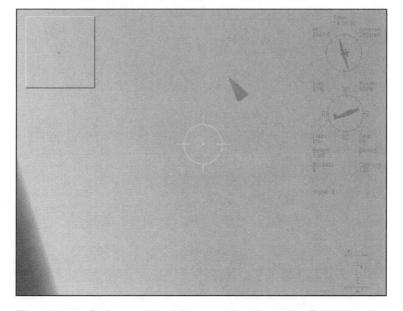

Figure 7-11 *Pull up and bank in same direction as the P-39. Note the direction of the enemy indicator and the lower airspeed from the climb.*

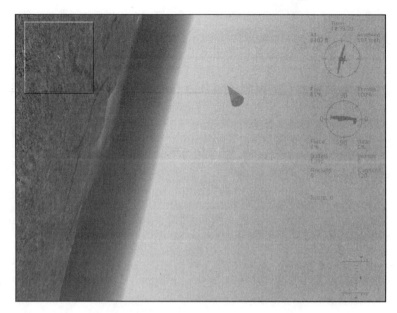

Figure 7-12   *Continue the roll, but pitch down to close on the P-39. Note the direction of the enemy indicator.*

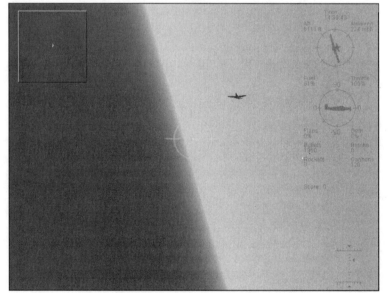

Figure 7-13   *Close on the P-39 with your speed reclaimed and a AOT of only 40 degrees.*

might start a scissors with you but catch you in your own trap by pulling straight up and hitting you from above while you're in a low-E state from all those turns.

Go to Quick Combat as with the lead turn, and maneuver to cross paths with the enemy at 90 degrees. Alternately, use the Slew function by pressing Y and put your opponent off your wing, as shown in Figure 7-14. Make an early turn toward your opponent as in Figure 7-15. Use your 45-degree up-forward view to see the enemy appear in your field of view. As soon as he appears, as shown in Figure 7-16, roll back into an opposite turn, as shown in Figure 7-17. Switch to your 45-degree up-forward view again,

and watch for your opponent. You should be moving to a position closer to the opponent's six o'clock with every cross. You can try reducing power at the crosses to speed up this progression, but don't reduce power so much that you stall in the turn. At some point, the enemy airplane will appear far enough ahead that when you roll in the opposite direction he'll drop into your forward field of view and you can set up a tracking shot, as shown in Figures 7-18 and 7-19.

Energy Tactics

To make energy tactics work, you need an E advantage before the attack. If you enter combat with equal E, you must maneuver to

Figure 7-14   *Start the scissors with your opponent off your wing.*

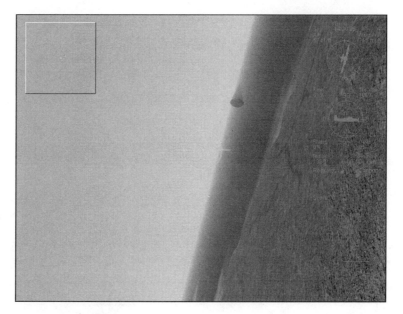

Figure 7-15   *Lead turn your opponent nose to nose.*

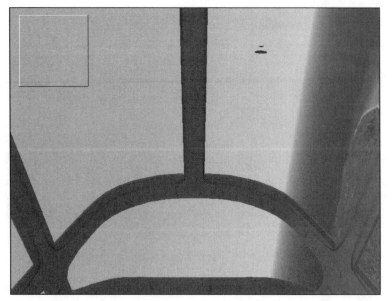

Figure 7-16   *Watch for your opponent in 45-degree up-forward view.*

gain E without letting your opponent do so, or you must get your opponent to lose E without losing too much yourself. What matters are the relative amounts of E you and the enemy have, not the absolute totals. Low-deflection tracking shots are unlikely. Be ready to act immediately if a brief high-deflection tracking shot or snapshot opportunity appears.

Overhead Attack

The overhead attack starts above your target, usually 2000 feet or more. The maneuver starts like a split-S, but when the nose points straight down you continue in a dive toward your prey. Use rudder to change nose position, keep the right lead, and fire at 200 yards or less. If you don't make a kill in the first pass, fly past the en-

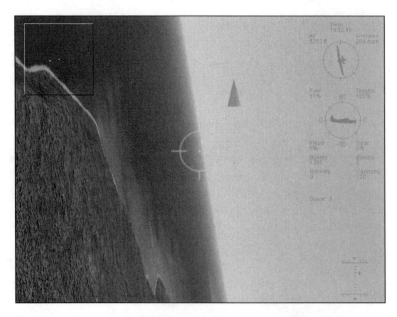

Figure 7-17   *Reverse direction as soon as you see your opponent appear.*

emy, pull up above him, and turn to hit again.

High Side Attack

The high side attack is similar to the over-head but requires less E advantage and works better if the opponent is off to one side rather than directly below you. Starting from a height of 1500 feet or more above the opponent, roll and dive at the same time to change heading 90 degrees. Give the necessary amount of lead, and hit at a 90-degree deflection angle. Again use rudder to keep the nose where you want it. If you don't make a kill on the first pass, you can climb and hit again from the opposite side or sometimes even slide in behind the target for a lead pursuit and deflection

Figure 7-18   *Continue reversals, and watch your opponent move ahead of you on each pass.*

Figure 7-19   *When the opponent is far enough ahead, your lead turn will put him in your forward field of vision.*

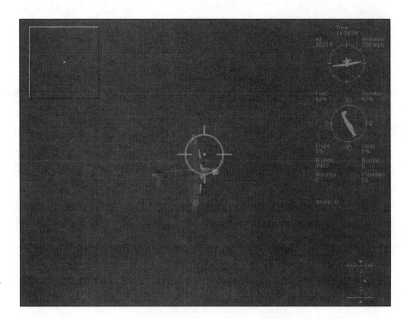

Figure 7-20 *With both the overhead and the high side attacks, you'll drop on your opponent from above for a snapshot with an AOT of about 90 degrees.*

shot. Figure 7-20 shows you what your Angle Off Tail (AOT) should look like in this attack.

The overhead and the high side attacks are both in the training missions. The AI instructor will help you learn these maneuvers.

Head-On and Extend

Crossing an opponent head-on and extending away can be an excellent way to build up enough E to escape or at least stay alive until help arrives. The goal is to cross head-on as close to your opponent as possible. The closer you are, the harder it is for the opponent to make an early turn without giving you a free snapshot. After the cross, you move away for as long as possible to gain E.

Go to Quick Combat, and fly a P-38 against a Zero. Set the tactical advantage to Neutral so that you cross head to head. After the cross, don't turn. Fly straight and climb shallowly. When the Zero has almost reversed course, start your turn with only 30 degrees of bank and a shallow descent. Cross again and repeat. The Zero will gain angular advantage, but the turns and climbs required to catch you will cost him a lot of E. Meanwhile, your shallow climbs, descents, and turns cost less E, thereby widening the gap. When you can go 2500 to 3000 yards before the Zero can complete his turn, you can dive shallowly and run. The Zero can't catch you.

Try the same exercise, but fly the P-38 against a George.

Situation Tactics

No two situations in aerial combat are identical, but some strategies apply to many situations:

- Attack from slightly above the enemy's wings. There's more airplane to see when you're at an angle above or below rather than dead astern; thus, you have a bigger target.
- When crossing head to head, your best defense is firing first.
- Don't get into a climbing-and-turning conflict with a Zero. It will always out-climb and out-turn you.
- If you turn to follow a tighter-turning opponent and start to overshoot before you get a tracking shot, point your nose in pure pursuit, dive at the enemy, and get at least a snapshot. Use a Yo-Yo to prevent the overshoot next time.
- If you have lots of E, try to entice an enemy to follow you in a climb. Watch for the enemy to lose forward momentum first. When that happens, turn around and dive on your opponent.
- If possible, keep all targets on one side of your airplane.
- When attacking a group, hit as many aircraft as possible without extra maneuvering and without going deep into the group.

Defensive Maneuvering

You go on the defensive in combat because your opponent has an angular or energy advantage that he can use effectively against you. The objective of all defense is to get into a better position in terms of angles, energy, or both, without getting shot while getting that position. The best defense for the energy fighter is an altitude sanctuary. This means the E fighter must start with an altitude advantage and should climb back up to altitude whenever not pressing an attack. A good energy fighter should be able to engage and disengage combat at will. If you're on the defensive against an energy fighter, you must get him to bleed off E, which means getting him to dive or turn. Getting yourself close to the ground will force your attacker to also come down and thereby lose E. Maneuvering close to the ground also prevents your attacker from zooming down on you for a shot, passing by, and zooming back to altitude: if the opponent overshoots close to the ground, he crashes into the turf.

The best defense for the angles fighter is cornering speed. The closer you are to cornering speed, the tighter your turns are. Time your turns so that you come out of the turn with a shot opportunity. In general, turn to meet your attacker head-on. The best defense in a head-on confrontation is firing first. The angles fighter can also use out-of-plane maneuvering by performing breaks, as described earlier. Faster but poorly turning energy fighters are unlikely to be able to follow, and even if they can, the high G-load would require an extremely large lead to make a shot. If you're on the defensive against an angles fighter, you must deny the shot while creating some other advantage. Angles fighters want to get tracking shots, so don't fly straight long enough to give them one. Uncoordinated maneuvers, such as a sudden skidding turn, help you evade fire. Forcing the fight to a faster speed by diving away in turns is effective. The high speed gets the fight moving faster than the angles fighter's cornering speed and thereby lessens the angles fighter's advantage.

Great Escapes

One of the most novel defensive maneuvers in World War II was successfully employed twice by the German fighter pilot Adolf Galland. With an enemy that he couldn't shake on his tail, Galland fired his guns into the empty blue sky ahead of him. The allied pilot saw the tracers and heard the shots but assumed they must be from a third airplane firing on the pursuer himself. The allied pilot would make an evasive maneuver against the nonexistent attacker and give Galland a chance to escape.

Chapter Eight

TARGETS OTHER THAN FIGHTERS

Surface Targets

Any combat pilot will tell you that ground weapons are much scarier than enemy aircraft. Ground targets can't move around as enemy airplanes do, but they more than make up for this deficiency with firepower. You usually don't have a choice about engaging them, either. When you get your orders to attack a surface target, you can assume the big guns are sitting around waiting for you. You can do little defensively against antiaircraft fire except try to get in and get out as fast as possible. Most antiaircraft weapons are ineffective at low altitudes, so a low approach can work. Low approaches usually mean you're moving slower than you are when diving in, so you're more vulnerable down low.

The most important things to practice with surface attacks are not hitting the ground, getting your airplane pitched downward to fire at the right moment, and dropping your ordinance with the correct amount of lead so that it doesn't overshoot or undershoot the target.

Flight Exercise: Zoom to the Deck

The objective of this exercise is to develop the timing to pull out of a dive and get exactly the result you want. There is a lag time between when you begin to recover from a dive and when you actually pull out. Many pilots died pulling out of a dive too late.

Go to Quick Combat with no enemies, and pick your favorite airplane. Start at full power in level flight. Roll to an inverted position, and pull into a power-on dive. Time your pullout so that you level off just a few feet off the ground or the surface of the water. Buzz along the beach for a few minutes, and then pull back up and level off at full-power level, maintaining your speed. Repeat this exercise for as long as it's fun. See how close you can come to the ground without hitting it.

Flight Exercise: Strafing

The key to successful strafing is having a clear plan of attack and keeping your speed up. Pay close attention to the intelligence reports about where the defensive batteries are located. When strafing, get down extra low and then "pop up" just before your target. This maneuver allows you to point your guns down a bit at the targets and increase the damage you inflict. While strafing often doesn't have a large impact strategically, it does have a big impact on enemy morale.

Flight Exercise: Rockets

Air-to-ground rockets are available on some of the American airplanes. These rockets are used against ground targets only and can be thought of as high-power strafing tools. Unlike a bomb, which simply drops from the airplane, the rocket is self-propelled and will travel some distance before striking a target.

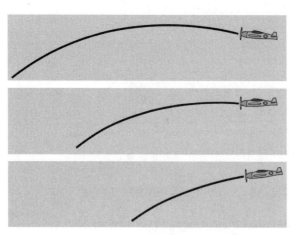

Figure 8-1   *The path of an air-to-ground rocket depends on the angle at which it's launched.*

The rocket's trajectory droops, so it won't hit exactly where you point it. How far the rocket travels is dependent on the angle at which it's launched, as shown in Figure 8-1. From 500 feet above the ground and at 300 mph, a rocket fired while your gunsight is level on the horizon will hit about 1.5 miles away. Raising the nose to place the bottom of your gunsight on the horizon will increase the range to 2.5 miles. Lowering the nose to place the top of the gunsight on the horizon will drop the range to half a mile. As you practice with rockets, use the Bomb/Rocket View command (the A key) to see exactly how the rocket travels.

Flight Exercise: Dive-Bombing

Both the U.S. and Japanese forces used dive-bombers to great effect in World War II. Dive-bombing did fatal damage to the Japanese aircraft carriers at Midway. While both sides employ specialized dive-bombers, fighters often make an initial bomb attack and then move back into a fighter role. The beginning of a dive-bomb run is a lot like an overhead attack. The only differences are that you're lining up on a much slower moving target and you'll release a bomb rather than fire your guns. A nearly vertical dive is much more likely to hit the target than a shallow dive, as shown in Figure 8-2. The dotted line represents the fighter's line of sight; the solid line represents the actual bomb trajectory. The

Figure 8-2   A steep dive will put your bomb on target.

more vertical the dive, the easier it is to hit the target. Just don't forget to pull up after you release the bomb.

One of the biggest errors when dive-bombing is a late pull-up. It's a shame to destroy your target only to crash into the ocean immediately afterward.

Torpedo Runs

Although not as versatile as bombs and slightly easier to defend against, torpedoes were deadly weapons from the beginning of the war. The torpedo airplane, however, has a tough job in that it must come in low over the water and close to the target. It must then release the torpedo close enough to the target to be fairly confident of a hit but far enough out to allow the torpedo 10 seconds in the water to arm before impact. Then the airplane must climb away in danger because it has much less speed than a dive-bomber.

The training missions include practice for both strafing and dive-bombing. Player-flyable airplanes cannot carry torpedoes.

Attacks on Bombers

The weaknesses of specific bombers are covered in Chapter 11, "Non-Player-Flyable Aircraft," but there are a few general rules for attacking the "heavy metal." The most important thing to remember is that what the bombers lack in speed and maneuverability, they make up for in armament. The B-25D carries ten .50 caliber machine guns, six of which can fire in many directions. A tracking shot on a bomber is very difficult to accomplish without getting your nose shot off. A clean tracking shot from behind a bomber is also difficult because the air behind and below the bomber is turbulent from the wake the bomber creates as it moves through the air. This means you'll need to hit the bombers with a series of slashing attacks from the sides above or below the aircraft. Bombers are also capable of taking much more damage than fighters and still remaining airborne. To make the most of your attacks, hit the same area of the bomber repeatedly rather than hit several different areas once or twice. The bomber's tail, as seen in Figure 8-3, is usually a good target since it can be targeted from almost any angle.

Figure 8-3 *Make high-speed diving attacks on one area of a bomber, and then zoom up to turn around and attack again.*

Chapter Nine

Understanding the Artificial Intelligence

The computer plays several roles in Combat Flight Simulator 2 in which it must emulate the behavior and decision-making abilities of people. The most complex of these roles is as an enemy pilot, which I'll discuss in this chapter. Some of the other behaviors, such as the movements of ground units, look like artificial intelligence (AI) but really aren't.

> *"The aircraft model and the AI are the two hairiest parts of getting it right."*
> *—Tucker Hatfield, Program Manager for Microsoft Combat Flight Simulator 2*

Tanks, trucks, and ground-based weapons look as if they're being controlled by people thinking about their tasks, but they aren't. The movement of each of these units is defined in the Mission Builder. (See Chapter 13, "Using the Mission Builder," for more information on the Mission Builder.) The ground units follow a script that tells them to move from waypoint to waypoint, sit still, or fire on any enemy targets. The only variation on this script is that their movements might be linked to mission events. For example, ground units might not start moving until the first bomb is dropped. The many possible links and variations of the script make these movements look like AI, but no real decision making is happening.

Ship movements are also controlled by scripts in the Mission Builder. Similar to ground units, ships move from waypoint to waypoint or sit still. Ships will automatically respond to attack, though, and switch from waypoint mode to defensive circle. In defensive circle, the ships move in a circle and fire on all enemy aircraft. The ships' guns will traverse as well, following the motion of an attacker through the sky.

Aircraft are the one component of Combat Flight Simulator 2 that are controlled by a decision-making algorithm that can truly be called AI. This part of the program is crucial to the game—the better the AI, the more realistic the game. Understanding how this AI works will definitely give you an edge.

Decision-Making Hierarchy

The AI uses a hierarchy to make its decisions. The highest item on the list is the mission goal. The AI pilot will attempt to achieve the mission goal above all else. If the mission is Combat Air Patrol, in which the goal is to engage the enemy immediately, the AI pilot will attack as soon as it sees you. If the mission is to drop torpedoes, the AI pilot will not engage unless attacked. If attacked, the AI pilot will fight back and might drop its torpedoes early to have a better chance. This maneuver allows you to have a chance to achieve a mission success if your goal is to foil the enemy mission.

The next AI action is to choose its first target. Included in this decision is the following information:

- Which targets pose the greatest threat to mission success.
- Which targets are of the greatest strategic value. For example, bombers are better targets than fighters.
- Which targets are easiest to kill. The AI uses its knowledge of aircraft performance figures and armament.
- Which targets are closest.

These factors are all weighed, and a decision is made. Once a target is selected, the AI pilot's next action is to put the aircraft guns on the target. Thus, if you're the target and the AI pilot is anywhere in your forward hemisphere, it will turn and face you. If it's anywhere behind you, it will point its nose on a spot directly off your tail. The AI pilot also knows about energy management and will seek height and speed advantage over you. (See Chapter 7, "Combat Maneuvers and Aerobatics," for more information on combat tactics.) And it knows key flight model numbers and will keep the airplane maneuvering at the optimum speeds for turning ability and responsiveness. These tactics apply at all three enemy experience levels: Rookie, Veteran, and Ace.

Inside the Head of the Enemy

Rookies are easier opponents than Aces, but it isn't tactics that separate them, it's execution. The AI pilot skill level works much the same as the aircraft Flight Model Realism setting. The computer is programmed to simulate the highest,

Chapter Nine: Understanding the Artificial Intelligence

most difficult opponent, and then the model is degraded from that point to produce the easier opponents. In those cases, the AI pilot model is degraded in four areas:

- **Marksmanship**   Rookies are less likely to get the right angle to make a shot, and they are less canny about when to shoot to make a kill.
- **Aircraft control**   Rookies have less precision control than Veterans and Aces. Since the AI pilot flies the aircraft just as you do, poor control inputs will equal poor performance.
- **Reaction time**   Rookies won't respond as quickly, and they might start one move and then change their minds and try another. Changing your mind in an airplane usually means a change of direction. A change of direction means the airplane's flight path straightens momentarily, and that's an opportunity for the opponent to make a kill.
- **Aggression**   The higher the rating of your opponent, the more aggressive he'll be. Aggressive moves include head-to-head passes with guns blazing, erratic turns to prevent a tracking shot, and firing at every shot opportunity no matter how brief. These are traits you should emulate. Rookies are the least aggressive, so be aggressive with them. When fighting one on one, the level of aggressiveness can actually make a Veteran a harder target than an Ace because the Veteran is less likely to get into a risky situation. If you ever get two Aces trying to attack you at the same time, however, call for help or run. Without assistance, you won't last long.

Sound like a tough opponent? It is. Add the fact that the AI pilot sees you as soon as you get within 5000 yards, even if you come from a blind spot, and you have your work cut out for you.

Of course, the AI pilot does have some weaknesses that can be exploited, as described in the following list. (For a full explanation of the combat terms used in the list, see Chapter 7.)

- The AI pilot takes the shortest route to get its guns on you. This means you can usually predict which way it will turn after a cross.
- The AI pilot tends to turn for too long. This makes it a sucker for a lead turn if you can get into position. If possible, break slightly above the enemy to keep the airplane in sight and prevent giving it a quick shot opportunity. A high or low Yo-Yo can also be effective against a turning AI pilot.

- The AI Rookies think horizontally. Vertical moves such as an Immelman or a split-S usually allow you to escape the AI. Making an attack or attempting a reversal by using the vertical dimension is usually more effective than using the horizontal dimension. The AI Aces almost always use a vertical move after a cross. This makes them somewhat predictable.
- The AI pilot won't push the airplane to the edge of the performance envelope. The AI pilot knows its stall speed at all angles of bank and load factors and will keep a margin above the stall. If you push your plane to the limits of its abilities, you'll see more performance out of any given airplane than the AI pilot will.
- The AI pilot strongly prefers tracking shots and won't take snapshots very often. The AI pilots can and will deflection shoot but only at relatively low angles. You're basically safe crossing in front of an AI pilot with Angle Off Tail (AOT).
- The AI pilot doesn't plan far ahead. This allows you to lure the AI pilot into an area where your squadron can finish it off.
- The AI pilot will always fly in coordinated flight, although many good escape maneuvers require uncoordinated flight.

A final factor is the fact that the AI pilot controls the airplane just as a human pilot would. This means that if the AI pilot needs to bank left to avoid your fire, the computer won't just redraw the enemy aircraft in a bank. Instead, the AI pilot recognizes it's under attack, chooses a maneuver to get out of danger, and sends the stick and rudder inputs to fly that maneuver to the aircraft model, and then the model computes the results of those stick and rudder commands. This might seem like a trivial difference, but it can work strongly to your advantage. Suppose that in the turn example I just described, the AI pilot's plane had damage to its ailerons. The airplane would not roll as well, and the normal control inputs would not be enough to get a rapid turn. A human pilot might add more input or try a different escape all together. The AI pilot is unable to make that adjustment and will simply keep using the normal control inputs. The wounded airplane now becomes an easy target.

AI Maneuvers

The process by which the computer calculates its desired path explains some of the AI pilot's limitations. The computer-controlled aircraft almost exclusively fly ellipses. For example, let's say you're following close behind an enemy airplane and it begins to turn. Remember that the first priority for the AI pilot is

guns on target. This means the AI pilot wants to put its airplane in a position directly behind your tail. As illustrated in Figure 9-1, the AI pilot will try to fly an elliptical path to reach that spot.

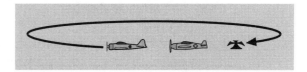

Figure 9-1   *The AI pilot will usually fly an elliptical path to place its airplane in a spot just off your tail.*

That ellipse can be parallel with the horizon, or it can be canted slightly up or slightly down. In a low-powered airplane with a tight turn, such as a Zero, the angle is usually slightly down. With a P-38, watch for the path to be slightly up. Starting an ellipse that's almost perpendicular to the ground is not done by the AI pilot because of the large speed penalty and the high G forces.

The important point to remember is that once the AI pilot has committed to one of these turns, it will stay in the turn for at least several seconds before trying something different. This is often enough time for you to maneuver for a deflection shot, especially if you can anticipate the turn and roll first. Watch for long constant turns after a head-to-head pass, after a quick escape climb or dive, or when close to the ground.

The AI pilot does have a few maneuvers in its bag of tricks. It will make high and low sloping turns, such as high and low Yo-Yos, but it uses these turns most often to turn around quickly rather than strategically. The AI pilot will also turn and face you, given enough room, but again, if you can break first, you can often catch the other airplane while it's still turning.

One final weakness is that the AI pilot is more of an angles fighter than an energy fighter. This technique has an advantage when the AI pilot flies maneuverable airplanes such as the Zero, but it serves the AI poorly when flying heavier, faster fighters, especially the P-38.

AI and Your Wingmen

Your wingmen use the same algorithm that the enemy pilot uses, so they have the same strengths and weaknesses. What's important to remember is that wingmen tend not to make head-on shots, which are essential to make in many team combat maneuvers, such as the famous Thach Weave. However, your wingmen make great bait to draw the enemy pilot into a crossing maneuver, letting you take a near-head-on shot.

Using Wingmen in Combat

In Combat Flight Simulator 2, you can issue commands to your wingmen, allowing you to coordinate your efforts. The four basic commands are Attack, Split Formation, Rejoin Formation, and Help Me. The Attack command is linked to the padlock. If you padlock a target and press Shift+7, two members of the squadron will attack that target. If you press Shift+7 twice, the entire squadron will attack that target. These targets can be ground vessels too, so you can specify the attack order on ships. You can combine commands to create events to trap enemy aircraft. For example, you can split formation into two groups of four and then split again into four groups of two. Next you would padlock a target

Note: *Pressing Shift+7 without a padlocked target will send the other pilots off to attack the mission goal target.*

between you and the next nearest group and press Shift+7 while simultaneously performing your own attack. This will trap the enemy between you and your wingmen.

The most important thing to remember when flying in a squadron in Combat Flight Simulator 2 is that the rest of the formation follows you. No matter what you do, they'll try to hold formation with you. Combat with squadrons in formation has several drawbacks: they're easier to see, they have less maneuvering room, and they make surprise more difficult. Also, attention given to collision avoidance means less attention given to the enemy.

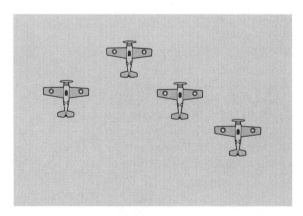

Figure 9-2   *The Finger Four formation.*

Squadron Formations

Mission designers use the Mission Builder, described in Chapter 13, to choose the initial formations that a squadron will fly. The following sections describe the most common formations.

Finger Four

Finger Four is the default formation. Its name comes from the relative position of the fingers on your hand, as shown in Figure 9-2. The pilots in the

Finger Four are ready at any time to break into two units of two airplanes. Each unit of two has a lead pilot who guides the attack and one wingman to defend him.

Shotai

The *shotai* formation was used by the Japanese and the Americans and consists of a group of three airplanes in a V, as shown in Figure 9-3. The Allies called this formation the Vic and stopped using it because of their success with the Finger Four. In the Japanese *shotai,* the rear two pilots weave back and forth to protect their leader. The Japanese fighter pilots would often hold formation only until battle and then split up in separate attacks.

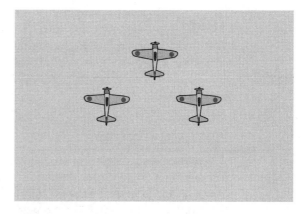

Figure 9-3   *The* shotai *formation.*

Echelon Right and Echelon Left

The Echelon Right and Echelon Left formations are formed by a diagonal line of fighters. (The Echelon Right formation is shown in Figure 9-4.) These formations are most useful when all the airplanes will follow a leader in a ground attack, such as when dive-bombing.

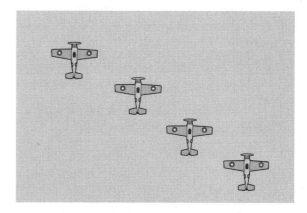

Figure 9-4   *The Echelon Right formation.*

Line Abreast

In the Line Abreast formation, all the airplanes fly in a line wingtip to wingtip. This can be useful for strafing wide areas.

Trail

The Trail formation has all the airplanes flying in a line nose to tail. Defensively weak because only the lead airplane can fire his guns while the squadron is in formation, this formation is useful for sustained attack on a specific ground target.

Box and Diamond

A Box formation consists of four airplanes flying two in front and two behind, forming right angles. The Diamond formation also consists of four airplanes, but only one is in the lead, two follow side by side behind the lead plane, and the fourth airplane brings up the rear. The Box formation and Diamond formation are useful for air shows and little else.

Chapter Ten

PLAYER-FLYABLE AIRCRAFT

The airplanes in Microsoft Combat Flight Simulator 2 were created to reproduce as closely as practical the real World War II fighters. Just like the pilots in the Pacific, if you want to survive, you need to know your plane like the back of your hand, and you need to know as many details about the enemy as possible. Different airplanes fly differently, requiring different

> *"This publication shall not be carried in aircraft on combat missions or where there is a reasonable chance of its falling into the hands of the enemy."*
> *—Printed on pilot operating handbooks containing information on airplane performance, weaponry, and armor*

tactics. Different airplanes have different procedures for takeoff and landing. Different airplanes have different ranges and weapons options. If you don't know what your aerial mount can and can't do, it's just a matter of time before you run out of fuel, bullets, or luck.

The information presented in this chapter is specifically for the airplanes as they are implemented in Combat Flight Simulator 2, but it matches pretty closely to the real thing. When the game's designers had to make compromises, they did so in the interest of playability. For instance, the management of fuel from different tanks varied widely between the real airplanes. The P-38 could have up to eight fuel tanks to draw from. Drop-tanks also rarely had fuel gauges. The pilot simply used the tank until the point at which (by his calculations) no fuel was left. To simplify matters for play, the airplanes in Combat Flight Simulator 2 all have similar fuel selectors and the fuel gauge always shows the amount of fuel in the selected tank. Some of the gauges scattered about the cockpit in the real aircraft have also been moved into the Cockpit view in Combat Flight Simulator 2. The Corsair flaps indicator was actually down to the left of the pilot on the flap control. The indicator is now up on the panel where you can see it. Even though it's been moved, the control retains the original look.

> **Note:** The speed limits for flap and gear extension mentioned in this chapter apply only when using the Hard (that is, realistic) flight realism model. On the easier flight models, you can extend flaps and gear without any fear of damage to your airplane.

Teaching Aircraft Recognition

One of the great dangers in aerial combat—both air-to-air and ground-to-air—is the danger of misidentification. At closing speeds of 240 mph, or four miles a minute, the time between first seeing an airplane and deciding whether to fire on it is measured in seconds. When the Hellcat was still fairly new, a group of seven Hellcats departed the carrier Essex to intercept an attacking formation of 40 Japanese fighters and 20 bombers. These weren't good odds, but the rest of the carrier's fighters were out on a mission. The seven Hellcats managed to disrupt the attackers enough that they gave up and turned around. The battle had used up too much fuel for the Hellcats to get back to the Essex, so they made for another carrier, the Hornet, which was much closer. The Hornet crew was unfamiliar with the Hellcats and fired on them. The seven Hellcats eventually landed on the carrier Langley, refueled, and headed home to the Essex.

The matter of recognition is further complicated in air-to-air combat when the aircraft in question might be seen from any angle and perhaps only for a brief moment through a gap in the clouds. Distinguishing a friendly airplane from the enemy is obviously important, but pilots needed to know the exact type of aircraft. A rear attack on a Zero from above could be an easy kill. Trying the same attack on a Val, a pilot would find himself face to face with a tail gunner. The only clear difference between the two aircraft when seen from above might be the more elliptical wings on the Val.

The central feature of the Navy's recognition training program is the three-view silhouette. These silhouettes appeared everywhere, even on packs of playing cards issued to the troops, as shown in Figure 10-1. Key distinguishing marks were pointed out and the aircraft were given easy-to-remember, usually one-syllable names such as Zeke, Pete, and Val.

One conscious design decision in the creation of the cockpits is the use of correct markings and units. The Japanese planes are labeled in Japanese, and the units can be obscure to Americans. ToolTips help to solve this problem. If you place the cursor over an instrument on the panel in Cockpit view, you'll see a pop-up ToolTip that gives the name of the instrument in English and the reading of the instrument in familiar units. This feature allows you to immerse yourself in the experience of the pilot without needing to learn Japanese.

What's in a Name?

The U.S. Army and Navy used different naming systems for their aircraft, but logic of the names is similar. The first one or two letters in the navy system identify the role of the aircraft. The next number and letter indicate the aircraft's design and the name of its manufacturer. The final number designates major modifications to that design. The codes for U.S. Navy airplanes in Combat Flight Simulator 2 are as follows.

Aircraft role (first letter group):

- **F**   Fighter
- **TB**   Torpedo/Bomber
- **SB**   Scout/Bomber
- **PB**   Patrol/Bomber
- **R**   Multiengine transport

Manufacturer (second letter group):

- **F**   Grumman Aircraft Engineering Corporation
- **U**   Chance Vought Aircraft
- **D**   Douglas Aircraft Corporation
- **Y**   Consolidated Aircraft Corporation
- **J**   North American Aviation

Under this system, the Wildcat F4F-4 is a fighter (F) that is the fourth fighter design (4) from Grumman Aircraft Engineering Corporation (F), and this particular model is the fourth major modification (-4). Not every design gets approved. The Grumman F5F was a twin-engine fighter that never made it past an early flying prototype. The first number is also omitted for the first design from a company. The SBD-1 was the first SB design from Douglas Aircraft Corporation.

The army system uses a letter for the type of aircraft, a number for the number of those designs accepted by the army,

Figure 10-1   *The silhouettes and names of both friendly and enemy airplanes appeared everywhere, even on playing cards, to train the troops in quick recognition. (Courtesy of U.S. Games Systems)*

and a final letter to designate the modification model. There is no information about the manufacturer. The P-38F modeled in Combat Flight Simulator 2 is a Fighter (P for pursuit) that was the 38th design accepted by the army (-38) and is the 6th (F) modification to that model.

The Japanese Navy employed a system similar to the U.S. Navy's. The first letter signified the type of aircraft, and the next number and letter designated the model number and manufacturer. The last number indicated major modifications to the design. The A6M2 is a fighter (A) that is the sixth design from Mitsubishi Heavy Industries (6M) and the second major modification.

Mitsubishi A6M Reisen (Type Zero Fighter)

The Zero—Allied codename "Zeke"—was designed to meet the Japanese Navy's explicit requirements for speed, takeoff, and climb performance; long-distance endurance; and maneuverability. (Figure 10-2 shows four views of the Zero.) Meeting these requirements set the stage for the Zero's greatest successes—and its worst failures. Japan's only engine choices for the Zero were under 1000 hp. By using an innovative design, and by reducing weight as much as possible, the designers of the Zero were able to meet the Japanese Navy's tough criteria. The low weight meant that the Zero had to go without pilot-protective armor or self-sealing fuel tanks, and structurally it was not as tough as U.S. fighters.

In its first bouts of combat, the Zero's extreme speed and maneuverability made it so hard to hit that its lack of protection was irrelevant. Two months after the Zero's introduction, 13 Zeros took on 27 Russian-built Polikarpovs and shot down all 27 without a loss. Zero pilots began comfortably winning aerial battles when outnumbered even two to one. Nearly a year after the Japanese Navy accepted the Zero fighter design, only two Zeros had been shot down, both by ground fire.

By the time of the Pearl Harbor attack in 1941, two-thirds of the Imperial Japanese Navy (IJN) fighters were Zeros. (The A6M2 Zero Model 21 with folding wingtips was the Zero used at Pearl Harbor.) The attack on Pearl Harbor went well for the Japanese, with only nine Zeros lost. This single-battle loss was four times the Japanese losses in China in the previous year, indicating that battling the Americans was going to be a different experience than air combat in China.

Experience in combat brought changes to the Zero. A power increase from the 950-hp Sakae 12 engine to the 1130-hp supercharged Sakae 21 turned the A6M2 into the A6M3. The plane's designers added modified flaps and ailerons, thickened the wing skin to improve diveaway speeds, installed better

ammunition feeds, and added some limited armor. With these modifications, the airplane was designated the A6M5. Originally, the A6M5 was seen as a stopgap fighter while Mitsubishi's next generation fighter, the A7M, was built. Persistent technical problems kept the A7M from being placed into production, and the A6M5 was produced until the end of the war.

Although about 150 A6M7 Zeros were produced with War Emergency Power (WEP), the Zero's initial design as a lightweight fighter sealed its fate. By 1943, U.S. pilots were flying improved airplanes. They had improved their tactics and knew the Zero's weaknesses. The price of the Zero's lightweight design and maneuver-ability was its poor diving ability and its inability to withstand much damage. Japan began to experience heavy losses to its pool of experienced pilots. By the end of the war, the Zero was a tool for the Kami-kaze Forces. Its reign as queen of the sky was over.

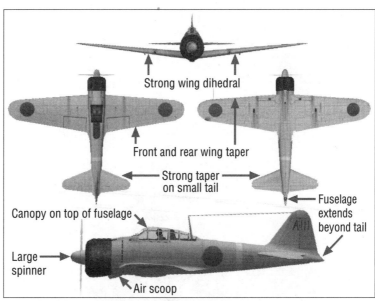

Figure 10-2   *The A6M Zero Fighter (A6M2 version shown).*

Cockpit Notes

Figure 10-4 shows the layout for the A6M2 cockpit with key items indicated, and the following sections describe those items. The A6M5 cockpit is essentially the same. Both Zero cockpits very well laid out, with the key navigation and flight reference instruments grouped together as found on much more modern airplanes.

Note: *The major visible difference between the A6M2 and the A6M5 is the engine cowl, as seen in Figure 10-3, indicating the switch to the more powerful engine in the A6M5. Note the large propeller spinner, characteristic of many Japanese designs. In Combat Flight Simulator 2, all the A6M2s are silver and all the A6M5s are green and grey.*

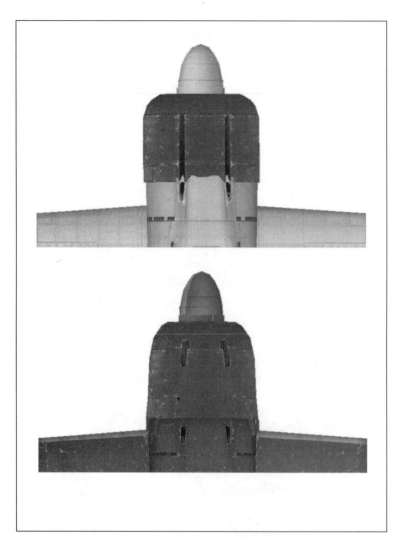

Figure 10-3   *The A6M2 (top) and the A6M5 (bottom).*

[1] Artificial horizon (vacuum-powered)   The instrument is the only player-flyable airplane horizon with a blue sky.

[2] Good luck charm   The small red bag is a token for good luck. There are similar amulets for good health, for safe driving, for passing examinations, and for love.

[3] Landing gear position indicator   The light shows the position of the two main gear and the tailwheel. Green means gear down and locked. Amber means gear in transit. Red means gear up. The Zero's gear is hydraulically controlled, so loss of the hydraulic system will prevent lowering the gear normally. You might still be able to pump the gear down manually with Shift+G.

[4] Fuel tank selector   The fuel tank selector is marked in Kanji, but the ToolTips will help you read it if you have any trouble. Clockwise from the top,

the settings are: forward tank, right tank, drop-tank, stop (fuel off), aft tank (beneath pilot), and left tank. The fuel capacity of the Zero is 141.33 gallons without a drop-tank; 228.5 gallons with a drop-tank.

[5] Low hydraulic pressure warning light This light will come on any time hydraulic pressure is too low. Since the engine runs the hydraulic pump, the light will come on any time the engine is turning very slowly or is stopped. If the light comes on in flight, you will not be able to move your flaps and will have to try and put down your gear manually.

Figure 10-4   *The A6M2 cockpit. The A6M5 cockpit has essentially the same layout.*

[6] Magneto control switch   The switch positions are in Kanji. From left to right, they read Both, Left, Right, Stop.

[7] Starter contactor   Pull out on the knob to engage the electric starter.

[8] Flap position indicator   Flaps positions indicated with the Kanji for flaps "Up" and "Down." The Zero has four-position split flaps that are hydraulically controlled. They are normally used only for landing. As with the gear, loss of the hydraulic system will affect the flaps. However, there is no back-up system for extending the flaps. Be prepared to make a flaps-up landing if the hydraulics give out.

Note: *Fuel management is important to airplane performance. If you use all the fuel in your right wing tank and none of the fuel from your left, the airplane will constantly try to roll to the heavy (left) wing. Likewise, in the Zero, the amount of fuel in the forward tank will change how nose-heavy the airplane will be. The aft tank is located near the center of the airplane so if has little effect on the balance of the airplane.*

[9] Machine gun magazine The machine guns are manually armed by the pilot. Combat Flight Simulator 2 arms the guns automatically.

[10] Engine controls Don't be fooled. The red knob is the Zero's propeller (engine speed) control, even though it's the exact same color and in the same position as an American mixture control.

Flight Notes

The Zero is a fun, responsive airplane to fly. It takes off and lands at some of the lowest speeds among the Combat Flight Simulator 2 airplanes. When using the Hard flight realism model setting, be careful during high performance turns because the Zero is easy to spin.

Takeoff

- Setting two steps of right rudder trim before takeoff will help keep the airplane straight on the takeoff roll.
- Leave your flaps up for takeoff, even from carriers.
- Hold the stick halfway back to fly off the ground in a three-point attitude or keep the stick forward in a wheeled position and rotate for takeoff 70–75 kts (81–86 mph).

Initial Climb

- Make your initial climb at 117 knots (135 mph) and full power.

Cruise

- The fuel burn in cruise at 65 percent power is 21 gallons per hour (gph).
- The fuel burn at 100 percent power is 91 gph.

Combat

- Cornering speed (V_c) for the A6M2 Zero is 164 knots (188 mph). (Remember that V_c is the speed at which a given airplane gives its best turn performance.) V_c for the A6M5 Zero is 186 knots (214 mph).

- Be careful when dive speeds exceed 250 knots (288 mph). Your roll rate will get very slow and your rate of turn will deteriorate.
- You can use your machine guns for most of your shots and to line up the best shots, but they do little damage to most American airplanes. Use your cannon to make a kill.

Approach and Landing

- Full flaps can be safely extended below 140 knots (161 mph).
- Landing gear can be safely extended below 135 knots (155 mph).
- Make your final approach with full flaps at 80 knots (92 mph) for carrier or runway landings.

Tactics

When you're flying the Zero, it's essential to maximize your strengths and account for your weakness. The Zero can maneuver well but can't withstand much damage. It's essential that you work to keep the Zero behind any enemy airplanes.

Preferred Tactics

The Zero is practically the definition of an angles fighter.

Advantaged Position

Don't lose this advantage. Use lead pursuit or straight pursuit to close on your opponent, and then use lag pursuit to get right behind. Fire your cannon when you are confident you won't miss. If you do miss, lure your opponent into a low-altitude turning fight at 200 knots or less. Under these conditions the Zero can be flown successfully against any American fighter.

Neutral Position

Turn as soon as possible to get a position on your opponent's tail. Make nose-to-tail turns in most cases to take advantage of the Zero's excellent turn rate. If you get particularly slow, make nose-to-nose turns to maximize your small turn radius. Slanting loops can be effective to get behind the enemy or just away from his line of fire.

The Genesis of the Zero

On October 6, 1937, the IJN published the requirements for its next-generation carrier-based fighter, the prototype 12. The list of requirements included a takeoff distance of less than 230 feet with a 36-mph (approximately 31 knots) wind, the ability to climb to 10,000 feet in 3.5 minutes, a true air speed of 310 mph at 13,000 feet, an endurance of between 1.2 and 1.5 hours in combat with no external fuel tank and an endurance of 6 to 8 hours with an external fuel tank, and an armament of two 7.7mm (.30 caliber) machine guns and two 20mm cannon. And this fighter had to be at least as capable a dogfighter as the IJN's current fighter, the AM5. At that time, no such fighter existed anywhere in the world.

To Jiro Horikoshi, the chief designer for the Zero, meeting all these requirements seemed impossible. To have good takeoff and climb, a large lifting wing is necessary, but a large wing reduces top speed. To fly so far requires carrying a lot of fuel, which in turn requires a big heavy airplane, but a big heavy airplane requires a big motor, which requires even more fuel, resulting in an airplane too heavy to dogfight well. The engine was the biggest obstacle to Horikoshi and his team. The only engine available in the size and weight he needed produced only 875 hp. (The first Spitfires were more than 1000 hp, the Wildcat was 1200 hp, and the Corsair was 2000 hp.)

The only way to make up for the lack of horsepower was to reduce weight. Horikoshi's team studied which parts of an airplane experienced the lowest stresses in flight and reduced their thickness. The team also used a new aluminum alloy that would later become one of the standard aircraft aluminum alloys. Finally they examined each part of the Zero that weighed over 1.7 grams (about the weight of two paper clips) to see if it could be lightened in any way.

(continued)

Disadvantaged Position

Use left-turning climbs and a tight turning radius to deny the enemy a tracking shot. If you have the flight model set to Hard, the Zero will make poor right-climbing turns because of P-factor. If you can lure your attacker into chasing you in a turn, do so. Make passes with horizontal separation whenever possible and turn toward the enemy's tail as soon as you are safe from a shot. If a high-E attacker is closing on you, use lead turn to cause an overshoot and allow you to slip in behind for a shot. The A6M5 will have slightly better performance than the A6M2, but tactics are unchanged. Figure 10-5 illustrates a position that you don't want to get in.

Kawanishi N1K2 Shiden-kai (Violet Lightning)

Like the famed Supermarine Spitfire, the *Shiden-kai* (Allied codename "George") traces its history to a floatplane, the N1K1 *Kyofu*. The *Kyofu* was the most capable float-equipped fighter of its time, with a 1460-hp engine and a

Laminar-flow wing analogous to the wing used in the P-51. The floatplane design had the wing mounted in the middle of the fuselage to help keep it out of the damaging water spray on takeoff and landing. Only about 100 of the floatplane fighters were produced, but the basic design was put on wheels as the N1K1 *Shiden*. The N1K1 had a bigger (1990 hp) engine and the same combination of guns and cannon as the Zero. More than 1000 of the N1K1 were produced, but the mid-fuselage wing was a problem. It required overly long landing gear legs that bent easily, and its place-ment reduced pilot visibility. The design-ers of the N1K2 *Shiden-kai* corrected these problems by moving the wing down the bottom of the fuselage. Other changes to the N1K2 included a redesigned tail, engine attach-ment, and a reduction in total parts, thereby reducing construction time. These changes also reduced the weight by 500 lbs. The N1K2 also used a sys-tem for combat flaps that decreased its

The Genesis of the Zero *continued*

The Zero also employed two new technologies to help eke out a better performance. One was the constant-speed propeller; the other was the flexible control cable, which balanced the controls so the pilot could more easily handle the airplane over a wide range of speeds.

Horikoshi's team's final product was the 3000-lb A6M1. (By comparison, the American Wildcat weighed just under 6000 lbs, and the Hellcat and the Corsair both weighed about 9000 lbs.) Even at that weight, the 875-hp Mitsubishi engine wasn't enough. The new 950-hp Nakajima Sakae 21 engine was bolted on the front of the A6M, making it an A6M2. Now Mitsubishi had a fighter that met the requirements for IJN prototype 12 and had no equal anywhere in the world.

Figure 10-5   *The Zero's unprotected wing tanks are excellent targets, especially for cannon fire. Don't give your opponent a chance for a shot.*

Unlocking the Mystery of the Zero

Reports of the Zero were sent to Washington by American observers in China in late 1940, but these reports were apparently ignored. American personnel in Pearl Harbor were actually told to expect an attack by biplanes if the Japanese started any trouble. The appearance of the Zero was a rude awakening to many and unlocking the mystery of its design and performance became a high priority for U.S. military intelligence.

The breakthrough came with the battle of Midway. Part of the Japanese plan was a feint to the north by attacking the American base at Dutch Harbor in the Aleutian Islands of Alaska. In the first wave of the attack, an A6M2 was hit by a single bullet, which ruptured an oil line. The pilot, Petty Officer Tadayoshi Koga, had to land on the small island of Akutan, where he would later be picked up by submarine. Landing on a soft bog flipped the Zero, breaking Koga's neck. Weeks later an American patrol plane spotted the flipped Zero. American forces retrieved the airplane and had it flying by September 1942, allowing U.S. pilots to gain important insights into the Zero's strengths and weaknesses.

turning radius, making it more difficult to stall in a turn in battle. (Figure 10-6 shows four views of the NIK2.)

Entering production in 1944, the N1K2 was a formidable opponent to any U.S. fighters, but because of U.S. bombing of Japanese factories, only 428 *Shiden-kai* were produced.

Cockpit Notes

The George's cockpit, illustrated in Figure 10-7 and described in the following sections, has many similarities to that of the Zero but isn't organized quite so well as the Zero.

[1] Low hydraulic pressure warning light   This light will come on any time hydraulic pressure is too low. Since the engine runs the hydraulic pump, the light will come on any time the engine is turning very slowly or is stopped. If the light comes on in flight, you will not be able to move your flaps and will have to try and put down your gear manually.

[2] Manifold pressure gauge   As with the Zero's gauge, the numbers show centimeters of mercury over or under sea level pressure. Plus 50 cm Hg would equal plus 18.5 inches Hg. Full throttle on the George is about 48.4 inches Hg.

[3] Landing gear position indicator   The light shows the position of the two main gear and the tailwheel. Green means gear down and locked. Red means gear up. The George gear is hydraulically controlled. The gear on the N1K2 is not as long and flimsy as on the N1K1, but it's still liable to bend if mishandled. Be careful in the George not to land while drifting sideways, such as

during uncoordinated flight, and do not drop the George hard on its gear or you might find the George riding on its belly.

[4] Fuel selector valve These settings are identical to those of the Zero. Clockwise from the top, the settings are: forward tank, right tank, drop tank, stop (fuel off), aft tank (beneath pilot), and left tank. The fuel capacity of the George is 189.2 gallons without a drop tank and 298.8 gallons with drop tank.

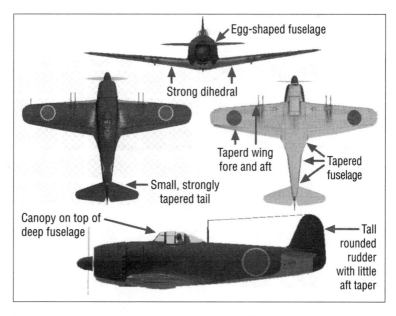

Figure 10-6   *Recognition features for the N1K2 George.*

[5] Artificial horizon (vacuum-powered)   No one is certain why the George has a black-over-black horizon. The George was manufactured later than the Zero, which has a blue-over-black system.

[6] Compass   The George had no DG.

[7] Flap position indicator   Flaps positions indicated in Kanji for flaps up and down. The George has three-position, hydraulically controlled slotted flaps that you can use for takeoff as well as landing. The George had a system for automatic combat flaps in which the flaps would extend slightly during high G-loads. This feature is not modeled in Combat Flight Simulator 2, but you can extend one notch of flaps to improve turn performance at speeds up to 250 knots without any damage.

[8] Magneto control switch   The switch positions are in Kanji. From left to right, they read Both, Left, Right, Stop.

[9] Starter contactor   Pull out on the knob to engage the electric starter.

[10] Engine controls   Note that the propeller and mixture controls are arranged like the Zero.

Flight Notes

Takeoff

- Set three steps of right rudder trim and three steps of right wing down aileron trim before takeoff.
- Set flaps to 1/3 down for all takeoffs.
- If you fly the George off in a three-point attitude, it will become airborne at 75 knots (86 mph), but the George has very poor roll control at such a low speed. The safer technique is to perform a wheeled takeoff and not to rotate and climb until reaching 90 knots. As you climb, retract the gear first and the flaps second.

Initial Climb

- Make your initial climb at 125 knots (144 mph) and full power.

Cruise

- The fuel burn in cruise at 65 percent power is 55 gph.
- The fuel burn at 100 percent power is 290 gph.

Combat

- V_c for the George is 175 knots.
- Combat flaps (1/3 deployed) can be used up to 250 knots (288 mph). The combat flaps will result in better cornering and a decreased likelihood of a spin. However, they must be retracted in dives over 250 knots or they will be damaged.
- Be careful making steep, high-g turns. The George will enter a spin with little warning, even with the combat flaps deployed.
- The George cannon require more lead than machine guns, and you have less ammunition than with machine guns.

Approach and Landing

- Landing gear can be safely extended below 150 knots (173 mph).
- Full flaps can be safely extended below 140 knots (161 mph).

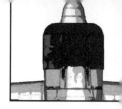

• Make your final approach with full flaps at 105 knots (121 mph) or more. The George has very poor roll control at low speeds and can easily roll over at the last minute. Expect to use approximately 40 percent power to maintain your speed until you raise the nose (flare) for landing.

Figure 10-7   *The George cockpit.*

Tactics

Preferred Tactics

The preferred tactics for fighting with George are either energy tactics (above 250 knots) or angle tactics (below 250 knots).

Advantaged Position

The George carries serious firepower with its four 20mm cannon. The down side of all that muscle is that you will run out of ammunition faster in the George than in any other fighter. With an advantaged position, fly the George much as you fly the Zero, but at a higher speed. As you close, move to a lag pursuit. When you think you are close enough to fire, get even closer, and then open up with all four cannon. Fire in repeated short bursts so you can make quick adjustments to your aim as needed.

Neutral Position

Your best bet is to get your opponent into an angles fight. While the George has the speed and power to be an energy fighter, its lack of armor puts you at a disadvantage. Cross your opponent with horizontal separation whenever possible and turn to get on his tail. The only Allied fighter that can match you in high-power, high-speed turns is the Hellcat. A George vs. Hellcat fight is an interesting match. The Hellcat is a little less maneuverable but is harder to kill. The George has a little edge on maneuverability and firepower, but is more vulnerable. The match will go to the better pilot, or go against the pilot who makes the first mistake.

Disadvantaged Position

Your number-one priority is to avoid getting hit. The only real protection you have is the large engine sitting in front of you, so turn into the enemy whenever you can. You are probably more maneuverable than the enemy, so try radical lead turns and out-of-plane maneuvers to force an overshoot. If your opponent starts turning with you, the situation will probably start to even out. Use full power, and WEP if needed, to keep your E up even in tight turns. Use the first notch of flaps if you are slower than 250 knots.

Grumman F4F Wildcat

The Wildcat actually began its existence as a biplane. The XF4F-1—X denotes the experimental prototype—was a biplane based on the existing F3F biplane fighter built by Grumman and used by the U.S. Navy. The performance of the biplane simply wasn't good enough to serve as a front-line fighter. The basic fuselage wasn't changed, but a new wing was designed and the airplane became the XF4F-2. This design still didn't meet the U.S. Navy's needs, but it was promising enough to keep in development. The wings were revised again, along with the tail and the engine, resulting in the XF4F-3. This design was finally accepted and the F4F-3 was put into production. The F4F-4, shown in Figure 10-8, is distinguished by the addition of better pilot protection and armor plating, self-sealing fuel tanks, and folding wings. General Motors used the Grumman plans to build 7808 Wildcats during the war.

Despite the Wildcat's stubby, bulldog-like appearance, Wildcat pilots genuinely loved their aircraft. The Wildcat was tough and could take a lot of damage and still get home. It was easy to fly, allowing even new cadets to feel confident in the sky. However, the Wildcat was no match for the Japanese

Zero. Where one Wildcat might fail, however, two or more could succeed. John "Jimmy" Thach is credited with inventing the Beam Defensive Maneuver, also known as the Thach Weave. The maneuver was created specifically to give the Wildcat a fighting chance against the Zero. The basis of the maneuver is that two pairs of Wildcats would weave as they flew, crossing each others' paths head to head

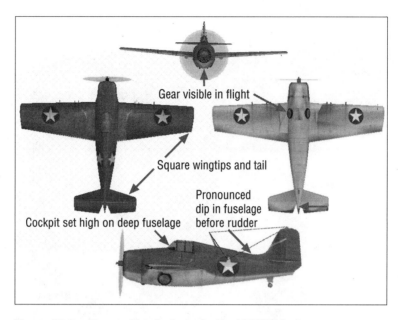

Figure 10-8   *Recognition features for the F4F Wildcat.*

every 20 seconds or so. This prevented the Zero from gaining enough time to get behind one Wildcat for a shot before the other half of the weave turned to get a head-to-head shot at the Zero.

The Thach Weave got its first test during the Battle of Midway in 1942. While flying in a group of four, Thach and three other Wildcat pilots were attacked by Zeros. One Wildcat was shot down right away and a second had his radio destroyed. Luckily the one remaining pilot with whom Thach had radio contact knew of Thach's plan. Thach ordered the remaining pilot to begin weaving. Within 20 minutes the three Wildcats had shot down four Zeros. The use of team tactics spread, and formations of weaving Wildcats became tough opponents for the Japanese.

Note: *A version of the Wildcat was tested on floats. This airplane, dubbed the Wild Catfish, never went into production.*

Cockpit Notes

Figure 10-9 illustrates the Wildcat's cockpit, and the following sections describe some of its components.

Figure 10-9   *The F4F-4 Wildcat cockpit.*

[1] Start switch
When the pilot held this switch, an explosive cartridge about the size of a 20-gauge shotgun shell was fired. The expanding gases spun the engine several times. If the engine failed to start, a crew member would load a fresh cartridge by reaching through the wheel well to the back of the engine.

[2] Magneto control switch   This switch has the following settings: both magnetos on, left magneto on, right magneto on, or both magnetos off.

[3] Fuel selector valve   The Wildcat had one self-sealing main tank holding 126 gallons of fuel and an additional 58 gallons for each drop-tank. In Combat Flight Simulator 2, the two drop-tanks are treated like one 116-gallon tank.

[4] Low fuel warning light   The light will come on when the level in any tank selected on the fuel selector drops below 30 gallons of fuel. Thirty gallons is about 30 minutes of flight at normal cruise power in the Wildcat.

[5] Landing gear indicator   The Wildcat gear is tough; there is no airspeed limitation for raising or lowering the gear. The gear is raised and lowered with a hand crank. Twenty-seven turns of the crank were required to get the wheels up or down. The system was simple but it worked well and was standard on Grumman fighters since 1931. Luckily, the designers of Combat Flight Simulator 2 decided to let you lower the gear by pressing G once rather that 27 times. The

crank actually turned a set of three bicycle chains that ran gears attached to the landing gear mechanism. The main gear are quite close together, making the Wildcat more difficult to handle on the ground and more prone to ground loop. Avoid high-speed turns on the ground—you could lose control of the Wildcat.

Note: *Wildcat pilots who tired of cranking their gear down by hand could release the gear crank lock and pull a sudden high-G turn. Under the stress of the turn the gear would swing down under its own weight, spinning the gear crank rapidly as it moved. This type of abuse didn't seem to hurt the tough little Wildcat one bit.*

[6] Flap position indicator The flaps on the Wildcat were pulled down by engine vacuum and brought up by springs and the pressure from airflow if the Wildcat was flying. As a result, even if the pilot forgot to raise his flaps after takeoff, the airflow would bring them up automatically by the time the airplane reached 150 mph. Likewise, if the pilot tried to bring the flaps down while the airplane was going too fast, the flaps simply wouldn't move. This meant the pilot could not damage the flaps by flying too fast with flaps extended. The Wildcat flaps in Combat Flight Simulator 2 will not automatically go up above 150 mph; however, to simulate the safety inherent in the real Wildcat, the flaps will incur no damage from overspeed up to the airplane's never-exceed speed. The Wildcat flaps could be lowered to any position the pilot wanted. To simulate this in Combat Flight Simulator 2 you have eight flap positions to choose from.

[7] Propeller control The F4F-4 used a Curtis Electric Propeller Control. The system is controlled the same as conventional propeller controls: push in to increase engine rpm and pull out to decrease engine rpm.

Flight Notes

The Wildcat is a responsive, pilot-friendly airplane that many World War II veterans remember fondly. It isn't very fast but it can dive well. The Wildcat is trickiest on the ground where its narrow gear make it easy to tip over if you turn too sharply.

Takeoff

- Set three steps of right rudder trim before takeoff.
- Set flaps to 1/2 for runway takeoffs and full down for carrier takeoffs.

- Take off in the Wildcat by holding the stick halfway back and letting the airplane lift off on its own from a three-point attitude at 70 to 75 knots (81 to 86 mph). Due to its narrow gear, the Wildcat can be difficult to control on the ground. A wheeled takeoff is possible, but is more difficult.

Initial Climb

- Make your initial climb at 125 knots (144 mph) and full power.

Cruise

- The fuel burn in cruise at 65 percent power is 52 gph.
- The fuel burn at 100 percent power is 170 gph.

Combat

- V_c for the Wildcat is 178 knots (205 mph).

Approach and Landing

- The landing gear in the Wildcat can be extended at any speed.
- You can select full flaps at any time, but they will not extend until your speed drops below 130 knots (150 mph).
- Make your final approach with full flaps at 85 knots (98 mph) for runway landings and 82 knots (95 mph) for carrier landings. Due to the narrow gear, a wheeled landing can cause you to weave down the runway like a drunken sailor. Three-point landings are a bit easier.

Tactics

Preferred Tactics

Use energy tactics with team tactics if possible.

Advantaged Position

Don't lose this advantage. Drop in on your enemy with the best speed possible to make a shot. After the shot, turn airspeed back into altitude by climbing away from the enemy. Turn and attack again from above. Since you will overshoot the enemy because of your greater speed, do not hit the enemy from behind and then regain your altitude in front of him. This gives a more

maneuverable enemy airplane a perfect opportunity to climb into a tracking position behind you. Try to cross the enemy at 90 degrees or more. Expect to make several passes before getting a kill.

Neutral Position

When you fly the Wildcat, all the Japanese fighters can outclimb and out-turn you. In a dive, the George can outdive you, and even the Zeros can almost keep up. Your goal is to keep your speed high, prevent the enemy from getting behind you, and take snapshot opportunities whenever they appear. The more turning you can get the opponent to do without making sharp turns yourself, the better off you will be as his E is reduced. Time that the enemy spends turning around is time you can use to get out of gun range before you need to turn around. Cross the enemy with as little horizontal separation as possible to prevent the enemy from taking an early turn. If the enemy does make an early turn, you will get a perfect snapshot. If he doesn't turn, rely on the sturdiness of your airplane and its armor to keep you safe while you fire head to head. Try to avoid a collision.

Disadvantaged Position

You didn't take everyone's advice and you got into a turning dogfight with a Zero. Now you are low on speed and altitude, and the Zero is clinging to your tail like a shadow. Your only hope is to build up some speed to get distance between you and your opponent. Continuously change your direction and angle of bank to prevent giving your enemy a tracking shot. Try to limit your bank angle and try not to pull too many Gs while maneuvering, as this will cost you E. Maneuvering close to the ground will limit your opponent's options for setting up a shot. Get help from one of your wingmen if possible. If all else fails, try to get at least 500 feet of altitude before getting your tail shot off so that you have enough time for your parachute to open after you bail out.

Honor in a Wildcat

Don't let the Wildcat's shortcomings keep you from flying this plucky little bird. Many Wildcat pilots were very successful in the Pacific, even before the introduction of the Thach Weave. Between December 1941 and January 1943, eight Wildcat pilots earned the Medal of Honor, the highest American award for bravery.

Combat Flight Simulator 2

Grumman F6F Hellcat

Grumman received the order for the Hellcat in June of 1941, five months before the attack on Pearl Harbor. The design took into account the U.S. Navy's experience with the Wildcat and the experience of the British fighting the air war in Europe. The big changes were more armor for protection, a lower wing for visibility, wider gear to improve ground handling, and larger ammunition magazines. All that additional weight necessitated a bigger engine. The Hellcat, shown in Figure 10-10, received the 2000-hp Double Wasp, the same engine found in the P-40 and the Corsair. The design was not specifically put forth as an answer to the Japanese Zero, but it turned out to be a good match. The Hellcat was extremely maneuverable and could actually out-turn a Zero above 25,000 feet. The rugged construction could also take enormous abuse and still keep flying. The Hellcat first saw action on September 1, 1943, on Marcus Island and began to replace its little brother, the Wildcat, over the course of the following year. Hellcats served in both war theaters, but their time in the sun was short. The Hellcat's performance was eclipsed by the even more capable Grumman Bearcat. The Bearcat never saw combat in World War II, but it was the platform for the U.S. Navy's Blue Angels soon after the war.

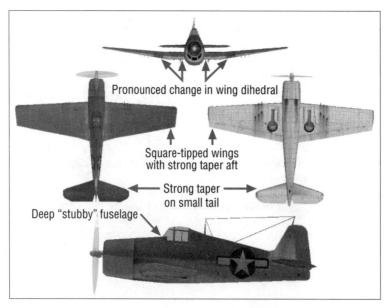

Pronounced change in wing dihedral

Square-tipped wings with strong taper aft

Strong taper on small tail

Deep "stubby" fuselage

Figure 10-10   *Recognition features for the F6F Hellcat.*

Cockpit Notes

Figure 10-11 shows the layout of the Hellcat's cockpit, and the following sections describe the items in the cockpit.

[1] Low hydraulic pressure light   The light will come on whenever hydraulic pressure falls too low. In the Hellcat, the wing flaps, cowl flaps, landing gear, wing-folding, and gun-charging systems all were hydraulic.

[2] Starter switch Like the Wildcat, the Hellcat used an explosive cartridge starter.

[3] Combined landing gear/ flaps indicator The Hellcat flaps move in increments of 10 degrees from full up to 50 degrees down, and the position is read across the top of the gauge. The flaps on the Hellcat extend both back and down from the wing, making them very effective even though they are fairly

Figure 10-11 *The F6F Hellcat cockpit.*

small. The Hellcat had a system similar to that of the Wildcat, in which the flaps wouldn't go down at speeds greater than 195 mph. In the Hellcat, a switch actually sensed airspeed and retracted the flaps if the pilot forgot. Once the airspeed dropped below 195 mph, the flaps would extend again.

Landing gear indicators are shown below the flap indicator with three lights representing the wheels of the aircraft. Three red lights indicate the gear are up and locked and three green indicate the gear are down and locked.

[4] Tachometer The Hellcat tachometer is unique in using an odometer-like indicator for thousands of rpm.

[5] Fuel selector The Hellcat can draw fuel from four different sources: the left wing, right wing, reserve, and drop-tank.

Flight Notes

Takeoff

- Setting two steps of right rudder trim before takeoff will help keep the airplane straight on the takeoff roll, but directional control is quite good in the Wildcat even without trim.
- Leave your flaps up for runway takeoffs, and use half-flaps for carrier takeoffs.
- Take off from a three-point attitude or from a wheeled attitude. From either position, you can get airborne at 75 knots (86 mph).

Initial Climb

- Make your initial climb at 130 knots (150 mph) and full power.

Cruise

- The fuel burn in cruise at 65 percent power is 55 gph.
- The fuel burn at 100 percent power is 290 gph.

Combat

- V_C for the Hellcat is 151 knots (174 mph). This V_C is very low, especially for an airplane with so much power and the ability to fight combat at high speeds. This means the Hellcat can maneuver well over a very wide range of speeds.

Approach and Landing

- Landing gear can be safely extended below 170 knots (196 mph).
- Full flaps can be safely extended below 135 knots (155 mph).
- Make your final approach with full flaps at 110 knots (127 mph) for runway landings and 100 knots (115 mph) for carrier landings.

Tactics

Preferred Tactics

The Hellcat is very versatile and, like the George, is capable as an angle fighter or an energy fighter.

Advantaged Position

Depending on your opponent, you might want to make repeated slashing attacks or establish a tracking position and shoot. You are still less maneuverable than a Zero, but due to your similar V_c you might be able to out-turn a Zero if a rookie is at the controls. You are slightly less maneuverable than a George at speeds above 175 knots and slightly more maneuverable below 175 knots. If you think you can get into a tracking position and finish your opponent in one pass, try for the tracking shot. You have six .50 machine guns, but no cannon, so you must make several hits to score a victory. Remember that Combat Flight Simulator 2 rewards accuracy. A relatively small number of hits delivered precisely will do the job. Since the Hellcat can follow an enemy in a turn, don't give up on a chase unless the target is getting higher and higher in your windscreen. If you are pretty sure you can't make a kill in a single pass, plan to keep your speed up and make repeated slashing attacks. Expect to make several passes before seeing that satisfying fireball.

> ## Lucky Lindy Once Again
>
> The Grumman Aircraft company and the Chance-Vought Aircraft company were located on opposite sides of Long Island Sound, and test pilots from both companies sometimes unofficially tested each others' airplanes. During the early stages of the Hellcat's development, Charles Lindbergh, who was doing some work with Chance-Vought, borrowed a Corsair to fly over to Grumman and take a look. At the invitation of some Grumman test pilots, Lindbergh took a new Hellcat up for about half an hour. When he returned to land, the gear would not come down. Losing Lindbergh in a bad, gear-up landing was not something anyone at Grumman wanted to see happen, so mechanics and engineers went up to the control tower to give suggestions. After a few dives with high-G pullouts, the gear dropped and locked into place. Lindbergh landed without any other problems.

Neutral Position

Again, the characteristics of your adversary determine the best tactics. For something maneuverable like a Zero or an Oscar, cross with no horizontal separation and try and make your kill head to head. Get far enough away after the cross to turn and face the target head to head again. If you're attacking something like a Betty, get lots of horizontal separation and turn early as you cross. Even if the enemy turns to meet you, you turn faster and can get a shot. Factor in altitude as well. Above 25,000 feet, a Hellcat will out-turn any other airplane in the game. If you do play the angles fight, leave yourself an escape route downward by keeping the fight up high. If you make a mistake and get into a jam, dive away with power and live to fight again.

Disadvantaged Position

As with the Wildcat, you're digging your own grave when you get low and slow in the Hellcat. Unlike the Wildcat you have a tight enough turning radius and the extra power to finesse your way out if you are lucky. Make turns to the right or left, repeatedly changing your angle of bank. Do not ever get slower that 150 knots. This makes getting a tracking shot difficult. Intersperse these maneuvers with shallow WEP dives to gain distance. Horizontal distance is your goal. If at all possible, cross your pursuer with little or no horizontal separation. Immediately after the cross, the enemy has no shot opportunity. Shallowly dive away and get more distance. It might take a few crossings, but eventually you will get an opportunity to run. Take it. Once you are out of firing range you can decide to keep running or return from a more even footing.

Chance-Vought F4U Corsair

The F4U Corsair, shown in Figure 10-12, was literally built around its engine, the 2000-hp Double Wasp. Harnessing all that power required the largest propeller ever bolted on a fighter to that date. But a long propeller meant long landing gear to prevent the propeller from striking the deck of a carrier. Long gear legs are more likely to bend on a hard landing, so they must be reinforced. Reinforcement adds weight, and weight is the enemy of a fighter airplane. The inverted gull wing was to give enough clearance for the propeller without very long gear legs. The same idea was actually employed on the German Stuka dive-bomber.

The Corsair unfortunately failed its first carrier trials because of poor controllability at low speeds and a tendency to bounce up in the air when landing hard. The Corsair was relegated to use as a land-based fighter, where it saw great success in the hands of many Marine Corps pilots. Once the landing problems were corrected, the Corsair was used off carriers beginning in January 1945. Together U.S. Marine and Navy Corsairs downed 2140 Japanese airplanes while losing only 189 of their own. The Corsair saw active service from World War II through the Korean War. In all, 12,571 Corsairs were made, with the last new Corsair rolling off the line in 1952.

Cockpit Notes

Figure 10-13 shows the Corsair's cockpit layout, and the following sections describe some of the cockpit's components.

[1] Low hydraulic pressure light The light will come on whenever hydraulic pressure falls too low. In the Corsair the wings flaps, cowl flaps, landing gear, and wing-folding and gun-charging systems all were hydraulic.

[2] Stall warning light This light will come on a few knots before the stall. The light was provided to give better warning in the landing condition, power on, when the normal warning is less marked and the Corsair was inclined to roll off to the left as it stalled. The light will come on approximately 5 mph before the stall. The light is designed for use in landing; do not rely on it to warn you of a stall in combat.

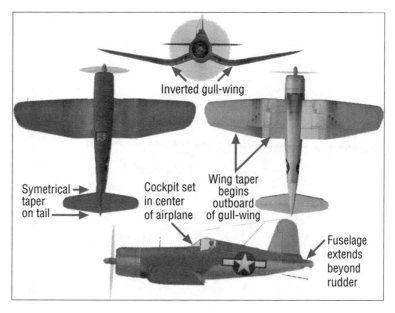

Figure 10-12   *Recognition features for the F4U Corsair.*

Labels in figure:
- Inverted gull-wing
- Symetrical taper on tail
- Cockpit set in center of airplane
- Wing taper begins outboard of gull-wing
- Fuselage extends beyond rudder

That's a Big Engine

The 2500-lb, 2000-hp Pratt & Whitney Double Wasp engine was the power plant for both the Hellcat and the Corsair. Each of the engine's 18 cylinders had a volume of 2.5 liters, or about the same volume as an entire modern 4-cylinder car engine. When the engine is building to full power, as during takeoff or combat, the Double Wasp guzzles 285 gallons of gasoline an hour. All that power isn't needed all the time. Running at normal cruising power of 2150 rpm, 34 inches of MP, and the mixture set for auto-lean, the Double Wasp is only producing about 1000 hp. At this setting, the Corsair's engine burns a mere 83 gallons each hour and has a mileage of about 4 miles to the gallon. Now you know why the fuel tanks are so big and drop-tanks are necessary for longer missions.

Figure 10-13   *The Corsair cockpit.*

[3] Carburetor air temperature warning light   The supercharger on the Corsair could create very high carburetor air temperatures and subsequent engine damage. In Combat Flight Simulator 2, this light will come on when a certain level of engine damage is reached or when CHT (gauge number 12) exceeds 260 degrees C.

[4] Flap position indicator   The Corsair flaps are hydraulically controlled and move in 10-degree steps up to 50 degrees. The Corsair also had safety flap retraction system designed to bring up the flaps if the pilot forgot. This system is not modeled in Combat Flight Simulator 2, so the maximum speed for 50 degrees of flap is 150 mph. The Corsair was approved to use up to 20 degrees of flap in combat for speeds under 230 mph. The actual airplane used a hydraulic reservoir to allow for three operations of the flaps in the event of hydraulic failure. This is modeled in the Combat Flight Simulator 2 Corsair: the flaps will actually slow down and eventually stop as hydraulic integrity decreases.

[5] Fuel selector   Each wing tank holds 63 gallons. The main tank holds 183 gallons, the reserve tank holds 50 gallons, and the drop-tank holds 172 gallons.

[6] Landing gear and tail hook position indicator   The Corsair gear is hydraulically activated and serves two functions. The main gear doors extend forward with the gear legs and act as dive brakes to increase the airplane's rate of

descent without increasing its airspeed. There actually was a separate dive brake control that extended only the main gear and not the tailwheel, since the tailwheel gcar door would be ripped off at high speeds. As a dive brake, the gear could be extended at up to 300 mph and could be left extended up to 400 mph. Because of this feature, the main gear and the tailwheel had separate position indicators. The Corsair in Combat Flight Simulator 2 extends all the gear together so that you can use the gear to slow down, but the maximum speed for deploying the gear is 230 mph. Since the tailwheel position indicator is not needed, it is a tailhook position indicator in Combat Flight Simulator 2.

[7] Hydraulic pressure gauge   The gauge shows the pressure in the hydraulic system and should maintain between 925 and 1150 lbs/sq. in.

[8] Starter switch   The Corsair also used a cartridge starter.

Flight Notes

Takeoff

- Set rudder trim 6 clicks right and aileron trim 6 clicks right for takeoff.
- Set flaps to 30 degrees for a normal or carrier takeoff. Takeoff can be made with any flap setting from 0 to 50 degrees. Thirty degrees provides a nice balance between not using a lot of runway, as happens with no flaps, and not getting airborne at a very low speed where the Corsair is difficult to control, as happens with full flaps.
- The Corsair can become airborne from either a three-point attitude or a wheeled attitude at 85 knots (98 mph).

Initial Climb

- Make your initial climb at 125 knots (144 mph) and full power.

Cruise

- The fuel burn in cruise at 65 percent power is 55 gph.
- The fuel burn at 100 percent power is 290 gph.

Combat

- V_c for the Corsair is 219 knots (252 mph). This is a very high V_c, so regardless of your chosen tactics, fly fast in the Corsair.
- The Corsair dives very well and can reach very high speeds. Use this diving ability to your advantage in combat.
- You can extend the 10 degrees of flap at any speed to help slow down or to achieve better turn performance below your V_c of 219 knots.

Approach and Landing

- Gear can be safely extended below 200 knots (230 mph). This high extension speed allows the Corsair pilot to use the gear to slow down or make very steep descents. On the Corsair gear extension causes a lot of drag. Extend the gear earlier if you need to slow down. Extend the gear just slightly before landing if you are already slow.
- You can extend to full flaps at 170 knots. This will help you slow down, without the steep descent that occurs when the gear come down.
- For a landing on the ground, final approach is 95 knots (109 mph) with 30 degrees of flap. For landing on a carrier, use 83 knots (96 mph) with 50 degrees of flap.

Note: *The inverted gull-wing of the Corsair made the airplane easier to safely ditch (perform a gear-up landing in the water) than other fighters. The wings would touch the water before the fuselage and plane across the water as the whole airplane slowed down. The fuselage would settle in the water without flipping over like many other fighters would.*

Tactics

Preferred Tactics

Energy tactics are best when fighting with the Corsair, but angle tactics are possible.

Advantaged Position

The Corsair and the Hellcat are similar fighters and can employ similar tactics. The Corsair is a little faster, both in acceleration and top speed, but it is less forgiving in hard turns, especially when the flight model is set to Hard. The same high-G steep turn that you can make in a Hellcat puts the Corsair into a spin. For these reasons, the better plan in a Corsair is to make repeated slashing attacks from above. Strike from above and with speed when possible. Blast right through enemy formations and don't look back until you turn around to do it again.

Neutral Position

Advantage in a Corsair means lots of E, so if you can't make a quick kill, work to build your E advantage. Whenever possible avoid steep high-G turns, but turn enough so that your opponent keeps turning hard and losing E. Beware of steep climbing turns during maneuvering—the Corsair will spin on the undisciplined pilot. The roll rate on the Corsair is good, though, so it is an excellent airplane for Immelman and split-S maneuvers. If you can get some altitude advantage, you can pass overhead and split-S into a diving attack.

Disadvantaged Position

The escape tactics of the Corsair are the same as the Hellcat. Work to deny a tracking shot while simultaneously increasing the distance between you and your pursuer.

Lockheed P-38 Lightning

In 1937, the Army Air Corps sought proposals for a high-speed, high-altitude intercept airplane. The Lockheed Aircraft Company put forth a radical new design—a twin-engine, twin-boom, tricycle-gear air-

Tips from a Master of the Corsair

Major Gregory R. "Pappy" Boyington met the Japanese and the Zero early on, flying for the American Volunteer Group in China (the famous Flying Tigers). As the colorful leader of VMF-214 (the "Black Sheep" squadron), Boyington flew the Corsair to great success. Boyington was known to go out looking for a fight. He once had his squadron fly high over a Japanese base in a bomber formation and spoke on the radio about bombing targets. When the Japanese climbed to intercept, the Corsairs returned to fighter formation and dove down on the Japanese. Boyington was shot down in January of 1944 and taken prisoner for 20 months. His final victory count was 28.

Here are some highlights from Boyington's suggested fighter tactics:

- *Tactics in the air should be studied and developed in comparison with time-tried tactics on the sea. The principles of scouting, out-flanking, ambushing, etc., all provide a basis for the development of air tactics. Of course allowances and modifications must be made for our speed, for the additional dimension in which we operate, etc. But land and sea experiences provide a starting point.*

- *Pilots must make a steady careful observation a habit. They must have a system and a routine for scanning the air both above and below, behind, on the flank and ahead. The vigil must be unceasing.*

- *All fighters must realize the critical importance of recognition in order to distinguish our planes from those of the enemy, in order to identify the enemy's different types so that his particular points of weakness can be exploited and his particular points of strength respected.*

(continued)

Tips from a Master of the Corsair continued

- *In normal combat, clouds might provide cover either for us or for the enemy and must be considered constantly in both connections.*
- *We must not climb into bogies. We must gain our altitude away in a position from which the action can be observed, and our climb must be made with a high forward air speed.*
- *We must not pull up when closely and dangerously attacked. Speed is our defense. With moderate loss of altitude and certainly without going all the way to the water and running for home, the enemy can be outdistanced, and then altitude and position recovered for further attacks.*
- *Our most successful runs against fighter opposition are from eleven to one o'clock ahead and from five to seven o'clock astern, from a level just above to a level just below.*
- *Fighters must hold their fire until within range, as indicated by the size of the target in the ringsight. Otherwise the [enemy] will be warned by the first over-anxious burst, will split-S and will be gone. On the other hand fire should be opened sooner in a head-on run because then we are closing faster and because the plane opening fire last usually turns away first and is a good target during that turn.*
- *In normal combat in enemy territory it is not desirable particularly for a single plane, to go below a base altitude, which might well be 10,000 feet. To go lower with a section of two planes might be desirable if both planes carry ample speed and are prepared to cover each other when necessary.*
- *When a plane drops out, the other member of the section should join up on some other single plane, if any is available. A one-plane section is about as useless as a three-plane section.*
- *Success in the air is a lot of little things. Most of them can be taken care of before takeoff.*

plane with counter-rotating propellers. They called it the Model-22. The Army would later call it the P-38, and the British would add the name Lightning. The P-38, shown in Figure 10-14, would become the first of many designs that would make the company a leader in defense aircraft.

Lockheed got the go-ahead to try and build a prototype Model 22, which had to climb to 20,000 feet in six minutes and cruise at a minimum of 360 mph. That demand was more than any one engine could muster, so the new design had two. Large radial engines experience cooling problems at very high altitudes, so the plane's designers selected the new version of the supercharged, liquid-cooled Allison engine.

Deliveries of the P-38 began in 1941 and U.S. Army Air Corps pilots soon found two problems. One concerned oscillation of the elevator. The balance weight you see on the tail of the P-38 was originally added to solve this problem. It turned out later that changing the shape of the wing connection to the engines was the solution, but the balance weights made elevator motion easier, so they were kept on all the

P-38s. The second problem was that the P-38 could dive at such speeds that some of the airflow created sonic shock waves, or mini sonic booms, forcing the nose downward and making the dive nearly unrecoverable. The phenomena ripped the tail off one P-38 before it was completely understood. Later models of the P-38 were equipped with a dive brake to prevent them from reaching that speed. Later

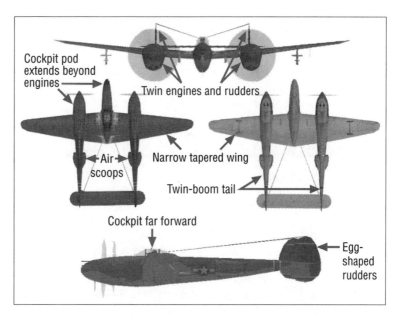

Figure 10-14 *Recognition features for the P-38 Lightning.*

models also had hydraulically boosted ailerons for easier control at high speed and 8 degrees of combat flaps to improve the P-38's less than spectacular turn performance. The P-38F modeled in Combat Flight Simulator 2 does not have any of these amenities, however.

In addition to its combat role, the P-38 was often used for photo reconnaissance. Most of these photo platforms were unarmed, even though they regularly flew over enemy territory. When danger approached, the P-38 pilots simply ran away. The enemy aircraft were unable to keep up.

Cockpit Notes

Figure 10-15 (on page 199) illustrates the P-38's cockpit layout; the following sections comment on the cockpit's components.

[1] Low hydraulic pressure light   The light will come on whenever hydraulic pressure falls too low. The P-38's wings flaps and landing gear were hydraulic.

Japan Helps Build the P-38

During the early design process of the P-38, Lockheed was on the brink of financial collapse. Ironically, Japan was integral in helping the company stay afloat. When Lockheed got the contract to develop the P-38, they had one product: the twin-engine, 10-passenger Electra. The Electra is most famous as the airplane Amelia Earhart and Fredrick Noonan were flying when they disappeared in the Pacific in 1937. Dai Nippon, the Japanese national airline, bought several Electras in 1938. Without that order, the Lockheed factory would have been empty when a British contingent came to visit and they probably would have dismissed Lockheed as a serious airplane company. Instead, the British placed an order for 250 reconnaissance/bomber versions of the Electra, giving Lockheed the cash they desperately needed to develop the P-38.

[2] Coolant temperature gauge This gauge shows the liquid coolant in both left and right engines. Desired readings are from 105 to 115 degrees C; the maximum is 125 degrees.

[3] Airspeed indicator This gauge is easier to read than the other American gauges, as the needle wraps around only once and the numbers are fully written out. Note that the numbers get closer together as the speed increases. The distance on the gauge between 300 and 400 mph is only one-third the distance between 100 and 200 mph.

[4] Tachometers Each engine has its own tachometer. Redline is 3050 rpm. Each engine also has its own MP gauge.

[5] Engine starter/magneto control switch The engine start switch—the on/off switch in the center—will start both engines, but the magneto controls are separate. To start just one engine, leave one magneto control in the off position.

[6] Fuel selector The original P-38 actually had two fuel selectors, one for each engine. The pilot was able to cross-feed tanks, so the left engine could draw from the right tanks if needed. For simplicity and to save panel space, both engines draw fuel from the same tank that you've selected via the selector. Except when you're using the drop-tank or the reserve, you want to have the setting on Both, indicating you are using both main tanks.

[7] Combined landing gear/flaps indicator The P-38 flaps have increments of down, 1/2, and up, shown across the top of the gauge. Flaps on the P-38 are hydraulic. Landing gear indications are shown below the flap indicator. Three red lights indicate gear up and three green lights indicate gear down and locked. The P-38 had tricycle gear rather than a tailwheel configuration.

[8] Engine controls There are separate throttle, propeller, and mixture controls for each engine. There are no cowl flap controls for the liquid-cooled P-38 engines.

Flight Notes

Takeoff

- Leave flaps up for takeoff. No rudder or aileron trim is needed.
- For takeoff, hold the brakes and bring the engines up 46" MP & 3000 rpm. Next release the brakes, and go to 54" MP.
- Do not lift off until reaching 120 mph (V_{mc}). After this speed pull back on the stick to lift the nose wheel.

Initial Climb

- Make your initial climb at 175 mph with both engines working or at 165 mph if one engine fails on takeoff.

Cruise

- The fuel burn in cruise at 65 percent power is 41 gph *per engine*.
- The fuel burn at 100 percent power is 180 gph *per engine*.

Combat

- V_c for the P-38 is 220 mph. With the P-38, even its best turn performance is really poor.
- One-half flaps can be used up to 250 mph to help improve turn performance, but the result is still far from stellar.

Approach and Landing

- Extending fifty percent flaps below 250 mph will help you slow down.
- You can safely extend your gear below 175 mph.
- You can safely extend full flaps below 120 mph.
- On initial approach, slow to 120 mph with gear down, flaps at half, and the engines at 25 percent power.
- Once you are near the runway and lined up extend the flaps to full and slow to 110 mph. Keep the power at 25 percent.
- Just before you reach the runway, cut the power and raise the nose just above the runway and let the speed bleed down. At approximately 80 mph, the main gear to touch down.
- For an approach with only one engine working, avoid turns into the dead engine, as the airplane can roll inverted if you are flying too slowly. Extend the gear at 160 mph, 1/2 flaps at 140 mph and fly at 130 mph and until landing is assured. Once the landing is assured, slow to 110 mph and extend the flaps to full. You will not be able to abort a landing from less than 500 feet with full flaps and gear down with only one engine operating.

Tactics

Preferred Tactics

Energy tactics are the only way to go with the P-38. Don't even try the angles fight.

Advantaged Position

The P-38 was designed specifically to get to high altitude quickly and perform well up high. When you are high above your opponent, you are in your element. You can dictate the terms of combat and, as long as you keep both engines running, no one can catch you. Dive for your attack and fly a pure pursuit. You will close quickly with your speed advantage, so don't lead your target until you are ready to fire. Fire with machine guns to check your lead and then let go with both guns and cannon in short bursts as you pass. Bank up and away to turn your speed back into altitude. When safely out of range, turn around for another attack.

Neutral Position

Don't get lured into a turning dogfight. You will lose. The minimum airspeed you want to see is 300 mph. Each time you cross the enemy's path look at your airspeed. If it is in the high 300s or the 400s, climb away, possibly with a right turn. If it is in the low 300s, make a shallow, diving exit and start climbing when at a safe distance. With your excellent rate of climb you can also climb to a position well above your target as you cross paths. Roll inverted at

Figure 10-15   *The P-38 cockpit.*

the cross and pull down into a high, slashing attack. Your success in gaining advantage in the P-38 will largely depend on how well you manipulate speed and altitude.

Disadvantaged Position

Run away. If you have better than 300 mph, you can turn hard right and up. Zeros can't make climbing right high-speed turns very well. This is especially true if you are in multiplayer mode and realism is set at Hard. If you don't have the speed, dive and turn left. If you are really desperate, you can use differential power to make tighter turns. If you have the engine control unit (ECU) showing, reduce the power on the engine inside the turn. So, if you wanted to break right even harder, you would reduce power on the right engine. Reducing one engine's power will reduce your total power and your climb rate will drop by close to 70 percent. If you use differential engine power, you're best off doing it while diving.

As long as you keep your speed up, you should be able to get far enough away to turn and face the enemy head to head in a neutral situation.

Chapter Eleven

Non-Player-Flyable Aircraft

A crucial component of success in combat is knowing your opponent's strengths, weaknesses, and tactics. This chapter gives you the low-down on the airplanes you can't fly yourself but will probably meet in battle. Some of these airplanes look alike but are actually very different. A common error is confusing a Zero and a Dauntless dive-bomber. If you have labels turned on, you won't make that mistake, but if you've turned them off for increased realism, the mistake could be fatal. Unlike the fighters, many of the non-player-flyable airplanes have rear-facing guns and multiple crew members trying to shoot you down. All the airplanes have some weak spots that you can exploit in combat, if you take the time to find out where those weak spots are.

Nakajima Ki-43 Hayabusa ("Oscar")

Like the U.S. armed forces, the Japanese Navy and the Japanese Army had separate air forces. The Hayabusa (Japanese for peregrine; Allied code name Oscar) is an army fighter and is in many ways analogous to the Zero. Though similar to the Zero, which was manufactured by Mitsubishi, the Hayabusa was a totally separate design by Nakajima Hikoki K.K. Faced with many of the same demands for fighter performance and constrained by many of the same limitations, the two companies produced very similar aircraft. When the Oscar first appeared, pilots complained that it was not maneuverable enough and was underpowered.

Many versions of the Oscar were made. The IIB version of the Oscar had a bigger Nakajima engine (1150 hp); shorter, stronger wings; limited armor; and a new canopy for better visibility. The IIB version was also one of the first Japanese fighters to have a reflection gunsight. A reflection gunsight is used in all the player-flyable fighters. It projects a gunsight on the front window of the cockpit so that the pilot doesn't need to look through a telescope-type

The Long-Lived Oscar

Unlike the Zero, the Oscar saw use as a fighter after World War II. Even though the Oscar was seriously outclassed by the new fighters of the late 1940s, a few countries used Japanese Army Air Force Oscars left behind after the Japanese defeat. Thailand and Indonesia both used Oscars to build their own air forces. The French used Oscars for a short time in what is now Vietnam. The Chinese People's Liberation Army also used quite a few Oscars in its own air force.

gunsight while flying. The various Oscars never got more than two 12.7 mm (.50-caliber) guns and never had cannon.

Figure 11-1 illustrates the features that make the Oscar easy to spot.

Combat Notes

Light and nimble like the Zero, the Oscar also lacks armor and structural strength. Unlike the Zero, the Oscar has no cannon, so it poses less of an offensive threat. The Oscar is also slower than the Zero, so it is a bit easier to simply outrun an Oscar that is closing on your tail. The Oscar wings aren't as likely to burst into flame, but a few repeated shots to the tail or a hit to the cockpit will usually take an Oscar down. The Oscar is very maneuverable, so expect angle tactics. You'll have trouble setting up a tracking shot on an undamaged airplane; your best bet are shots taken head-to-head. Once hit, the Oscar often loses maneuverability and can be tracked for an easy kill. Figure 11-2 illustrates a typical scenario.

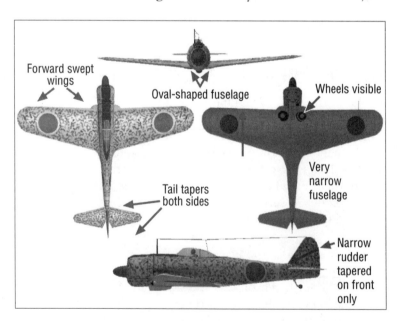

Forward swept wings

Oval-shaped fuselage

Wheels visible

Tail tapers both sides

Very narrow fuselage

Narrow rudder tapered on front only

Figure 11-1   *Recognition features for the Nakajima Ki-43 Hayabusa (Oscar).*

Nakajima B5N ("Kate")

The Kate was one of Japan's first all-metal, low-wing combat aircraft. In many ways similar to the Douglas Devastator, the Kate was a torpedo bomber with a crew of two or three and was capable of carrying light or heavy bombs or one heavy torpedo. The Kate did a great deal of damage at Pearl Harbor, with an estimated 50 percent of the torpedoes launched exploding on target. Faster than the Devastator on a torpedo run, the Kate was still slow and vulnerable. Like the Betty bomber, the Kate had a "wet wing" full of fuel that was a favorite target for American gunners. By 1944, the Kate was being replaced by the vastly superior Jill in combat. Figure 11-3 shows the unique features of the Kate.

Figure 11-2 *This Oscar is shot down after a single hit to the cockpit. The attacker was flying a Zero and following the Oscar to gauge the Oscar's maneuverability.*

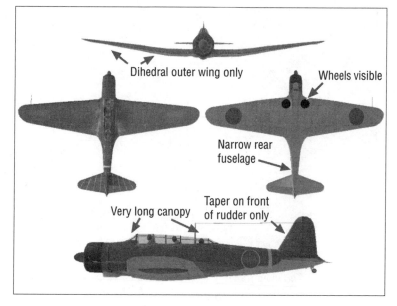

Figure 11-3 *Recognition features for the Nakajima B5N (Kate).*

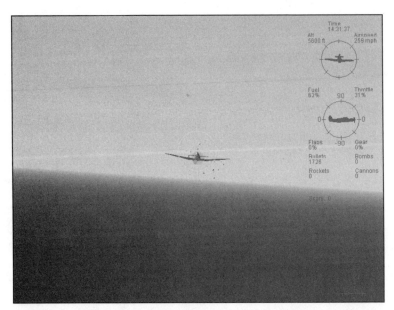

Combat Notes

The Kate is slow and has a weak armament of .30-caliber machine guns. The cockpit itself is an excellent target: one hit sends an apparently undamaged airplane rolling over into the sea with a dead pilot. You can avoid the Kate's tail gunner by striking the Kate from behind and below if it is still high in formation. Once on a torpedo run, the Kate is very low off the water and is best destroyed by a frontal attack just slightly above the angle of its forward-facing guns. The Kate is not very maneuverable compared with most fighters; as long as you can avoid the tail gunner, the Kate should be an easy kill. Figure 11-4 illustrates the Kate's more vulnerable features.

Figure 11-4 *The slow-moving, weakly defended Kate is especially vulnerable from behind and slightly below or from the belly.*

Aichi D3A ("Val")

The Aichi D3A "Val" dive bomber was designed in 1936 after extensive study of the German Heinkel dive bombers. The Val also resembles the excellent German dive bomber, the Junkers 87 "Stuka." Vals were used to devastating effectiveness in the Pearl Harbor attack, with an 80 percent hit rate. After dropping its bomb, the highly maneuverable Val would often take on the role of a fighter and do what damage it could with its .30-caliber guns. The Val is still fairly slow and vulnerable in level flight. Of the 29 Japanese planes lost in the Pearl Harbor attack, 14 were Vals. Dive-bombing is a difficult skill to master, however, and as experienced Val pilots were lost in combat, the Val's effectiveness declined. After the battle of Midway, where the Japanese lost a majority of their best Val pilots, the hit rate of the dive bomber crews fell to under 15 percent. Figure 11-5 illustrates the Val's unique features.

Note: *The term* dihedral *refers to how much the wings appear to bend upward as seen from the front. An airplane with a lot of dihedral will have wings that appear v-shaped when viewed from the front (see the Kate in Figure 11-3), while an airplane with no dihedral will have wings that appear flat.*

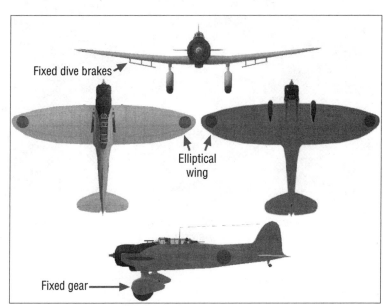

Figure 11-5 *Recognition features for the Val.*

Combat Notes

The Val is structurally reinforced to handle the stresses of high-speed dives and pullouts and therefore is stronger than many of the other Japanese combat aircraft. The Val is also lightweight and highly maneuverable, making it a much more difficult target than the Kate. The Val will readily out-turn the P-38 and can even give a Wildcat pilot a hard time. If the Val had more firepower, its maneuverability would be a real problem. With .30-caliber machine guns, the Val lacks any real hitting power. The rear gunner has only one machine gun, instead of the Kate's two. Try to get the Val before it begins its dive. As with the Kate, attack the Val from a spot behind the airplane and below it, or from a spot in front and above. With its single rear gunner, a Val can be attacked from above and behind, as seen in Figure 11-6, with less danger than the same attack on a Kate.

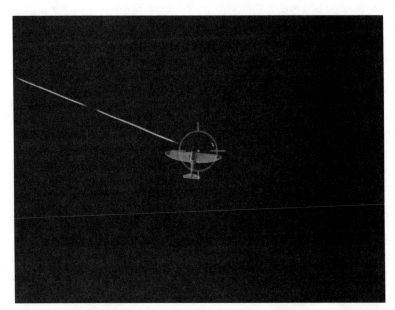

Figure 11-6 *The Val has the same undefended areas as the Kate and has only one rear-facing machine gun.*

Mitsubishi G4M ("Betty")

The Betty was designed to meet Japan's need for a long-range bomber capable of carrying up to 800 kg (1760 lbs) of ordnance. Mitsubishi's first designs were

for a four-engine bomber, but the navy rejected the design, demanding a two-engine airplane. Two engines limited the weight of fuel the airplane could carry, so Mitsubishi designers again had to cut weight at the expense of crew protection and structural strength. The Betty's "wet wing" design was its Achilles heel. The wings were filled with up to 6500 liters (1717 gallons) of fuel. This gave the Betty a range of 2535 miles, greater than that of a contemporary B-17 and almost twice the range of a B-25, but several well-placed incendiary bullets would detonate the wing. Making the wing tanks bulletproof would have reduced the fuel load by 45 percent, which the navy believed was unacceptable. Thick-skinned and reasonably well-armed, the Betty was not necessarily an easy kill. The Betty was the primary bomber for both the navy and army throughout the war. Figure 11-7 illustrates the Betty's unique features.

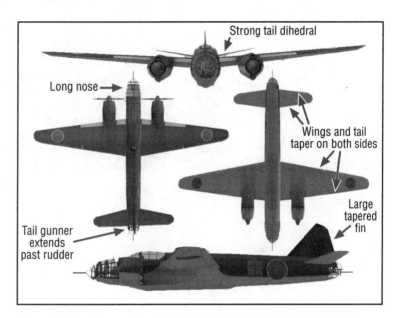

Figure 11-7   *Recognition features for the Mitsubishi G4M (Betty).*

Combat Notes

It's a mistake to think of the Betty as an easy kill. The least-defended approach is from the side, and even here you will get trouble from the top and

bottom gunners. The nose, top, and belly gunners don't pose a big threat with their .30-caliber machine guns, but the tail gunner has a 20 mm cannon and can cause some serious damage. As you can see in Figure 11-8, you'll find it difficult to get a sustained tracking shot on a Betty without giving the tail gunner your airplane as an easy target. Try to hit the Betty in the wings from side attacks or the cockpit from frontal attacks. Accuracy counts with the Betty, and repeated hits to one area will serve you better than several hits spread over the airframe.

Figure 11-8 *Attacking a Betty from behind might be the last thing you do in your piloting career unless you can get in a quick shot, as shown here.*

Bell P-39 Airacobra

The Bell P-39 Airacobra implemented many new design ideas. Some of those ideas worked well; some didn't. One of the Airacobra's greatest assets was the 37-mm cannon mounted right in the center of the propeller hub. A single well-placed hit from this cannon would down most any fighter and was devastating in strafing runs against ground equipment. The cannon was so powerful that the wing would momentary stall if the gun were fired at too low an airspeed. The P-39 was designed as a high-altitude interceptor, just like the P-38. Also like the P-38, the P-39 has the Allison inverted V-12 engine, but unlike the P-38, the P-39 was produced without the turbocharger. At the time, the turbocharged Allison was not very reliable and the army decided it wasn't necessary. They were wrong. Down low, the P-39 performed well and flew beautifully. Over

Yamamoto's Betty

In early April 1943, all the airplanes from the carrier task force commanded by Admiral Isoruku Yamamoto were stationed at Rabaul in preparation for a major Japanese counterattack on New Guinea and the Solomons. Yamamoto was the strategist who had brilliantly orchestrated the attack on Pearl Harbor and who had suffered massive defeat at Midway. The defeat at Midway was due in part to U.S. code breakers, who had broken the Japanese radio code and discovered Japan's true plans. The cracked code came into play again when the U.S. Navy learned that Yamamoto would leave Rabaul on April 18th on a Mitsubishi Betty bomber. Fourteen P-38s set out to intercept that bomber. Four of the Lightnings picked up the flight of two Bettys and six Zeros. Two Lightnings tore through the Zero formation and bore down on their principal targets: the Bettys. The Zeros followed but couldn't keep up. Capt. Thomas Lanphier slowed slightly, sent a long burst into the right wing of the first Betty, and watched the wing burst into flame and separate from the airplane. Lt. Rex Barber was slowing behind the second Betty when three diving Zeros came in around him. Lt. Besby Holmes dove on the Zeros at 425 mph, hitting two. Holmes's speed actually carried him past Barber, allowing both P-38s to fire on the Betty and send it crashing to the sea. Yamamoto was gone, and the huge counterattack never happened.

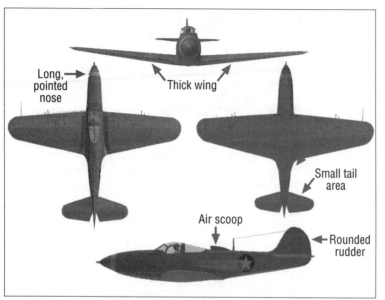

Figure 11-9   *Recognition features for the Bell P-39 Airacobra.*

10,000 feet, though, it was too underpowered to put up much of a fight. P-39 pilots could inflict serious damage if they had the element of surprise, but they suffered at the hands of the Japanese pilots in their Zeros. After the P-38 replaced the P-39, many P-39s went to the Russians, who used them successfully on the eastern front for low-level ground attacks. Figure 11-9 shows you how to spot an Airacobra.

Combat Notes

As you can see in Figure 11-10, the P-39 has a dangerous face, with seven weapons ready to fire on you. Avoid a head-to-head with the Airacobra at all costs. Once you're safely to the side, turn

Figure 11-10   *The business end of a P-39: four .30-caliber guns, two .50-caliber guns, and one 37 mm cannon. Stay away from here.*

and get on the P-39's tail. Lots of horizontal separation at each cross will help you get in position behind the P-39 and avoid the head-to-head confrontation. Expect the P-39 to turn well, especially at low altitudes, but not as well as any Japanese fighter. If you can move into a tracking position, the battle is basically over. The P-39 isn't as rugged as the Grumman fighters. Once you've established the proper lead, as shown in Figure 11-11, pull the trigger and wait for the fireball.

Figure 11-11   *This is the view of a P-39 you're better off looking for. Note the lead of the gunsight relative to the airplane.*

Douglas TBD Devastator

The Douglas TBD Devastator was the navy's first all-metal, single-wing airplane. In 1935, when the TBD first flew, it was a formidable airplane. Capable of carrying bombs, depth charges, or a torpedo, the TBD seemed an excellent weapon against sea and land targets alike. Most navy pilots wanted a chance to

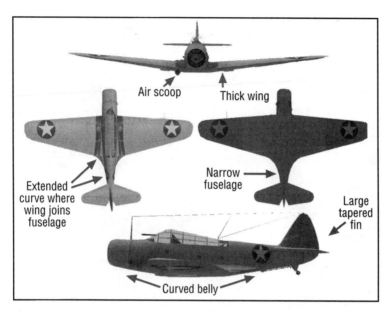

Figure 11-12 *Recognition features for the Douglas TBD Devastator.*

fly the big, sleek bird to a target and sink an entire ship. But the appeal of the TBD was short-lived. While the airplane was effective against ships that had no fighter defense, the slow-and-low attack profile and weak weapons made the TBD an easy target. After disastrous losses at Midway, the TBD was phased out and replaced with the new Grumman TBF Avenger. Figure 11-12 illustrates the TBD's unique features.

Combat Notes

Attacking the TBD is much like attacking the Kate. While the Kate is faster and better armed, the TBD can take more damage before falling. Like the Kate, the TBD's best strike points are above and in front or below and behind. The rear gunner's .30-caliber machine gun doesn't pack much punch, but if you're attacking in an unarmored Zero, avoid it. Slashing attacks from the side can wreak havoc on a squadron of TBDs, as can inside turns with a strong lead pursuit. The only time you might see a TBD moving quickly is during a dive,

just before it begins a torpedo run, but the TBD is surprisingly maneuverable and when piloted by an ace, can keep changing direction to prevent a tracking shot.

Figure 11-13 illustrates the best strategy when confronting a TBD. Using a tight turn for a high-lead pursuit will allow you to close on the target while staying mostly clear of the tail gunner. The higher the lead, the faster the closure and the safer you'll be, but the shot opportunity will be shorter and you may overshoot the target.

Douglas SBD Dauntless

Like the TBD, the Douglas SBD was a slow yet maneuverable airplane with the dangerous mission of making attack runs on ships defended by fighters and

The P-39 in Australia

Rick Durden relates the experiences of his friend Marion Franklin Kirby (or Kirby), a P-39 pilot in the early days of World War II:

The P-400 was the export version of the P-39 Airacobra. It had an Allison engine and an absolute ceiling of 23,000 feet so long as the pilot did not apply much rudder or aileron. Any control deflection meant the rapid loss of about 2,000 feet. The words Kirby uses to this day to describe the P-400 cannot be repeated in print. Suffice it to say he loathed the airplane.

Kirby was assigned to the 80th Fighter Squadron, the Head Hunters, in New Guinea, where he flew off both 12 Mile and 14 Mile Strips near Port Moresby. There, with his squadron mates, he fully came to understand just how awful the P-400 was. It did not even come near to performing with the Japanese Zero. U.S. intelligence had seriously underestimated the quality of the Zero, as well as the pilots who flew it.

The P-400 proved to be so bad that when Kirby's squadron would be scrambled on word of a bombing raid on Port Moresby, they would take off and climb in a direction away from the attacking aircraft in an effort to get to altitude. They would struggle up to 23,000 feet out over the ocean and only then turn back to face the enemy airplanes. The Japanese would come over at 27,000 feet and bomb unopposed because the U.S. fighters could not get that high. Fortunately for Kirby and his mates, because they could not threaten the bombers, the Zeros at that time in the war were under orders not to break close escort formation with the bombers and attack. Kirby remains convinced that had they attacked he would have been just another dead P-400 pilot shortly after it started.

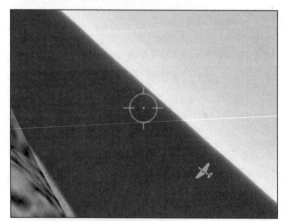

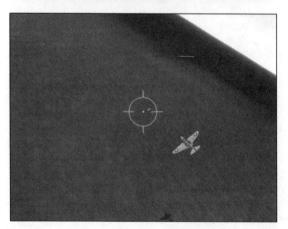

Figure 11-13   *Attacking the Devastator.*

antiaircraft fire. The SBD had a few advantages over the TBD. Where the TBD made its attack runs at 115 mph and flew low over the water to drop torpedoes, the SBD crews dove nearly straight down on the target at 275 mph and then used the accumulated energy from the dive to pull up and escape. To help mask their approach, the SBD crew would attack from the direction of the sun. Japanese gunners learned to watch for a flash high above their ship. The flash was the sun glinting off the SBD canopy as it rolled over to dive. If the gunners missed that warning, the next indication of an SBD attack might be the whine of the engine and the whistle of the dive brakes and flaps. By then, it was too late. Figure 11-14 shows the SBD's unique features.

Combat Notes

The SBD is much better armed than the TBD, with two forward-facing .50-caliber guns and two rear-facing .50-caliber guns for the tail gunner. The SBD is more stoutly constructed as well, so it will take more hits before it goes down. Unfortunately for you,

these improvements didn't cost the SBD much in terms of maneuverability. While the SBD can't out-turn any of the Japanese fighters, an ace pilot in an SBD can make for a hard target. The SBD is faster than the TBD, but it is no speedster. The same slashing attacks and high lead pursuits that work on the TBD also work on the SBD. Watch out for those .50-caliber guns when you attack from in front or from behind. The SBD is also vulnerable from below, which is an attack possibility in the climb-capable Zero. As with the Val dive bomber, try to catch the TBD before it begins its dive. If you don't, you might find you have no ship left to land on after the battle.

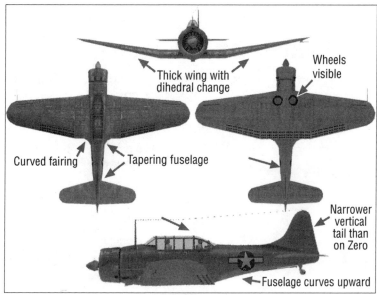

Figure 11-14 *Recognition features for the Douglas SBD Dauntless.*

Midway: The Final Battleground for the Devastator

During the battle of Midway, three Devastator squadrons, VT-8, VT-6, and VT-3, attacked the carrier group of Vice Admiral Chuichi Nagumo. Flying slow and low over the water, the Devastators were easy prey for defending Zeros and antiaircraft guns. Seven of the eight TBDs in VT-8 were shot down before they even got in torpedo range. The eighth airplane was shot down after its dropped torpedo malfunctioned and didn't explode. Five minutes later, VT-6 lost 10 out of 14 TBDs before they got into range; the remaining 4 missed their targets. Thirty minutes later, VT-3 attacked with 19 TBDs. Again ten were downed while still out of range, and the torpedoes that were dropped either malfunctioned or missed. In the end, 35 of the 41 TBDs were lost, all without scoring a single hit. The Japanese victory was short-lived, however. As the Japanese were finishing up the TBDs, a squadron of SBDs, the other Douglas two-man bomber, was beginning its bombing dives from above.

Grumman TBF Avenger

The Grumman TBF Avenger was designed to replace the aging Devastator before the horrible events at Midway demonstrated once and for all that the Devastator was no longer fit for combat. Chronologically, the Avenger was designed after the Wildcat and before the Hellcat. Some of the Avenger's design features also found their way into the Hellcat. The three big lessons of the Devastator were bigger guns, better protection, and more speed. The Avenger had all three and fared better than its predecessor. Even so, torpedo bombing was a dangerous proposition that fell out of favor after the war. Figure 11-15 illustrates the Avenger's unique features.

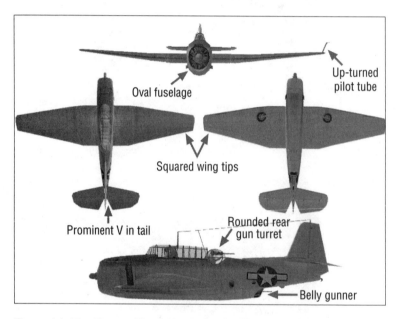

Figure 11-15   *Recognition features for the Grumman TBF Avenger.*

Combat Notes

The Avenger is the fastest, toughest, and best-armed of the American torpedo and bomb airplanes. The Avenger can also be confused with a Dauntless. As Figure 11-16 illustrates, this mistake will result in a nasty surprise from the extra

belly gun. The Avenger isn't as maneuverable as either of the Douglas airplanes and seems to be most vulnerable in the tail. Considering the rear-facing weapons, the tail might be a little tough to hit, but a long, concentrated burst of fire will probably result in victory.

North American PBJ/B-25 Mitchell

Figure 11-16 *When attacking from below and behind, make sure your quarry is an SBD (top) and not an Avenger with a belly gun (bottom).*

The B-25 was the first twin-engine bomber designed by North American Aviation, the same company that produced the famous P-51 Mustang. The bomber was built to meet the army's need for a fast attack bomber that would not require a fighter escort. The first B-25s were fast and quite maneuverable—so fast, in fact, that the Army declared their speed a national secret—but they lacked enough firepower to adequately defend themselves. Later versions of

Diving a Dauntless

Diving 5 tons of aluminum and high explosives almost straight down for 3 miles took skill, courage, and nerves of steel. A Dauntless pilot worked through the following steps to put the payload on the target:

1. *Establish an altitude of approximately 15,000 feet above the target.*

2. *Retard the throttle, and raise the nose slightly.*

3. *Pull the handle that deploys the dive-brakes and landing flaps.*

4. *Roll inverted.*

5. *Pull the nose downward, and assume a dive angle of 70 degrees.*

6. *While diving, look into the telescopic gun sight and carefully align the crosshairs on the target.*

7. *Keep the flight of the airplane coordinated.*

8. *Avoid the antiaircraft fire.*

9. *Release the bomb between 2500 feet and 1500 feet.*

10. *Immediately retract the flaps and dive brakes, and pull out of the dive with a 6-G pull-up.*

11. *While pulling out, repeatedly change bank angles to avoid enemy airplane and antiaircraft fire.*

12. *Run for home. The SBD carries only one bomb so you get only one shot.*

The whole process takes less than a minute. The rear gunner is firing at enemy planes throughout the dive, hoping the pilot can pull out.

the B-25 had more and larger weapons—all the way up to a 75 mm cannon in the nose. With this kind of armament and a load of either bombs or depth charges, the B-25 was a complete attack machine, capable of destroying airplanes and ships alike.

Figure 11-17 shows you how to recognize the Mitchell.

Combat Notes

The B-25 is one rough customer. It's quite well armed, so you can't count on a safe attack position. It's fast, so it is hard to catch up to except in level flight, and level flight makes you a sitting duck for the gunners. It's tough, so don't expect a victory after just a few hits. The bomber attacks I discussed in Chapter 8, "Targets Other than Fighters," are some possible scenarios. Regardless of what strategy you choose, keep your speed up and try to attack in waves. Bomber attacks in general go better when more aircraft attack,

spreading out the focus of the gunners. The B-25 can maneuver fairly well except while in formation. The top gunner on the B-25 is also limited at angles where he is firing directly at his rudders. This is a tough angle to close from, but it is a weakness that a skilled pilot could exploit. Figures 11-18 and 11-19 illustrate strategies for facing the B-25.

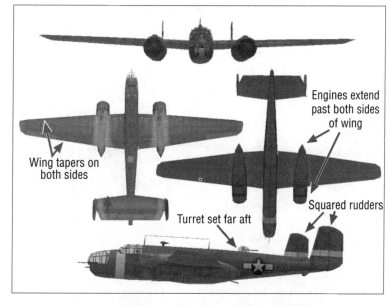

Wing tapers on both sides

Engines extend past both sides of wing

Squared rudders

Turret set far aft

Figure 11-17   Recognition features for the B-25 Mitchell.

Consolidated PB4Y/B-24 Liberator

The B-24 is an example of function over form. Compared to the B-17, the other heavy U.S. bomber, the B-24 looks like an

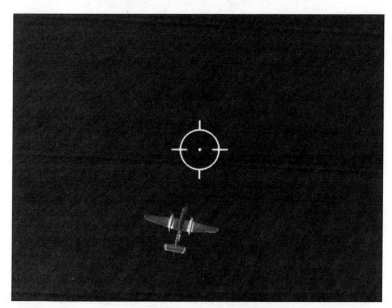

Figure 11-18   The B-25 is well defended from almost every angle. Attacking at high speed and from difficult-to-hit angles will improve your survival rate.

Figure 11-19   *Notice how the right rudder is between you and the top gunner. Attacks from this angle are hard to make, but will meet little resistance.*

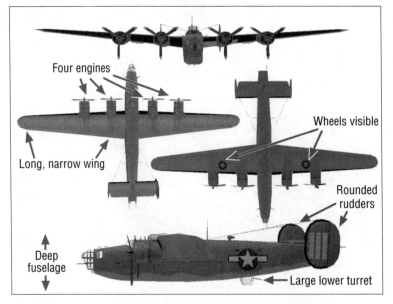

Four engines

Long, narrow wing

Deep fuselage

Wheels visible

Rounded rudders

Large lower turret

Figure 11-20   *Recognition features for the B-24 Liberator.*

ugly boat with wings. But looks are only skin deep, and the B-24 was a well-conceived design created to meet the army's need for a four-engine bomber capable of flying at 300 mph with a range of 3000 miles. The B-24 came close to these numbers while also carrying a massive load of bombs. Performance always comes at a price in aviation, though. The B-24's top-secret wing design was efficient but unstable at high altitudes. The B-24 also couldn't take the battle damage that a B-17 could withstand. Even with its shortcomings, the B-24 became the most produced airplane design of the war.

Figure 11-20 shows you how to recognize the B-24.

Combat Notes

Everything that's true about the B-25 is also true for the B-24, except that the B-24 is bigger and faster, and its tail gunner sits past the rudders so that he can fire in any direction. As illustrated in Figure 11-21, the B-24D has one potentially fatal flaw: the nose gun in the original B-24 fires in virtually every direction except straight ahead. This was remedied to a degree in the B-24D modeled in Microsoft Combat Flight Simulator 2, but the airplane is still not as well defended against a head-on run from slightly below. Make that shot count, though. As you can see in Figure 11-22, attacking a B-24 from behind is bad for your health. The B-24 is big, so you don't want to waste shots by

Modifying a B-25 for a Carrier-Based Attack

In early 1942, a select group of volunteer pilots and crew were trained for a top-secret attack on the Japanese homeland. Their airplanes were B-25s that were specially modified for the job. The B-25s had their bottom gun turrets removed and extra fuel tanks installed in the wings. Even more fuel was carried in the fuselage in five-gallon cans that would be pumped into the tanks during the flight. The top-secret Norden bombsight was replaced with a different sight. Finally, dummy wooden guns were added to the tail to discourage attacks from behind, where the airplanes were now weakly defended. The crews practiced taking off in overloaded bombers in a short a distance of 750 feet.

The modified B-25s were hoisted onto the USS Hornet, which sailed for Japan. Eight hundred miles off the coast of Japan, the Hornet was spotted by a fishing boat. Worried the boat might radio a warning to Japanese authorities, the bombers launched. The crews knew they didn't have enough fuel to reach their final destination airfields in China, but they took off anyway. Their mission was to bomb Tokyo, but the bombing raid did little actual damage, and all the B-25s were lost to crashes or capture in China. Most of the pilots returned home safely and discovered that their actions had been a huge boost to U.S. morale and had affected Japanese war strategy: it caused the Japanese to rethink their defense of the home islands. Front line fighter units were taken out of action in the South Pacific to defend the main islands. Lieutenant Colonel Jimmy Doolittle, the commander of the mission, was awarded the Medal of Honor, and all 79 volunteers received the Distinguished Flying Cross.

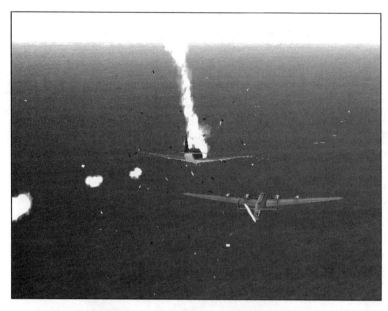

Figure 11-21 *Attacking a B-24 from dead astern will usually produce unsatisfactory results, as this fighter's discovered.*

hitting it all over the airframe. Concentrate your fire on vulnerable areas such as the cockpit or engines.

Douglas R4D/C-47 Skytrain

Ask a group of pilots to name the ten most significant airplanes of all time, and you'll probably find the C-47 on everyone's list. Most pilots would probably refer to the C-47 by its civilian name, the DC-3. Designed as a passenger and cargo carrier for the young but growing field of air travel, the DC-3/C-47 was pressed into service hauling heavy loads long dis-

Figure 11-22 *Only one gun points forward out of the nose on the B-24D.*

tances, often out of very rough airfields. Versatile and dependable, the DC-3/C-47 would continue to be used in military and civilian roles for many years. (Before the beginning of the war, there were 455 DC-3s flying. By the war's end, nearly 11,000 DC-3s had been produced. Of these, several hundred are still in use today.) Figure 11-23 shows you how to spot a C-47.

Note: *Cabin heat was not available on B-24s until 1944, even though the temperature around the cabin of a B-24 at altitude over the South Pacific was -20 degrees C (-4 degrees F).*

Combat Notes

The C-47 has no armaments and no armor. You are still best off concentrating your fire, just as with the bigger bombers, since the airplane is stoutly built and can take quite a bit of punishment without exploding. Sometimes the only indication that you have shot down

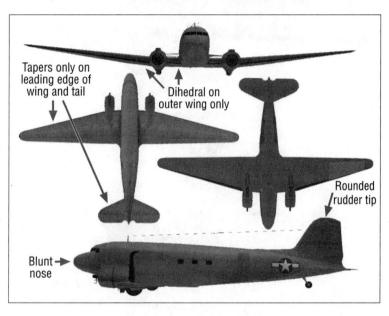

Figure 11-23   *Recognition features for the Douglas R4D/C-47 Skytrain.*

the C-47 is the message at the top of the screen telling you—or the sight of three crew members bailing out.

Chapter Twelve

MISSIONS AND CAMPAIGNS

Congratulations on completing your combat pilot training. Now that you know the moves and the machines, it's time to put your new knowledge to the test by flying missions. Unlike Quick Combat, in which the combatants are tossed into the aerial arena and left to duke it out, missions are carefully planned out and involve the actions of many participants. Missions also happen in real time. For example, a mission might call for you to fight off an attack on a distant airbase. After you launch, a small group of enemy fighters appears to the south, tempting you off course. If you choose to attack the fighters, you'll arrive at the air base too late to save it. If you stay with your mission goal, you'll arrive with time to climb high and wait for the enemy.

Missions also involve ships and ground troops, which add a whole new dimension to flying combat. Sometimes these items will be your direct targets and you must strafe or bomb them. Sometimes these items will be your indirect targets and you must protect bombers or torpedo planes so that they can destroy the ship or airbase. Don't expect the ground units to sit still while you attack. As you maneuver to get a shot at the enemy, you must also avoid flak and bullets from the ships and cannons below you. Flak appears as black puffs of smoke and as objects that look like spinning disks. Gunfire from below is lit by the same tracers that you see in aerial combat. Figure 12-1 shows gunfire and flak.

Mission Briefing

All missions start with a mission briefing. The briefing contains important information such as photos, background information, and a map of the mission as planned. To see most of this information, click the Advanced Info button on

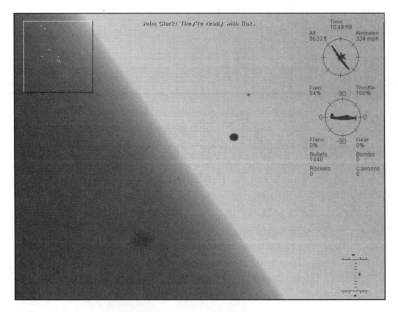

Figure 12-1 *When you fly a mission, you must maneuver to avoid flak and gunfire, as well as enemy fighters.*

Note: *When you select a mission, you can choose from three difficulty levels: Easy, Medium, or Hard. The difficulty affects the computer-controlled pilots. When you select Hard, your wingmen won't be as skilled and your enemies will be tougher than if you select Easy. Selecting Hard also holds you to a stricter standard for scoring. Your criteria for success are more ambitious, making it harder to get medals and promotions.*

the Briefing screen. In the Advanced Info screen, your mission briefing is described in a text area on the left side of the screen. Here you'll find a description of the mission, the aircraft you'll fly, and your area of operation. As you scroll down, you'll see the overview of this mission, background information explaining what led up to this mission or where it fits in the bigger picture, and intelligence reports that might give you valuable tips on the location of antiaircraft guns or the possibility of surprise attacks.

Mission Map

Missions are planned out on maps, just like the big tabletop maps surrounded by generals that you see in old war movies.

On the right side of the Advanced Info screen, you'll see the mission map. The map is dynamic; you can zoom in on specific areas that you want to examine in detail. What you see on the map are the routes of individual groups involved in the mission.

Mission construction starts with your squadron, which follows a planned route across the map. Along this route, the mission developers have designated specific waypoints where actions take place. The actions at waypoints are indicated by shape. The takeoff point appears as an airplane. Turn points—points where you change direction—appear as circles. Attack points appear as triangles. The landing point appears as a box. Figure 12-2 shows the Advanced Info screen for a simple mission in which the player intercepts and attacks an unescorted ship.

Combat Tip #10: *Although the Axis forces lost the war, history pays respect to the best World War II combat pilots irrespective of which side they flew for. In Microsoft Combat Flight Simulator 2, playing each side offers unique challenges and the overall victory or loss of the war should be considered immaterial. Be confident that whichever side you choose—I hope you'll play both—the skills you acquire will prove invaluable should the office LAN suddenly erupt into the next Combat Flight Simulator 2 war zone.*

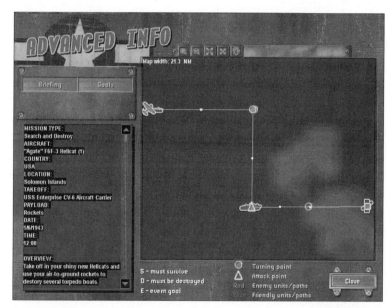

Figure 12-2   *This simple mission shows the player departing a carrier to the west, turning south, attacking an unescorted ship, and landing on an island.*

The mission briefing does not necessarily show all the groups of enemy forces you might encounter. Mission designers who want their missions to retain an element of surprise can prevent elements from appearing in your briefing. Furthermore, your actions can trigger new enemy units to appear or can cause a change in your route. The mission briefing can still give you clues that hidden events might exist. When a map shows a mission in which your route zigzags over a group of bombers you're escorting, each of these waypoints is a possible point for a surprise attack. As you study the map in the mission briefing, look for unusual turn waypoints as places where the mission designer might try to catch you off guard.

Mission Goals

"All missions must be flown as planned and briefed unless there is real justification to the contrary—there must be discipline. Along with realizing the purpose of the mission, each pilot must realize fully his responsibilities for its successful execution."
—Major G. "Pappy" Boyington

Each group of airplanes, ships, or ground units can be incorporated into the mission goals as elements that must survive, if they are on your side, or must be destroyed, if they belong to the enemy. Clicking the Goals tab on the Advanced Info screen will show you these goals. Your success in the mission is based on how well you meet these goals. You can down enough aircraft to become an ace but still fail in your mission. When you fly a campaign, missions are linked, so your success in one mission will determine what happens in your next mission. Your success in meeting mission goals will also influence promotion in rank and what medals you receive.

Flying a Mission

Now that you've read your briefing, it's time to fly. A mission can start with you already in the air, but you'll usually start on a carrier or an airfield. You need to start your engine and take off. If you have wingmen accompanying you on this mission, they fall in behind you once you're airborne. When you have built up some speed, you'll have the option of flying to the next waypoint in real time or using warp. When warp becomes available, a message will appear, offering to let you skip to the next action by pressing X. If you do so, warp will take you to the next waypoint and will account for the fuel and time it would have taken to get there. The airplanes, ships, and ground troops in the mission will also have moved as if time had passed.

Note: *Warp is not always available. The mission designer can disable warp at any waypoint. You are never allowed to warp out of combat.*

Once you get to an attack waypoint, you'll usually still have some distance to close between you and the enemy. Use this time to get yourself into an advantageous position. If you can, gain some altitude so that you can swoop down on the enemy from above. If you plan to attack from behind, maneuver so that you'll close on the enemy from behind. Unlike Quick Combat, in which the enemy's only goal is to shoot you down, in a mission, the enemy planes might not engage until you start the attack. This means you can sneak up on the enemy and attack from the best position, usually the rear. Figure 12-3 shows three Zeros flying in a triangular *shotai* formation. The pilot closed on the nearest airplane

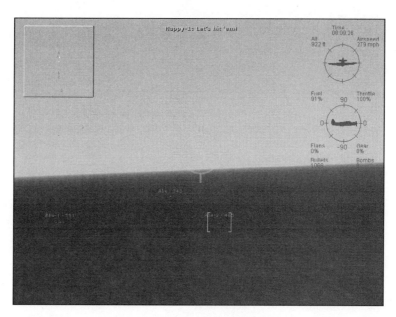

Figure 12-3   *Attacking a formation from behind gives you the opportunity to hit several airplanes in a single pass.*

first and didn't fire until the selected fighter was close enough to guarantee a quick kill. After the first Zero is dispatched, a quick adjustment will put the next Zero in the gun sights. The same method works on most airplane formations. This system is less safe on airplanes that have rear gunners, but the strategy is still effective, as shown in Figure 12-4.

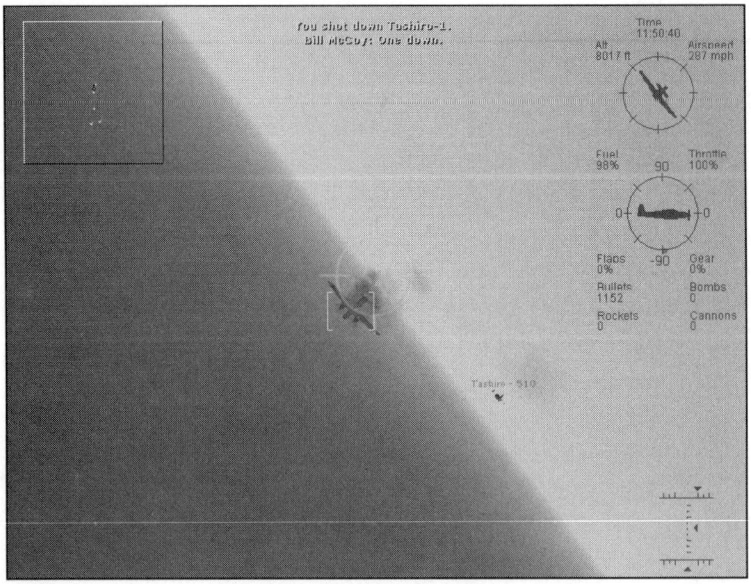

Combat can get confusing when you're in the air with a dozen other friendly and enemy airplanes. Always remember your mission goals. If part of your mission is to protect TBD Devastators, stay over the enemy ships and use your airplane identification skills to find the Devastators. If you have labels turned on, you'll notice that many airplanes have numbers after their unit names. Airplanes with the same name are always of the same type. Therefore, if you notice that one of the Devastators that you were supposed to protect is "Duckbill-4," you know any airplane labeled "Duckbill-x" is also a Devastator. Figure 12-5 shows a busy sky with a Devastator labeled "Pitchfork" in the upper right of the screen. The leader of any group of airplanes does not have a number after his name, so Pitchfork might be leading more Devastators labeled Pitchfork-1, Pitchfork-2, and so on. Pitchfork might also be a "group" of only one airplane.

Figure 12-4   *Attacking bombers from behind is dangerous but can yield the same advantages as attacking fighter formations from behind.*

After fighting in a busy sky for a while, you might have trouble seeing how many targets remain. Use Padlock (accent key ` or button 2 on your joystick) to count how many enemy targets are in the area. As shown in Figure 12-6, as you cycle through all the available targets by pressing Tab, the name of each target appears in the damage text at the top of the screen. In the situation you see in Figure 12-6, there are six targets in two groups of three.

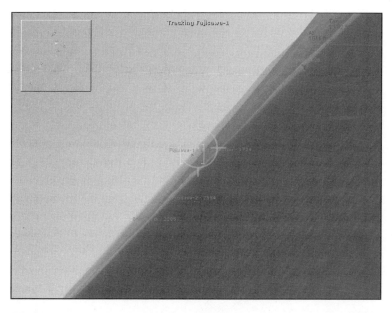

Figure 12-5   *When the action gets busy, stay with your mission. For example, if you're supposed to protect Devastators, keep watch over "Pitchfork" in the upper right of the screen.*

Responsibilities of Command

When you fly missions, you're usually in command of a squadron. The other pilots in the squadron are AI pilots who know the mission goals. If you completely ignored your squadron, they would still fly in formation with you to the scene of combat and do their best to accomplish

Note: *Padlock will lock on to the type of targets that appear in the tactical display only. If you want to use Padlock on ships, you must change the tactical display so that S (ship) or G (ground units) appears in the display. When a letter appears in the tactical display, you can't lock on to airplanes.*

Combat Tip #11: *The tactical display and the Labels option are great ways to maintain the "big picture" of what's going on around you. However, if you're interested in having a more realistic World War II combat experience, turn these features off and try a couple of missions. You'll soon see why good eyesight and the ability to quickly identify enemy aircraft played a crucial role in determining a fighter pilot's success.*

the mission goals. As the squadron commander, your role is to lead the squadron as you see fit. Your chances for a successful mission improve if you select key targets for your wingmen and send them off to attack. Your chances will also improve if you keep your squadron organized as the battle progresses. For example, if you're in tight formation when the fighting starts, you increase the probability of a collision between two of your own airplanes. This is especially true if you perform an evasive maneuver and your wingmen try to follow. If you're in a Finger Four or *shotai* formation and you reverse direction with an Immelman turn, the wingmen on your left and right will follow with level turns toward your position and collide head-on.

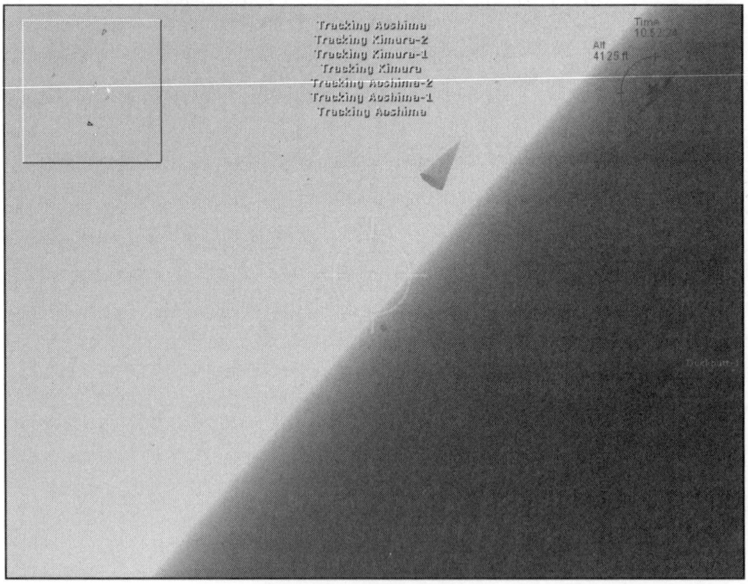

When you go into battle, issue the Split command to spread out your squadron. When you need to regroup to move toward a new target, issue the Rejoin command. You can also use the Rejoin command to call off a wingman from attacking the last enemy airplane so that you can make the kill yourself and get the credit.

Figure 12-6   *Use Padlock to count remaining enemy targets.*

Finishing a Mission

When the last enemy airplane has left the sky, you'll have the opportunity to warp to the end of the mission. Missions end with an optional landing, either at an airfield or on a carrier. It's frustrating to complete a tough mission only to die on the landing, so some gamers always press X to skip the landing. Other gamers believe skipping the landing is a cop-out. Real pilots couldn't just skip the landing because their airplane was shot up or they didn't feel like it. I suggest a compromise: try every landing you're offered, either on land or on the carrier, but have your finger ready on the X key. If you land successfully, you'll feel that extra satisfaction and you'll gain experience performing successful landings. If at any point the landing goes awry, press X and end the mission while you're still a success.

> **Note:** *To make two wingmen attack a target, padlock that target and press Shift+7 (A in the combat keyboard layout) to issue the Attack command. To make half the squadron attack a target, padlock the target and issue the Attack command twice. To return the squadron to pursuing the general mission goals, turn off padlock completely by pressing ~ and then sending the Attack command.*

You don't have to land back at home to end the mission successfully. If you meet the goals but lose the airplane, friendly forces can still pick you up, as shown in Figure 12-7. Bailing out of a shot-up airplane (press O twice) is usually safer than trying to land it with no engine or poor control. In some mission briefings, front lines will appear on the map. If they do, make careful note of their location. If you bail out over enemy territory, you're more likely to be captured than rescued. You must also deploy your parachute manually by pressing O a third time after you bail out. Bailing out can be done as low as 200 feet, but your chances of survival are better with at least 900 feet between you and the ground (or water). If your airplane goes into a spin, you probably won't be able to bail out because the G-forces will be too high. Be sure to cut your power to idle, and try to recover from your spin as described in Chapter 4, "Flight Theory and Practice for the Combat Cadet." Even if you can get the plane to stabilize for only a moment, you'll have enough time to "hit the silk."

Navigation over the Featureless Ocean

Asked what the most exciting thing about flying combat missions was, one Pacific Theater veteran answered, "Seeing land." Most of the combat missions in the Pacific took place over wide stretches of open ocean with no landmarks or emergency landing sites. The standard instruments for navigation were a compass, a clock, and a map. Pilots were taught to estimate the strength and direction of the wind by looking at the waves on the water below them (assuming the ocean wasn't obscured by clouds). Both sides lost many airplanes when pilots low on fuel came out of the clouds to the spot they hoped contained their ships or island bases only to find nothing but empty ocean.

In Combat Flight Simulator 2, you can use X to skip the tedious and stressful aspects of navigation or you can fly the same routes manually. Here are a few tips for flying the routes manually:

- *Your course to the next waypoint will appear on the tactical display.*
- *You can speed up the simulation rate to four times normal speed by selecting Simulation Rate under the Options menu. If you do speed up the simulation rate, note that the controls become much more sensitive.*
- *You can access your briefing map in flight by pressing I to verify your location.*

Campaigns

In a campaign, the player assumes the role of a named pilot and flies a series of missions strung together in sequence. During the campaign, the pilot can receive medals and promotions, as shown in Figure 12-8. If the pilot dies at any point during the campaign, the campaign is over. If the pilot survives to the end, he gets to retire.

Pilot Careers

When you create a new pilot, you choose your national allegiance and the level of difficulty for the entire campaign. At the beginning of the campaign, you're put in charge of a squadron. These seven pilots will accompany you through the campaign—assuming they don't die—and gain skill as time passes. Since the death of your pilot character ends your campaign, it's even more important to balance the risks of battle with the need for self-preservation. Remember: when in doubt, bail out.

Scuttlebutt

The scuttlebutt feature is unique to campaigns. Information you receive as scuttlebutt is determined by the current date in the mission. This information will have no specific bearing on any particular mission. Scuttlebutt can give you a sense of what to expect on your next several missions, however. You can get to the Scuttlebutt screen by clicking the Scuttlebutt button on the Squadron screen.

Campaign Structure

Combat Flight Simulator 2 has only one campaign, as opposed to the two campaigns in the original Combat Flight Simulator. The campaign is more dynamic

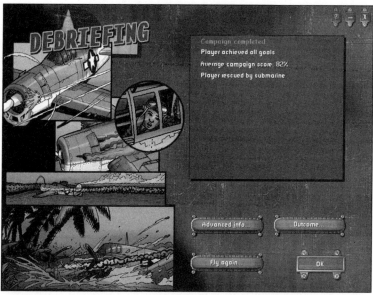

Figure 12-7   You can have a successful mission even if you don't bring your airplane back.

Combat Pilots Held for Ransom

In World War II, friendly battleships, destroyers, or submarines often picked up combat pilots who bailed out over the water. The rescuing ship would return the pilot to his aircraft carrier but wouldn't turn him over until the captain of the carrier paid a ransom. What was the standard price for one combat pilot? Seventy-five gallons of ice cream.

THE SECRETARY OF WAR
WASHINGTON

A grateful nation issues this commendation to you in recognition of
your having attained Ace status by destroying five or more enemy
aircraft. Your courage and determination are in keeping with the
highest standards of the United States Armed Services.

FOR THE PRESIDENT.

SECRETARY OF WAR

Figure 12-8 *One feature unique of campaigns is the chance to receive medals and promotions.*

than those in the original game, so it stands up to replay better. You can play the campaign from either the Japanese or the American perspective, and you can start the campaign from several different points. The campaign contains ten missions that correspond to actual battles of the South Pacific. Regardless of how well or how poorly a player performs in the game, the outcome of each Historical Mission is the same as the historical outcome. For example, the battle of Midway will always end with four Japanese carriers going down in flames. Between each of these Historical Missions, there are three Filler Missions, with one exception that I'll mention in a moment. The Filler Missions are not based on historical battles, but the airplanes, front lines, and events are realistic.

If you survive the entire campaign, you'll play ten Historical Missions but only some of the Filler Missions. Which Filler Missions you play depends on your success in the previous missions. Figure 12-9 shows how this branching system works.

The first mission in a new campaign is randomly chosen from four possibilities, so you won't always start with the same mission. There are seven filler missions between Historical Mission 7 and Historical Mission 8 to account for the large span of time between those two missions. An entire campaign is 44 missions from beginning to end. Due to the branching nature the campaign, you can play the same campaign repeatedly and experience a very different set of missions.

Note: *In the days of wooden ships, the scuttlebutt was the water barrel, around which sailors would gather when it was time to have a break and take a drink. As we well know today, water coolers are magnets for rumors and gossip. In the navy and Marine Corps, the term* scuttlebutt *refers to rumors and unofficial information that gets passed around by sailors and Marines.*

The following table shows a comparison of the American historical missions with the Japanese ones. Note that to prevent the early American missions from being too hard, the Zero must be removed from the picture. This favor is not returned at the end of the campaign, when it's much harder to succeed in the Japanese campaign due to the appearance of the Hellcat and the Corsair.

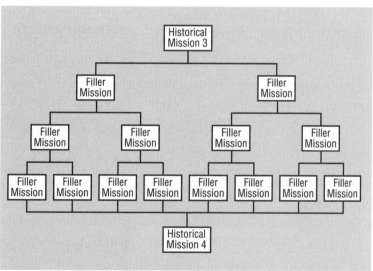

Figure 12-9   *Except for the first historical mission, you'll play the same ten historical missions each time you go through the campaign. You might play different filler missions, however, depending on your overall mission success.*

Combat Flight Simulator 2 Historical Missions

Imperial Japanese Navy	Historical Mission 1A	United States Navy
Rabaul	**Battle**	Rabaul
January 22, 1942	**Date**	February 20, 1942
Easy.	**Difficulty**	Easy, because there is no A6M escort.
	Status at end of mission	U.S. carrier group remains untouched.
	Historical Mission 1B	
Wake Island	**Battle**	Wake Island
December 21, 1941	**Date**	December 8, 1941
Easy.	**Difficulty**	Easy, because there is no A6M escort.
IJN fleet remains undamaged.	**Status at end of mission**	Some F4Fs must survive.
	Historical Mission 1C	
Houn Gulf	**Battle**	Maloelap Atoll
March 10, 1942	**Date**	February 1, 1942
Easy.	**Difficulty**	Easy, because there is no A6M escort.
All Japanese bombers on the ground are destroyed.	**Status at end of mission**	
	Historical Mission 1D	
Expansion into Baku	**Battle**	Makin Atoll
March 13, 1942	**Date**	February 1, 1942
Easy.	**Difficulty**	Easy, because there is no A6M escort.
	Status at end of mission	The Yorktown remains undamaged.
	Historical Mission 2	
Coral Sea	**Battle**	Coral Sea
May 8, 1942	**Date**	May 8, 1942
Medium; lots of interceptors.	**Difficulty**	Medium; lots of interceptors.
Shokaku only damaged.	**Status at end of mission**	The Yorktown receives light damage; the Lexington is listing when player is done. (The Lexington actually sank ten hours later.)

Imperial Japanese Navy	Historical Mission 3	United States Navy
Midway	**Battle**	Midway
June 4, 1942	**Date**	June 4, 1942
Medium; lots of interceptors of low skill.	**Difficulty**	Medium; lots of interceptors.
Four IJN Carriers destroyed.	**Status at end of mission**	
	Historical Mission 4	
Guadalcanal	**Battle**	Guadalcanal
August 7, 1942	**Date**	August 7, 1942
Medium; lots of interceptors.	**Difficulty**	Medium; lots of interceptors.
	Status at end of mission	All USN ships survive, some with only minor damage. No damage to USN carriers.
	Historical Mission 5	
Battle of the Solomon Sea	**Battle**	Battle of the Solomon Sea
August 24, 1942	**Date**	August 24, 1942
Medium.	**Difficulty**	Medium.
	Status at end of mission	No damage to the Saratoga, which was hiding behind a squall. The Enterprise takes three bomb hits but does not sink.
	Historical Mission 6	
Santa Cruz	**Battle**	Santa Cruz
October 26, 1942	**Date**	October 26, 1942
Medium.	**Difficulty**	Medium.
Four bombs hit the deck of the Shokaku, leaving it burning.	**Status at end of mission**	The Hornet damaged but floating; the Enterprise slightly damaged.
	Historical Mission 7	
Solomons	**Battle**	Solomons
February 1, 1943	**Date**	March 13, 1943
Medium.	**Difficulty**	Easy.
One destroyer sunk.	**Status at end of mission**	

Combat Flight Simulator 2 Historical Missions, continued

Imperial Japanese Navy	Historical Mission 8	United States Navy
Gilbert Islands	**Battle**	Mariana Islands
November 24, 1943	**Date**	November 18, 1943
Hard; IJN pilots are outnumbered, and USN has the new Hellcat.	**Difficulty**	Easy.
Japanese equipment on the island is destroyed.	**Status at end of mission**	
	Historical Mission 9	
Marshal Islands	**Battle**	Marshal Islands
January 29, 1944	**Date**	January 29, 1944
Hard; IJN pilots are outnumbered, and USN has the new Hellcat.	**Difficulty**	Medium.
Japanese equipment on the island is destroyed.	**Status at end of mission**	USN ships remain undamaged.
	Historical Mission 10	
Marianas	**Battle**	Philippine Sea
June 15, 1944	**Date**	June 19, 1944
Hard; IJN pilots are outnumbered, and USN has the new Hellcat and Corsair.	**Difficulty**	Medium.
	Status at end of mission	USN ships remain undamaged except for some light damage to picket line destroyers.

Chapter Thirteen

Using the Mission Builder

The new Mission Builder is a huge improvement over the earlier Microsoft Excel–based Mission Builder in the European version of Combat Flight Simulator. This tool, which allows you to create new missions or edit existing ones, takes you beyond just the placement of airplanes, ships, and ground personnel. You can actually link events to specific triggers, creating an interactive game in which the player's decisions affect how the mission unfolds. The Mission Builder included on the CD is exactly the same software that the Microsoft Combat Flight Simulator 2 team used to create the missions included with the game.

> **Note:** *"We almost certainly haven't thought of all the cool things you can do. Think of what it can be with ten thousand designers out there rather than four."* —*Tucker Hatfield, program manager for Combat Flight Simulator 2*

How the Mission Builder Works

Creating a new mission starts with an idea and an empty map. The mission designer—that's you—puts two types of objects on this empty map: infrastructure and routes for airplanes, ships, and ground personnel. Infrastructure objects include buildings, anti-aircraft guns, and airplanes under repair. (I'll discuss infrastructure more fully later in this chapter in "New Infrastructure.") Routes are the heart of mission design. You'll build your missions from routes. A route is a path taken by a vehicle, such as an airplane or ship. Routes consist of at least two waypoints

> **Note:** To launch the Mission Builder, first exit Combat Flight Simulator 2 if it's running. You must also set your screen resolution to 1024 x 768 in the Display Properties dialog box. This setting is required for the Mission Builder to run properly.

that define the path that the vehicle will travel. As shown in Figure 13-1, the simplest mission might be for the player to start at an airbase on one island (waypoint #1) and fly to an airbase on a second island (waypoint #2). To make this mission a little more exciting, you could add a second route consisting of

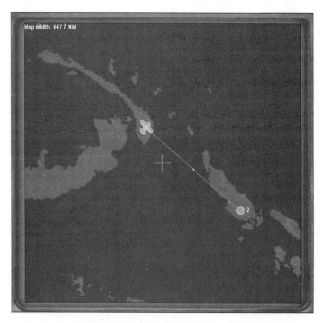

Figure 13-1 *The simplest of missions: one route consisting of two waypoints. The player takes off from one island and lands on another.*

an enemy aircraft that starts on a carrier and flies to the same airbase as the player. Of course, this second route has its own waypoints. The number of planes that can fly a route ranges from a single aircraft to a group of up to nine airplanes flying in formation.

You might make a simple mission even more exciting by increasing the player's group to four airplanes and the enemy's group to eight. Not only is there a fight when the player arrives at the airbase, but the player's flight is also outnumbered 2 to 1. Toss in some anti-aircraft fire, a couple of fuel ships in the harbor, and some bombers on the ground to defend and you're really cooking.

Starting a New Mission

When you install Combat Flight Simulator 2, a shortcut to the Mission Builder is placed on your desktop. To open the Mission Builder, either double-click the shortcut icon or from the Start menu, click Microsoft Games, click Combat Flight Simulator 2, and then select Mission Builders. When the Mission Builder opens, you'll see the map for part of the Solomon Islands and an airplane symbol connected by a line to a circle, as shown in Figure 13-2. The airplane is the starting waypoint for the player's aircraft group. The circle is the final waypoint.

If you want your mission to originate in the Solomon Islands, you can start right away. To plan a mission anywhere else in the Pacific, or anywhere in the world for that matter, use the buttons at the upper left of the screen.

Note: *Before running the Mission Builder, make sure you've closed Combat Flight Simulator 2.*

 The New Mission button will give you three options for the location shown on the map screen:

- **Current Map Location** Use this location if you want to work on the current map but you want to clear everything off the map and start fresh.

- **Exact Map Location** The Mission Builder uses the same landscape database as Combat Flight Simulator 2, so you can create a mission any-where in the world. If you're creating a mission out-side the Pa-cific, you'll need to load the scenery for that area to get high-resolution landscapes. See Chapter 1, "First Look," for instructions for importing scenery from Flight Simulator 2000.

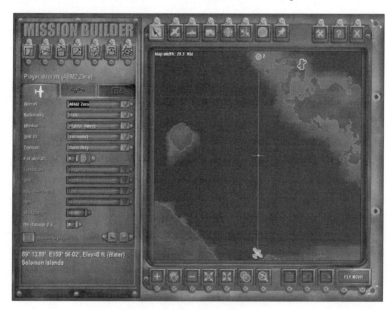

Figure 13-2   *The Mission Builder start-up screen.*

- **Airbase** All the airbases loaded in the scenery library should appear in the Airbase list box. If you choose an airbase from the list, you'll see a map that displays about 27 nautical miles (nm) north to south, with the airbase at the center.

- **Operating Area** The operating areas are for the Pacific Theater only, and the scale of the map window will adjust to fit an area up to 540 nm. If you choose the entire Pacific Theater, the map shows only part of it. Looking at an entire operating area is handy early on in mission development—you'll get the big picture of the island layout to help you decide where different events will occur.

The Load Mission button will allow you to open any saved mission, including all the missions shipped with Combat Flight Simulator 2. You have the choice of looking for standalone missions or missions that are part of a campaign. You can also load missions from Combat Flight Simulator version 1 by choosing Browse and finding the missions or campaigns folder in the \Program Files\Microsoft Games\Combat Flight Simulator directory. The Filters area of the Load Mission dialog box will let you choose the type of mission that you want to edit. If you decide to edit a mission included with Combat Flight Simulator 2, you should save it with a new name to keep the original mission intact, in case you ever want to go back to it.

The Save Mission button opens a dialog box that looks just like the Load Mission dialog box. You can save the missions that you build as either a Single Mission or as a Campaign Mission. The Mission Builder doesn't let you link missions in complete campaigns, so you'll probably save your mission with the Single Mission option. See "Editing Campaign Files" to see how to link missions in a campaign. When saving a mission, you need to assign both a mission name and a filename. The mission name appears in the Missions list box after the file is saved.

Once you've chosen your location on the map, the Mission Setup button lets you enter the setup parameters for your mission. The Alliances function allows you to determine who will fight whom. You can make the Germans and the British allies and have them fight the United States and the Japanese. Note that you don't need to set up an alliance if you simply want to pit a German airplane against a Japanese airplane. (Nationality in this case refers to the pilot, not the airplane.) You can leave the Alliances options alone and still have U.S. pilots fly Zeros.

The Mission Setup dialog box also includes options for the date, time of day, and weather conditions. The Date function is important in determining who controls what island, but it doesn't change how that island looks. For example, if you want to work from a U.S. airbase on Wake Island, you must choose a date on which the United States controlled Wake Island. If you aren't sure what date to choose, just try one and see how it works out. You can go back and change the date later. The airbase itself will look the same no matter what year you choose or who

Note: *One nautical mile is equal to the distance of one minute of longitude, or roughly 6000 feet. To convert nautical miles into the more familiar 5280-foot statute miles, multiply the nautical miles by 1.15. To convert statute miles into nautical miles, multiply by 0.87.*

controls the base. You can add features like extra buildings if you want to maintain a more accurate historical feel.

The Briefing area is where you give the player flying your mission the information needed to complete your mission successfully. To aid in the development of your mission, it's a good idea to jot notes down in these areas before you start putting your mission together. Then just remember to come back to the setup screen and revise the initial text to match the mission you created. You can see the Mission Builder Setup screen in Figure 13-3.

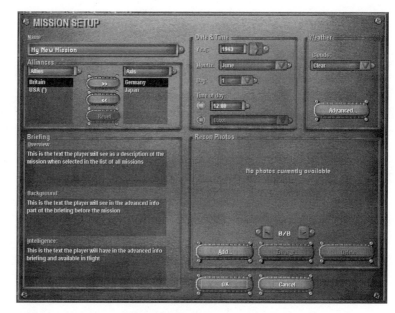

Figure 13-3   *The Mission Builder Setup screen.*

Notice that you can enter text in the Overview, Background, and Intelligence boxes in the Briefing area. You can even attach photos or graphics in the Recon Photos section to add a professional touch to your mission. Let's look at each of these options.

- **Overview**   This text will appear when the player is browsing the list of available missions. Your entry here should be brief but describe the point of the mission. Here is an example from the game: "Hello in Mili. Today on the menu we have a handful of bombers and some fighters for desert. Head south to Makin and off the coast will be enemy ships supporting an invasion. Take out their bombers and then their fighters. One last thing, you get to fly the Type 52." If the player doesn't choose Advanced Information, the overview will be all he or she reads about the mission, so try to be as complete as possible in your brief description.

- **Background** This text allows you to add some depth and historical authenticity to the mission and also gives you an opportunity to drop some hints about how to successfully complete the mission. For example, you might add that the American forces on Wake have been under continuous attack for five days and that this attack might be the final straw that collapses the American resistance.

- **Intelligence** This text is specifically for information that is supposed to help the player complete the mission. The supposed location of the anti-aircraft guns on the target island would be good intelligence. Don't limit yourself, though. Intelligence reports are often incomplete and are sometimes completely wrong. No one says you need to supply the player with the right information. The mission might take a nasty turn when it turns out that in addition to the antiaircraft guns there are eight warships waiting in the harbor as well. This intelligence information will be available to the player in flight after the mission has begun, via the in-flight briefing and map.

- **Recon photos** The recon photos can be a bitmap or JPEG graphics file, containing a photo, drawing, or even a graphic of text. Recon photos are usually photographs taken from high above an airbase or target from a reconnaissance aircraft. These photos are especially useful to pilots when they contain information about defenses and about the exact location of the target by showing it in relation to major landmarks. Regardless of what the image contains, you must put it in the \Combat Flight Simulator 2\Photos folder. The photos in this folder are available in both single missions and campaigns. You can add as many photos as you want to a mission.

Editing the Mission

To start editing your mission, click the Select Mode button in the upper left of the map window. Click any open area in the map. To the left of the map you'll see information pertaining to the overall mission. Click a waypoint from the player flight on the map—that is, one of the numbered circles. A three-tab information window containing an Aircraft tab, a Route tab, and an Information tab will appear. You use the options in these tabs to edit the settings for the selected waypoint and for the entire route.

Flight Tab

The default player aircraft for a new mission is the A6M2 Zero, but you can change this to any of the seven player-flyable airplanes in the game. After selecting the aircraft you want to use, you choose the player nationality. The nationality you assign to a group of airplanes determines who that group will fight. Unlike in real life, Americans flying Japanese planes will not fool the computer.

> **Note:** *To edit a mission from Combat Flight Simulator, click the Browse button in the Load Mission dialog box to find the Mission folder in the Combat Flight Simulator folder. Once you edit the mission, save it in the \Combat Flight Simulator 2\Mission folder. Keep in mind that edited missions will not work when launched from Combat Flight Simulator.*

After choosing airplane and nationality, you select the type of mission from a list of eight options. The mission type you choose affects the availability of later attack options, so pick the type that best matches the mission you want to create.

> **Note:** *To add a new nationality to the list, see "Adding Nationalities" at the end of this chapter.*

The following sections provide an overview of the different missions.

Nothing

This means just what it says. If the mission you want to create doesn't fit any of the other categories, select Nothing. With this mission, you won't have the option of attacking specific targets in your mission goals.

Escort

In this mission, you escort bombers to meet their target. The main goal of this type of mission is usually to protect bombers. You aren't given the option of attacking ground targets.

Combat Air Patrol (CAP)

This is a search-and-destroy mission for enemy aircraft, with no option to attack ground targets.

Intercept

To "intercept" means to meet and destroy enemy aircraft at a known location. Most commonly, these aircraft will be escorted bombers. You have the option of attacking all the airplanes or focusing on the bombers, with no option to attack ground targets.

Fighter Sweep

This is another search-and-destroy mission for other aircraft, but this time the player wouldn't know the location of the enemy planes, with no option to attack ground targets.

Strike

This is a mission to attack known land and sea-based targets such as airfields and ships.

Anti-Ship

This is a mission to attack known ships.

Search and Destroy

This is a search-and-destroy mission for land and sea-based targets. Use Search and Destroy when the player will discover the location of the enemy sometime during the mission rather than at the initial briefing.

CAS (Close Air Support)

Close Air Support missions place the flyer in the position of supporting ground troops at the battle lines. This was a common type of mission for Marine aviators during the war in the Pacific.

Your next choices on the Flight tab are the Unit ID, Payload, and the number of aircraft in the unit. If the player is going to fly alone, the Unit ID isn't really necessary. If you set the number of airplanes in the group higher than one, the Unit ID is handy. The Unit ID is a name shared by all the airplanes in the group. If the player is in a group with only four airplanes and the Unit ID is Bulldog, the player is Bulldog, and the others are Bulldog-1, Bulldog-2, and Bulldog-3, respectively. Other groups of airplanes are named in the same way.

Note: *Be sure you know the range of the airplanes in the mission. If you send them on a long mission without enough gas, they'll run out of fuel before the mission ends. Use long-range drop-tanks when necessary.*

The Payload options depend on the aircraft you select. For example, a Zero can't carry rockets. Choose the payload that best suits your mission. Long-range missions require that you use drop-tanks, which often means you can't carry bombs or torpedoes.

If you have more than one airplane in the group, the airplanes will fly in formation following the player's airplane.

The player's aircraft is always the group or squadron leader. (Chapter 9, "Understanding the Artificial Intelligence," contains descriptions of the different formation types.) You can choose the skill level and aggressiveness for the computer-controlled aircraft. The less aggressive the player's squadron is, the less likely it is to engage the enemy when combat is not the mission goal.

The only other setting that applies to the player flight is Pre-Damage, which allows you to create a mission in which the player begins play in a damaged airplane.

For our mission, set the player aircraft to an A6M2 and the nationality to Japan. Make the Mission Strike, make the Payload Bombs Light, and put eight planes in the player's group. Have the airplanes fly in Echelon Right, as shown in Figure 13-4.

Route Tab

The Route tab shows information for each waypoint along the route. Click the Route tab, and then click the first waypoint on the route. Information about the route is displayed on the tab. Each waypoint has an action associated with it. The action could be as simple as turning in a new direction or it could involve an attack, a takeoff, or a landing. The choices for an action are limited by the available options. If no enemies are in the area, attack is not an option. The first waypoint is set to Turn. This means the player will start the mission with the airplane already in the air.

Figure 13-4 *Aircraft settings for a player flight of eight Japanese Zeros.*

Speed and altitude at the waypoint are set near the bottom of the tab. Don't give the airplanes an altitude higher than 0 and with 0 speed unless you want them to start the mission by falling toward earth. The Route tab also shows the distance and bearing to the next waypoint and provides arrows to scroll to the next waypoint. Click the next waypoint arrow, and you'll see the information about the second waypoint. Since this is currently the last waypoint in the route, the options for landing are now available.

Information Tab

The Information tab gives you the specifics on the vehicle for the chosen route. In our example, you'll see the details for the A6M2 Zero that the player is flying, along with a model of the aircraft.

Moving Around on the Map

The distance across the map at startup is less than 25 miles. Since most missions take place over hundreds of miles, we need to zoom out to see larger areas.

The three basic buttons that change the map view are the Zoom In, Zoom Out, and Pan buttons. Click the Zoom Out button (-) three times to zoom out to more than 200 miles. Now use the mouse to move the two waypoints. First move them to the bottom of the map, and then place them further apart and to the south part of the map, as shown in Figure 13-5.

You can add waypoints to a route two ways: you can right-click a waypoint and select Insert, or you can click and drag on the small square at the midpoint between two waypoints. The waypoints will automatically renumber. Add another waypoint to the player route by dragging the small box in the center of the route north to the American airfield on the north part of the island, as shown in Figure 13-6. (If the

Figure 13-5 *Once the map is zoomed out, you can reposition the waypoints to a more realistic distance.*

American airbase shown doesn't appear on your screen, select any American airbase in the Solomon Islands.)

Insert Mode

We now need to add some items to the map to make the mission more interesting. We'll do so by using the insert buttons at the top of the screen.

New Aircraft

The New Aircraft button lets you create a new group of between one and nine airplanes that will move as a unit. You add new aircraft by clicking the New Aircraft button and then clicking anywhere on the map. To set the course of the aircraft, click the map. You'll notice that a new path and waypoints are created. When you're finished, right-click the map.

With the new aircraft selected in the map, you can set the options for the aircraft as you would for the player aircraft. You can select from any of the player-flyable or non-player-flyable airplanes, but each group can contain only one kind of airplane. If you want to create bombers with a fighter escort, you must insert two new airplane groups.

Since this is an air combat game, adding some enemy aircraft seems in order. Click the New Aircraft button, and put a squadron of American airplanes near the American airfield. We want these airplanes to stay near the airbase, so click once over the airbase, a second time close by the airbase, and a third time over the airbase. Right-click to finish the insertion.

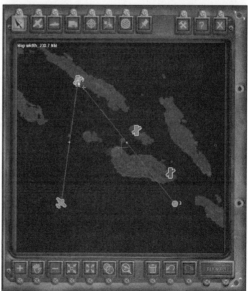

Figure 13-6   *Click and drag the midpoint of a route to add another waypoint.*

Note: *When you finish making the mission, the map you create will be the mission map. However, you have the option of hiding some elements to prevent the player from getting the entire picture before beginning the mission.*

While you select the route, it appears with a green outline. Using the Flight tab on the left, you can set the type of airplane. Since these are computer-flown, you have a wide range of airplane choices. Set the flight to eight P-39s so that they aren't too hard to kill, and then give them a unit name and set the mission to Intercept. In this case, they'll intercept the player's attack squadron.

The Mission Goal setting is now available as an option. Mission Goal always refers to the goal of the player's squadron, *not* the goal of the American P-39s. Setting the goal to Must Be Destroyed means that the player has to destroy the P-39s. Setting the goal to Must Survive means the player must protect the P-39s so that they survive to the end of the mission—clearly the wrong choice here. Setting the goal to None means that the mission success has nothing to do with the fate of the P-39s but the player still gets points for shooting them down as targets of opportunity. Leave the goal setting to None. We also don't want the player to know beforehand exactly where the P-39s will be, so check Hidden To Player in the bottom left. Hidden objects won't appear in the player briefing. Your Flight tab should look like that shown in Figure 13-7.

Note: *As in the mission briefing, objects and vessels allied with the player are blue; enemy objects are red.*

Note: *If you make a mistake, such as adding a flight accidentally or an extra waypoint, correct the problem by using the Trash, Undo, and Redo buttons at the bottom right of the screen. The Undo and Redo functions remember up to 25 steps.*

Next click the Route tab, and give these American planes their flying instructions. Use the right and left arrow buttons on-screen to get to the first of the three waypoints. Set the action to Takeoff. The airbase for takeoff will default to the nearest available airbase, which is what you want in this case. You could also have the flight take off from whatever airbase you wanted by choosing

one from the list. Click the right arrow on the next waypoint, and set the action to Intercept All. This should make the P-39s take off and intercept the player. The waypoint symbol changes from a circle to a triangle to indicate that an attack happens at this waypoint. In this case, the P-39s will attack the player's flight of Zeros. Set the third waypoint action to Land At Airbase. The waypoint symbol changes to a square to indicate the landing. Of course if the player has good aim, there won't be much left of the P-39 flight to land.

Insert Ship

The Insert Ship button lets a player add naval vessels to the map. Click the Insert Ship button, and then click player waypoint #1 to place a ship. (We'll make this ship the home carrier for the player.) After you click, a dotted line representing the ship's route will extend from the ship to the cursor. Since the carrier will move while the player is away, place a second waypoint to the east, and then right-click to finish the insertion.

In the Options panel, go to the Ship Type list and select one of the Japanese carriers. Make sure the nationality is Japan, or the player might have a rather unfriendly welcome upon landing. Select a Unit ID for the carrier so that you can identify it later.

Ships cannot be inserted as groups, so you must enter any carrier escorts separately. Add two more ships to escort the carrier using the Insert Ship button. You must also set the speed of each vessel. Not all vessels have the same top speed, so be sure to select a speed that all the ships can keep up with. Figure 13-8 shows what your screen should look like.

Figure 13-7 *Once you place the defending group of airplanes on the map, select Intercept as their mission.*

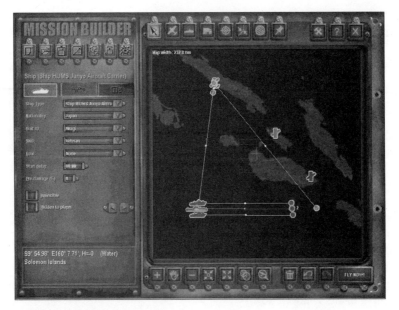

Now go back and select the player's route by clicking it, and then choose the Route tab. You can reset the action for the first waypoint to Takeoff; you can set the base to be the carrier you placed. If the carrier does not appear as an option, make sure both the player and the carrier are set to the same nationality.

The carrier also needs to be in the right place for the aircraft to land. It could get complicated trying to calcu-

Figure 13-8 *The carrier is now the takeoff point and has two escorts. The whole group is moving east.*

late exactly where the carrier will be by the time the player is done fighting. Luckily you don't have to. Take the final waypoint for the player's flight of Zeros, and drag it over the carrier. Go to waypoint 3 on the Route tab, and select Land At Base. The carrier will appear as one of the bases. The player won't actually land in the exact position shown on the map. Instead, when the mission is over, the player will be guided to his carrier at some position along the carrier's route. Figure 13-9 shows what the screen will look like at this point.

Now zoom in on the American airfield by clicking the Zoom In button and then clicking the map. Zoom in to a view of less than one mile across so that you can accurately place elements around the field.

Chapter Thirteen: Using the Mission Builder

New Ground Unit

Use the New Ground Unit button to add items such as jeeps, trucks, and tanks to your map. Zoom in on the American airfield so that the map is approximately two miles across. Place a few ground units with weapons around the airfield to fight off the attack. Set the options for these new units in the Options panel. The ground units will move during combat, so assign them routes. Be sure to insert these items on dry land, and name them so that you can identify them later.

Figure 13-9   *The player flight will take off from and land on the same carrier.*

New Infrastructure

While you're zoomed in on the airfield, add some infrastructure by using the New Infrastructure button. Infrastructure objects are stationary objects in the mission, such as buildings and boxes of supplies, as well as active objects such as stationary anti-aircraft guns. Insert three or four anti-aircraft guns to keep things interesting.

You can also use the New Infrastructure button to add any airplanes, ships, and ground units that do not move during the mission. A group of airplanes parked by the side of the runway that will not take off are inserted as infrastructure, not as airplanes. Put seven stationary B-25 Mitchell's on the grounds of the American airbase by the runway. Use the New Infrastructure button, since these B-25s will not move.

Figure 13-10 shows what your screen should look like now. You're ready to set up some mission goals.

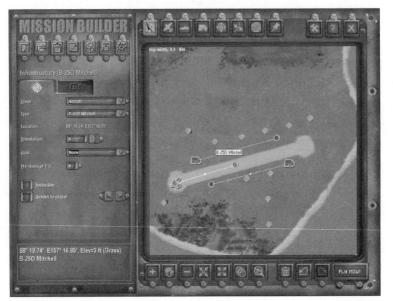

Figure 13-10   *Zoom in tight on the airfield for attack to place the targets.*

Setting Mission Goals

When the player gets the mission briefing, he will need to see the mission goals. Achieving goals is how a player's success on a mission is judged, so you want to make sure the player has at least a chance at succeeding. To do this, you must tell the player what the goals are in the beginning of the mission and make sure you assign the goals to the correct objects in the Mission Builder. The goal for our mission will be to destroy at least two B-25s. Set the goal for each B-25 to Must Be Destroyed.

The briefing will inform the player that all seven B-25s need to be destroyed, but the computer-controlled pilots in the player's squadron won't know what to do until you tell them. Find the #2 waypoint in the player's flight, and drag it over one of the B-25s. Select the #2 waypoint, and go to the Route tab on the left. Set the action to Attack With Bombs. The waypoint changes from a circle to a triangle, which represents an attack waypoint, and the waypoint centers on the nearest target, as shown in Figure 13-11. Right-click the attack waypoint to insert a second attack waypoint. Drag this

waypoint over a second B-25, and select Attack With Bombs. Since each airplane only carries two bombs, you won't be able to specify an attack on any other B-25s. Once the initial two targets are destroyed, however, the AI pilots will automatically look for similar targets. Given that there are sixteen bombs between all eight airplanes, it's conceivable that all seven B-25s could be destroyed in the mission.

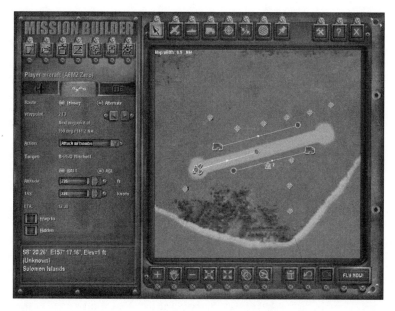

Figure 13-11   *Put the player waypoint over the target and select Attack With Bombs.*

Once you've completed the detail work, click on the map to deselect any objects and zoom back out by clicking the Zoom To Fit button to see the big picture.

Triggers and Events

Two of the best features in the Mission Builder are triggers and events, which allow you to make the mission much more interactive and player-driven. The controls for triggers and events are flexible, so the possibilities are nearly limitless. Triggers and events are sophisticated if-then statements: if condition A happens (Trigger), then perform action B (Event).

> **Note:** *If several waypoints are on top of one another, right-click the pile and select the waypoint you want. If you need to edit that waypoint often, move it to one side of the pile of other waypoints and then move it back when you're done.*

> **Note:** *If Attack With Bombs is not an option or the target remains unassigned when you choose Attack With Bombs, make sure you have the correct mission chosen on the Aircraft tab.*

Note: *The Zoom To Fit button works in two ways. If nothing is selected, Zoom To Fit will set the scale of the map just large enough to fit the entire mission on the screen (up to 500 nm). If a point or waypoints are selected, Zoom To Fit will zoom to fit only those waypoints on-screen. If you want the view to go out as large as possible, use the No Zoom button.*

Triggers

The Trigger button calls up the list of available triggers. Select New to create a new trigger. Each trigger must have a name, and it's best if this name identifies the details of the trigger. Name this trigger something like "Zeros arrive on target." Next select the trigger category from the following four options:

- **Aircraft**   Aircraft refers to any of the aircraft that are flying a route. The Zeros and the P-39s are the only options in our current mission. The B-25s don't fly in this mission, so they're considered infrastructure.
- **General**   The General options allow you to base a trigger on elapsed time or to have the trigger happen as a random occurrence.
- **Infrastructure**   Infrastructure allows you to set a trigger based on the status of a particular object, such as whether it has been destroyed.
- **Moving Object**   Moving Object refers to all moving objects except airplanes, so ships and ground units fall into this category.

Note: *It's helpful to give a Unit ID name to each group of airplanes. Later on, when you set up triggers and events, this allows you to identify groups from the various lists.*

Each of these four categories can be evaluated to test for up to 31 different parameter values, but each trigger can contain only one parameter. For example, you could have a trigger for "If the airplane reaches the second waypoint" and another one for "If the airplane is flying at more than 4000 feet in altitude," but you couldn't have a trigger for "If the airplane has reached the second waypoint and is flying at more than 4000 feet in altitude." Individual triggers are combined in more complex scenarios when you create an event.

For our example mission, use the aircraft category for the trigger and select the name of the player's group. The 31 different parameters to choose from cover everything from the health of the pilot to where on the map he has flown. We want the trigger to trip immediately when the Zeros arrive, so set the trigger parameters to: Status, Waypoint Reached, Equals, 2. The whole trigger reads like a sentence: *When the airplanes of the player's group status is that*

the waypoint they have reached equals number two then set off this trigger. It's not a very good sentence, but it is understandable. Figure 13-12 illustrates how to create a trigger.

Events

Triggers aren't useful by themselves—they must cause some event. In our case, we want the P-39s to take off when the Zeros are overhead. Click the Events button to create a new event. The event should have a descriptive name so that you can remember what each event does. You'll see the trigger for Zeros On Target in the left box. Select it and move it over to the right by clicking the >> button.

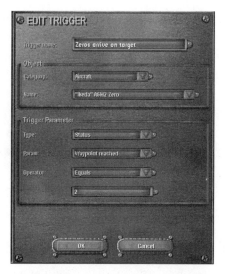

Figure 13-12 *You can attach triggers to almost any situation that might occur during play.*

The most common event is a spawn. This means that the object you placed on the map doesn't exist (and therefore won't begin to move) until it's triggered. Select Spawning as the type of action, highlight Spawn, and choose the name of the P-39 squadron. Now the P-39s will take off when the Zeros arrive overhead, but not before. Click OK, and close the Events dialog box. The effect will be as if the airplanes were scrambled by the attack. If you created any mobile ground units, add them to the event actions as well so that they actually spawn at the same time the P-39s take off.

To make the effect even stronger, you could add a second type of action to this event. Click the Events button to open the Event dialog box. Select the event you just created, and click Edit. In the Actions area, you'll see the Spawn Unit action in the In Use list. Choose Display Text from the Type list, and click the >> button to add it to the In Use list. This will pop up a dialog box that lets you enter any message you like. A good message here might be: "The American airfield is right below us, and it looks like they are sending up some planes to welcome us." You can see how the Actions area should look in Figure 13-13. Now when the event is triggered, the P-39s will launch and the text will appear as if it came over the radio.

Each event can have multiple triggers. Multiple triggers are sometimes necessary to make the mission flow smoothly. For example, the ability to warp to the next waypoint—without having to fly it yourself—is automatically disabled

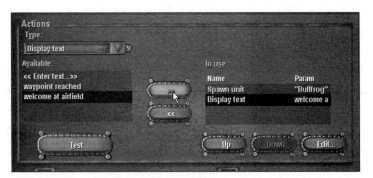

Figure 13-13 *The same event can have multiple actions.*

Note: *Events can also launch .wav files. The action type is either Play Sound or Play Priority Sound. Play Sound will play the .wav file, but it might get cut off if a second .wav file plays soon after. Play Priority Sound will play the .wav file uninterrupted.*

Note: *You could have made the B-25s into a single target by making them a flight of airplanes; however, you would have had less control over their placement and you would have had to set a delay for their takeoff to keep them on the ground.*

until you turn it on or use the Route tab to specify that it stay on. We want to give the player the ability to warp back to the carrier if all the B-25s are destroyed or if the flight runs out of bombs. To do this, create several more triggers. One trigger is for the player flight running out of bombs. Create this trigger by choosing the player's flight as the trigger object and set the parameters to "stores-bomb count-equals-0". Save this trigger as "Zeros out of bombs". To detect whether the B-25s have been destroyed, you must create a separate trigger for each B-25. Create triggers for each by setting the object to "Infrastructure- B-25D Mitchel" and the parameters to "Status-Heath-Equals-0". Save each of these triggers as "Mitchell 1", "Mitchell 2", and so on.

Event Areas

The Mission Builder lets you define areas of the map by name and use these areas as part of triggers. To create an area, click the Area button and then click and drag a circle starting in the center of the part of the map you want to define, as shown in Figure 13-14. Let's make it a six-mile circle around the airbase. Name the area something like "Area 51."

Now create a new trigger called Leaves Airbase. The trigger should have the player flight as the object and the parameters set to "Status-Area-Leaves-Area 51". This trigger will trip when the player's flight leaves the area you just created. Save the trigger as "Leaves airbase area".

Finally, create a new event called Enable Warp, as shown in Figure 13-15. Select two items from the list of triggers: "Zeros out of bombs" and "Leaves airbase". Now

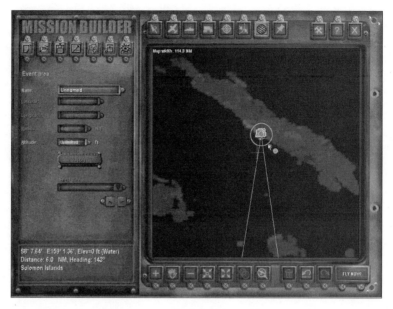

Figure 13-14 *Define an area by dragging from the center of the space you want to name.*

press the Or >> button to get a second window for triggers. Put all the Mitchell X triggers and the Leaves Airbase trigger in this second window. Set the action to Miscellaneous, and select Enable Warp. Warp will now only be enabled if either the player runs out of bombs and leaves the airbase or the player destroys all the B-25s and leaves the airbase. Without completely meeting one of these requirements, the player can't warp away.

Alternate Routes

Each ship, ground unit, or flight of airplanes can have an alternate route in addition to its primary route. The alternate route allows you to have two different possibilities for how a route will progress based on some trigger. Computer-controlled vehicles can also have alternate routes, thereby allowing the enemy to go different directions depending on the player's actions. We'll create an alternate route designed to get the player lost on the way back to the carrier.

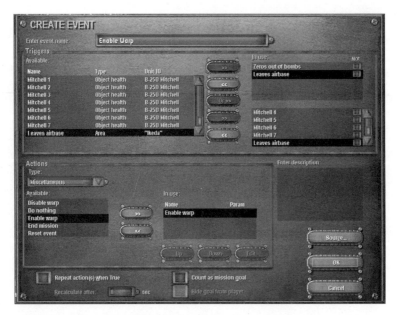

Figure 13-15 *And/or statements and multiple triggers allow you to design very specific events.*

First add a waypoint to the player's flight halfway back to the carrier. Hide it by checking the Hidden To Player check box in the Flight panel. (We don't want the player to see this waypoint in the briefing or they will suspect that something will happen to them on the way back to the carrier.) Next select the player flight at any waypoint, and go to the Route tab. Click the Alternate Route button. If you move the mouse over the map, it now displays an airplane cursor. Click next to the waypoint you just added, and then click to the east near the Japanese airfield but a few miles away. Right-click to end the insertion. Two kinds of dotted lines will appear. The long dashes show where the flight began—in this case, on the carrier. The short dashes show the alternate route. Drag waypoint #1 of the alternate route over waypoint #9 of the primary route. Figure 13-16 illustrates what this looks like when it's complete.

Now create two new triggers. Call the first one "Reach Waypoint 9", set its object to the player flight and the parameters to "Status-Waypoint Reached-Equals-Nine". Call the second trigger "Random 50-50", set the object to general and the parameters to "Percentage-Random Number-Equals-50". Next create a small text file that says "Excuse me sir, but I think we're off course." Save this file as off course.txt in the Missions directory in the directory called Text. Alternately, you could create a .wav file of someone saying the quote and save it in the directory called Sound. Now you'll create two events. The first event will occur when the player reaches waypoint 9 and the random number value is

true. This event consists of three actions, shown in the In Use list of Figure 13-17.

1. Text will appear (or a .wav file will play) saying that another pilot thinks the flight is off course.

2. The route will switch to the alternate route.

3. Warp will enable, allowing the player continue, but

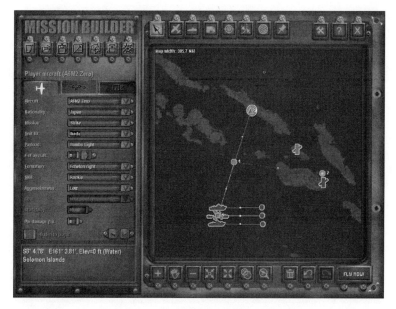

Figure 13-16 *An alternate route allows you to branch off the primary route and give the player a bit of a surprise.*

in the wrong direction. So as not to be too cruel, the player comes out near a friendly airbase and can complete the mission successfully if he finds the airbase before running out of fuel.

To create this event, make a new event called "Switch to alternate course". Choose the two triggers "Reach Waypoint 9" and "Random 50-50". Then choose the action "Change Waypoint", and double-click "Alternate Route". Next add the action "Display Text" (or "Play Sound"), and choose the text "off course". Finally, add the action of enabling warp.

The final effect will be that when the player warps home from the battle, he will come out of warp halfway home. Fifty percent of the time the player will be switched to the alternate route but he won't know that this has happened. The "off course" text will appear and warp will enable, but since the player is on the alternate route, instead of warping home to his ship, he'll warp to the small island off to the east and be quite lost.

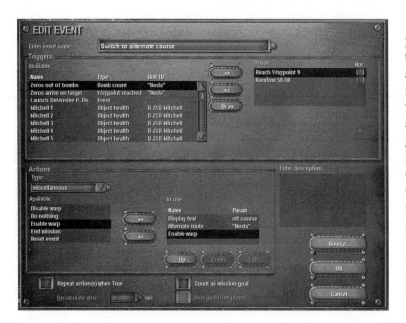

The other fifty percent of the time the player will not switch to the alternate route but his warp will be disabled at waypoint 9. To give the player a way home in this case, create a new event called "Stay on course" with the same two triggers as "Switch to alternate course", but this time check the Not checkbox by the trigger "Random 50-50" as shown in Figure 13-18. The "off course" text will appear as before, but the player will stay

Figure 13-17 *Any trigger can launch the alternate route. The airplane proceeds along the shortest route to reach and follow the alternate course.*

on the primary route. Then warp will enable and the player will continue home to the carrier, blissfully ignorant of how close he came to getting lost.

Ending a Mission

Two situations automatically end a mission: If the player dies, the mission is over. If the player completes all the mission goals and survives to land at the final waypoint in the route, the mission is completed successfully. In our mission, however, if the player does end up off course and lands, the mission won't automatically end.

To finish this mission design, you should create one more trigger and one more event. Create a trigger called "Zero airspeed", set the object to the player flight and the parameters to "Status-Speed-Less than or equals-0". Create an event called "End mission", and choose two triggers. The first trigger is "Reach waypoint 9" and the second is "Zero airspeed". Set the event action as "Miscellaneous-End Mission". Now when the Zero gets past waypoint 9 and lands, the

mission will end
when the airplane
comes to a stop. If
you used only "Zero
airspeed" as the trig-
ger, the event would
occur at the beginning
of the mission, when
the Zero is waiting to
take off from the car-
rier and has no air-
speed. The mission
would start and im-
mediately end.

Another case in
which you might want
an event to end the
mission is a bomber
escort mission where
all the bombers are
destroyed. The mis-
sion won't end, how-

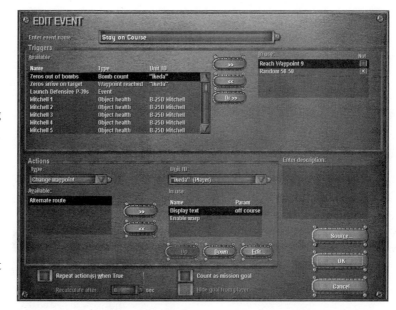

Figure 13-18   *Events can be based on triggers executing or specifically not executing.*

ever, if there are still enemy fighters in the air. You can create a trigger for the
condition of all bombers are destroyed and link it to the Miscellaneous action
for End Mission. Then, when the player allows the last bomber to fall under
enemy fire, the mission will immediately finish.

Front Lines

As I mentioned in Chapter 12, "Missions and Campaigns," landing behind enemy lines greatly increases your chances of being captured.
The Front Lines button allows you to place the front line, using as
many points as needed to weave around islands. You create a front
line by clicking the New Front Line button and then clicking the map
once for each bend in the front line. As you do this, you'll see the line
continue off the screen in both directions. (The front line actually continues
around the world, but it applies to this mission only, so it won't affect front
lines you create for other missions.)

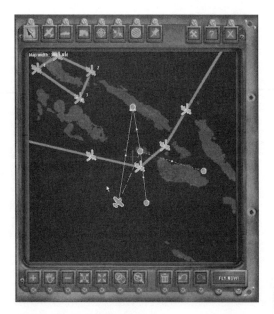

Figure 13-19   *The New Front Line button allows you to place the front line and to create pockets of enemy-held land inside friendly territory. If Japan controlled the south section of this map, Japan would also control the small diamond-shaped area in the north.*

You can also have isolated pockets controlled by the enemy behind friendly front lines. To do this, right-click to complete the main front line and then make a new front line in which the points actually form a complete circle. This situation occurred numerous times in the Pacific when the Allies hopped over Japanese-controlled islands that were not of strategic value. As Figure 13-19 illustrates, you can create as many front lines as you like, as long as the lines don't cross.

Filters and Chart Labels

The Filter button allows you to select certain items and make them invisible. This feature is helpful when you're designing a complex mission. You can filter by nationality, type of object, or both. For example, you could set the filter so that you see only the Japanese items or only the Japanese aircraft. The check boxes in the Filter dialog box show the items that will remain visible. You can also temporarily filter individual objects by right-clicking them and selecting Filter from the pop-up menu. Figure 13-20 illustrates one use of the Filter button.

Chart labels, illustrated in Figure 13-21, are also helpful for keeping track of items during complex missions. The labels are much more helpful, however, to the players who fly the mission. Without labels, the players have no way to distinguish items on the chart. The labels can get in your way when you design a mission, so it helps to filter them out.

Sharing Missions

One exciting aspect of the Mission Builder is that you can share your missions with Combat Flight Simulator 2 players all over the world. (See Chapter 14, "Playing Well with Others," for more information.) Here's what you need to do to get your mission ready to share:

1. Copy the mission file (.mis) and the dynamic mission elements file (.dyn) from the Missions folder, and put them in a new folder. The two filenames should be the same except for the suffix.

2. Copy any text or sounds you use in your actions from the Sounds folder and the Text folder in your Missions folder, and put those items in the new folder.

Figure 13-20 *This filter allows only American airbases and aircraft to appear, along with the front lines.*

3. Copy any graphics you use from the Photos folder, and add those graphics to the new folder.

4. Add a readme.txt file to the folder telling the reader where the files should be placed, and note any special airplanes you use, such as airplanes from Combat Flight Simulator, aircraft from Flight Simulator 2000, or third-party aircraft. (Without a heads-up from you, this could be confusing for someone playing your mission.) If the person playing your game does not have an aircraft you specify, an A6M2 Zero will substitute regardless of nationality.

5. Compress the new folder you've created with an application such as WinZip to create a single file.

6. Send the mission off, and wait for the compliments to come pouring in.

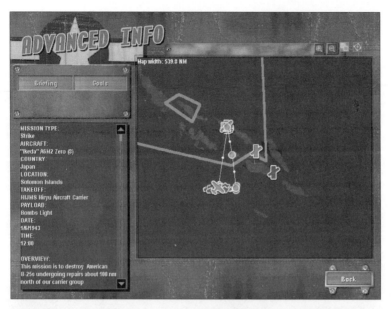

When you get someone else's mission, you'll need to do these steps in reverse, opening the folder and putting the files in the appropriate places. You can also look at somebody else's mission in detail by loading it into the Mission Builder.

Editing Campaign Files

There is no tool to weave your missions into a complete campaign, but you can create campaigns manually by creating a campaign file. The campaign file is just a text file that resides in the campaign folder and has the suffix .cmg. Here's a sample campaign file for a campaign with only two missions:

Figure 13-21 *Without labels (top), the advanced info in the mission briefing isn't very helpful. With labels (bottom), it makes much more sense.*

```
[Campaign Global Info]
campaign_name=%campaign_name_string%
overview=%campaign_overview%
soundfile=welcome_to_war.wav
imagefile=first_look.jpg
moviefile=
allegiance=3

[Strings]
"campaign_name_string"=Small USN campaign
"campaign_overview"=This is a short campaign consisting of one or two mis-
sions.

[node.0]
imagefile=off_to_war.jpg
true_branch=1
false_branch=2
percent_true=50
filler=0

[node.1]
mission_name=wake_usn
true_branch=2
false_branch=4
goal_count=2
filler=1

[node.2]
mission_name=marshals_usn
true_branch=3
false_branch=4
goal_count=2
filler=1

[node.3]
moviefile=medal-of-honor.avi
percent_true=100
filler=1
```

```
[node.4]
moviefile=court_marshal.avi
percent_true=100
filler=1
```

> **Tip:** If you find yourself creating a lot of well-received missions, consider using an installer program to place the files in the appropriate folders automatically. People installing your missions will appreciate it immensely.

Campaign Global Info and Strings

The global info sets up the basic and default information for the campaign. This includes the player's nationality, the name of the campaign, and the information the player sees when deciding which campaign to play. The allegiance of 3 means that this is an American campaign. The allegiance numbers are listed in the country.cfg file in the main Combat Flight Simulator 2 directory. See "Adding Nationalities" for more information on the country.cfg file. The soundfile, imagefile, and moviefile are links to the files that will play before the campaign begins. In this example, the image first_look.jpg will appear on-screen while welcome_to_war.wav plays. An .avi movie file could also be run here. When these files are finished playing, the first mission will appear.

> **Note:** Sound, Movie, and Image files must reside in specific places to appear in campaigns. Sound files can be in the Sound directory or the Campaign directory. Movie files can reside the Video\Trasit directory or the Campaign directory. Image files must be in the Campaign directory.

Nodes

Each mission is assigned to a node. The campaign starts with node 0 and progresses in a branching structure. In our example node 0 has no mission attached to it. It only has a true branch and a false branch with a 50 percent chance of each. What node 0 does is randomly send the player on the mission in node 1 or the mission in node 2. The *filler=0* line means that the player can begin a campaign at this node.

Node 1 is tied to the mission wake_usn, which is a search-and-destroy mission on wake island. Wake_usn is the filename of the mission minus the .mis suffix. (Don't use the title of the mission to identify it.) If the player completes the mission successfully, the next mission will be the mission in node 2. If the player is unsuccessful, he will proceed to node 4. The number of goals

achieved determines success. In this case, if the player achieves two or more goals, he is successful. The *filler=1* marker means that the player cannot go directly to this node at the beginning of the campaign. For very long campaigns, it's nice to offer the player a choice of entry points so that he or she doesn't have to play the entire campaign just to reach a choice mission near the end of the campaign.

After a success in node 1, the player will move to node 2 and a mission in the Marshall Islands. Completion of two or more goals in the Marshalls will result in success, and the player will move on to node 3. Node 3 has no mission, but it does have a movie file of the player receiving the Medal of Honor. After the movie plays, the campaign will end and the player's pilot character will retire.

> **Note:** *The different medals and the requirements to receive them are edited in the country.cfg file.*

If the player fails on either mission but doesn't die in the process, he will move to node 4 and see a film of his court marshal. Once it is done, the pilot character will be retired.

Adding Nationalities

If you want to add more nationalities to the game, you must edit the country.cfg file. Save a copy of this file before you start, just in case. To add a nationality to the game, you need to enter the information in two places. First add the following lines to the file:

```
[country.5]
name=Uzbekistan
short_name=Usb
nationality= Uzbeki
```

The country number must be a unique number that no other country has, but other than that you can make the name and country anything you want. Next you must give the new county an allegiance. This is done by country number. To add Uzbekistan to the Allies, change the following text (country 1 is Great Britain and country 3 is the U.S.):

```
[alliance.0]
name=Allies
country.0=1
country.1=3
```

to read:

[alliance.0]
name=Allies
country.0=1
country.1=3
country.3=5

The country.cfg file also establishes the requirements for different medals and getting promoted. Editing these features is beyond the scope of this book, but if you're feeling adventurous, read the section for a country like the U.S. and try some variations.

Scuttlebutt

As mentioned in Chapter 12, scuttlebutt is based on the mission date and is not part of the mission file. You can edit the scuttlebutt to create custom scuttlebutt for your campaign. The details of reworking the scuttlebutt file are fairly complex and are not covered in this book. You'll find the scuttlebutt file in the Info folder. The file is called scuttlebutt.dat and contains a brief explanation of how the scuttlebutt file works.

Troubleshooting and Tips

The Mission Builder has a context-sensitive help system that will answer many of your specific questions. To help you get off to a smooth start, however, here a few tips for working in the Mission Builder:

- If the attack or landing options you want are not available, make sure you have the correct nationality set and that the mission type allows the kind of attack you want.
- Use appropriate airplanes for the task at hand. For example, the P-39 has terrible performance at high altitude. Use the P-38 to fly up high with bombers.
- To measure a distance on the map, click and drag an empty space. A yellow line will be visible as long as you drag. The distance and direction of the line will appear in the lower left of the Mission Builder screen.
- Use the Hidden To Player function in conjunction with Random events to create many different variations on how the mission proceeds. This will keep the mission interesting, even after playing it several times.

- Study the historic battles of the Pacific Theater to get new mission ideas.
- Picking apart the missions that came with Combat Flight Simulator 2 is a great way to learn more about how missions work. Whenever you edit one of these mission or config files, make a copy of the file before you change anything. That way you can always go back and undo any really bad blunders.

Chapter Fourteen

PLAYING WELL WITH OTHERS

No matter how sophisticated the AI pilots might be, and no matter how realistic the mission might seem, nothing is quite like flying in combat against a real person. Real opponents will make more creative maneuvers, as well as more mistakes. Human pilots are also much more vulnerable to surprise. Performing a surprise attack from the sun or clouds is a real possibility, especially if all players agree to turn off their tactical displays. Multiplayer flight also allows you to use real team tactics. With three other players in your squadron, for example, you can fly an actual Thach Weave. Squadron flying with human pilots requires some new skills as well. Your AI squadron pilots already know how to fly perfect formations, and you're always the lead pilot. In multiplayer, you might fly as a wingman and face a whole new challenge of staying close to your leader without colliding. The Multiplayer feature in Microsoft Combat Flight Simulator 2 is a combat arena (just like Quick Combat) containing two or more aircraft flown by players communicating over an office network or over the Internet.

> **Note:** Currently, there's no way to fly missions with other players; you can, however, exchange custom missions via the Internet. See Chapter 13, "Using the Mission Builder," for information on exchanging custom missions.

Getting Started in Multiplayer

Multiplayer games require one person to act as the game host. The host computer doesn't need to be a particularly fast or powerful machine since the bulk of the computer processing happens on each player's individual computer, but the faster the connection host computer has, the better the quality of play. A host that with a slow connection will cause poor frame rates for all the players in the game. The host decides the ground rules for the game and determines how many people can play. Clicking the Multiplayer button on the main screen opens the Multiplayer Connect screen, as seen in Figure 14-1. Your computer will look for all available hosts on the selected network. In most cases the Protocol Type you want will be TCP/IP, which is the common communication protocol for the Internet and is also used in many office networks. Even if you're connecting to the Internet via modem, you should choose TCP/IP for the protocol type. Choosing Modem in the Protocol Type drop-down list box works if you want to call another player's telephone line modem directly and play one on one.

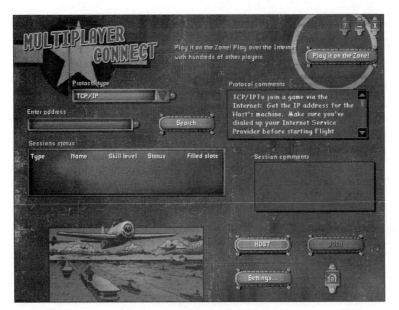

If no hosts appear on your network, or if you simply prefer to do so, you can host a game yourself. Click the Host button on the Multiplayer Connect screen to open the Multiplayer Host screen, as shown in Figure 14-2.

Figure 14-1   *The Multiplayer Connect screen shows you the games available on the selected network and allows you to host a game yourself.*

You choose the ground rules for the game, including the realism setting, the maximum number of players, and whether it will be every pilot for himself or team play. You also choose the victory requirements that determine when the game ends. Here are the Victory Requirement options:

- If you choose not to have a victory requirement (None), the game will go on indefinitely.
- If you want victory to be determined by reaching a certain number of kills (First Player To Destroy), each player's aircraft will respawn after dying until someone achieves the desired number of kills.

- If you choose Last Player Alive as the victory requirement, players are out once they are killed or bail out. Players who are out of the game then wait until a final victor emerges and the game restarts.

You can also set a password for entry to the game so that only your friends around the office can join the fun. Once enough players have joined in, the host can start the game.

Figure 14-2   *If you host the game, you choose the ground rules for play.*

Playing in the MSN Gaming Zone

The MSN Gaming Zone allows you to play Combat Flight Simulator 2 over the Internet with thousands of other Combat Flight Simulator enthusiasts. If you want to try your hand at multiplayer but don't have a particular person in mind as an opponent, the Zone is a great place to go to find a game. The Zone also hosts tournaments in which Combat Flight Simulator players from all over the world compete for prizes.

> **Note:** To host a private game with friend over the Internet, you need to know the IP address of the host computer. To determine the IP address of your computer, make sure you're already connected to the Internet and then go to a command prompt and type **ipconfig**. Your IP address will appear in the window. Once you know this IP address, tell your friends to type it into the Enter Address text box and click Search. Your host computer should appear on their screens.

Game Voice

Microsoft Sidewinder Game Voice is a new piece of gaming hardware that can add another dimension to Combat Flight Simulator 2 by letting you talk to other players over the Internet while you play. Each player must have the Game Voice hardware, a control box and headset, and Game Voice software installed on his or her computer. Once the Game Voice system is up and running, players can talk to the entire group or they can speak to each other over private channels. In Combat Flight Simulator 2, Game Voice gives you the ability to conduct real-time radio communication with other members of your team. Game Voice comes with its own headset, so your hands are still free to fly the airplane. The Game Voice control box also allows you to access frequently used commands via voice recognition. Players without the Game Voice hardware can still participate in conversations by installing Game Voice Share, which is available as a free download. To find out more about Game Voice, go to http://www.gamevoice.com.

Note: *You can also go to the MSN Gaming Zone directly. The address is http://www.zone.com.*

The easiest way to get on the MSN Gaming Zone is to connect to the Internet and then launch Combat Flight Simulator 2. On the Multiplayer Connect screen, click the Play It On The Zone! button, which will launch your Web browser and take you to the Combat Flight Simulator – Game Rooms page, as shown in Figure 14-3. This page contains the latest news about Combat Flight Simulator 2 on the Zone and lets you see the rooms available for game play. I'll describe the four types of room in this section. Please note that the screen shots in this chapter are from the Combat Flight Simulator area on the MSN Game Zone. By the time you get Combat Flight Simulator 2 set up, it will have its own, very similar area.

Standard Rooms

Most of the players on the Zone spend their time in standard rooms. You'll see more than one type of standard room, but there aren't big differences between them. Click the room of your choice to see all the games available in that room. Figure 14-4 shows a standard room with multiple games in progress.

Inside the room, you'll see all the games available. Some games will be full, so you can't join them until someone else leaves. Other games will be open to new players; these rooms will have a button marked Info. Clicking the Info button shows you the ground rules for that game and any messages the

host has added—for example, "Free for all or teams. No modifications but Abacus add-ons okay. Rookies, come get your wings…"

Clicking Join puts you in the game and brings Combat Flight Simulator 2 into focus. It might take a few minutes for your machine to make its connections and to completely get into the game. Don't cancel the process unless six or seven minutes pass without any apparent progress.

Some of the available games will have no players and a Host

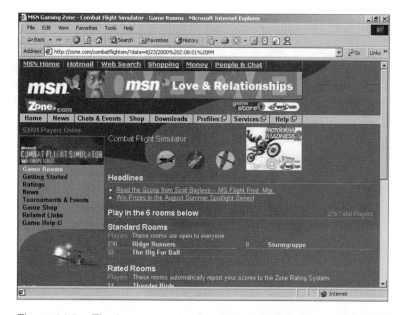

Figure 14-3 *The home page for Combat Flight Simulator on the MSN Gaming Zone hosts multiplayer games and tournaments, provides tips and news concerning Combat Flight Simulator, and contains links to other Web sites dedicated to combat flight simulation.*

button will replace the Join button. Selecting Host allows you to choose the ground rules and location for the game. The Zone will allow others to connect to your computer via the Internet. The Zone only acts as the connection between you and other players. When you host a game on the Zone, your computer still does the actual hosting.

Rated Rooms

Rated rooms are just like standard rooms except that your performance is scored and kept on the Zone for other players to see. These ratings are used for tournaments and MSN Gaming Zone events.

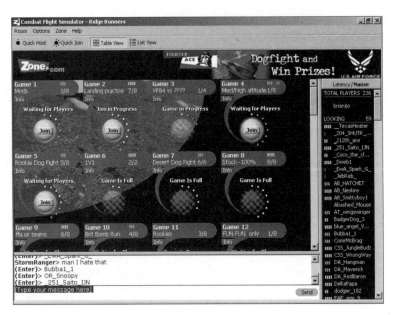

Microsoft
Combat Flight Simulator 2

Tournament Rooms

Tournaments are hosted by both individuals and the MSN Gaming Zone. Tournaments often award prizes to the winners and can be a satisfying experience after you gain some skill in playing the game.

Ladder Rooms

Ladder play keeps a continuing ranking of players. The exact rules vary from ladder to ladder, but usually if you defeat a player above you on the ladder, you move up in the ranks. Defeating players who are ranked high on the ladder will move you up faster than defeating low-ranked players. Unlike tournaments, in which the second-best player could be eliminated in the first round if he or she was unlucky enough to draw the best player as a challenger, ladders tend to ensure that the best players all get to the top. Ladder play might or might not have prizes attached.

Figure 14-4 *Once you enter a specific room, you have many different games to choose from.*

Latency Indicator

The MSN Gaming Zone will display the latency of all the players in the game. Latency is a measure of the speed that information travels from that player's computer to the server. The lower the latency, the less time it takes a computer to communicate with the server, and the better the game performance. In some games, high latency is just an annoyance. (In a game of cards, for instance, a player with high latency simply causes longer pauses during his or her turn.) In Combat Flight Simulator, high latency affects everyone's quality of play. The

airplane belonging to the high-latency player will move in erratic jumps. This makes the airplane hard to target and greatly reduces realism.

The latency indicator consists of four bars next to each player's name in the Web browser window used to connect to the game. Four green bars are ideal and will result in good game play. Three green bars indicate satisfactory latency. Two yellow bars or one red bar indicate high latency. If your latency is high and degrades the game as a whole, it's good etiquette to quit the game. You can reduce your latency with a faster modem or a better Internet connection.

If You're New to the Zone

If you've never played on the MSN Gaming Zone before, you need to sign up with a username and password. The Zone has many members, so your favorite username might already be taken. If you end up with a long username and password that you don't want to retype every time you play, check the box instructing your Web browser to remember your name and password. Once you sign up, you'll be prompted to download the basic MSN Gaming Zone software. The software will install automatically. Whenever you play a game for the first time, you'll be prompted to download software for that game. The first time you play Combat Flight Simulator 2 on the Zone, you'll download the appropriate module. The game downloads are small and rarely take more than four minutes to download.

Game latency—a measure of every player's speed relative to the game itself—is also displayed using the four-bar indicator. Again, high latency will result in a poorer gaming experience. The game latency indicators appear to the right of each game name, as shown in Figure 14-4 earlier.

Etiquette, Honesty, and Hacking

When you use the MSN Gaming Zone to play and communicate with other Combat Flight Simulator enthusiasts, you'll find a whole community of people excited about flying with or against you in combat. These people are also often the best folks to answer your questions and provide tips to improve your play.

Unfortunately, the same open architecture that allows people to create new airplanes and missions also allows people to modify their airplanes to give them an unfair advantage in combat. The original Microsoft Combat Flight Simulator had almost no protection against this sort of hacking. Combat Flight Simulator 2 has a few more safeguards, but players must still rely on the honor system. If you're playing against another player whose aircraft seems to be doing impossible things—his Zero can climb straight up at 300 mph, for instance—the best thing to do is to leave the game and find someone else to fly with. Keep in mind this popular saying about online flight simulation: play Combat Flight Simulator with friends; play Fighter Ace (a subscription-based game available on the MSN Gaming Zone) with strangers.

The Autofollow Bug

When Combat Flight Simulator was released, a development command was inadvertently included in the game. The command (autofollow) allowed a player to lock on to another airplane and follow it automatically. This made for an unfair cheat, but once the game shipped, there was no way to remove it from circulation. Combat Flight Simulator 2 has no autofollow bug.

APPENDIX

System Requirements

Any game simulation contains a delicate balance between realism and playability. The challenge is to provide the highest quality graphics possible without slowing down the game so much that it interferes with your ability to play. In Chapter 2, "Behind the Screens," you'll find recommendations for optimizing Microsoft Combat Flight Simulator 2 for a given computer system. The better your computer hardware, the better your gaming experience. If possible, take a look at your current system before you install Combat Flight Simulator 2, and see if you might want to do a little shopping.

The official system requirements are a Pentium II 300 MHz or equivalent processor, 32 MB of RAM, and a 4x CD-ROM drive. (There is no official requirement for a graphics accelerator card.) While this will be enough to run Combat Flight Simulator 2, it really isn't enough to play enjoyably. A better suggested minimum is a Pentium III 450 MHz or equivalent, 128 MB of RAM, a 4x CD-ROM, and a 3D graphics accelerator card.

Graphics Accelerator Cards

When you look at a graphics accelerator card, use three criteria to determine how well it will handle the demands of running a simulator:

- How fast data is exchanged between the computer and graphics card
- How much memory is available to use for graphics processing
- What built-in features the card has to speed processing

Graphics cards can plug into one of two slots inside the computer, PCI or Accelerated Graphics Port (AGP). PCI slots are the most common expansion slots and are where most modems, network cards, and sound cards are installed in the computer. Older graphics cards usually plug into one of the PCI

Graphics and Graphics Acceleration

When you play Combat Flight Simulator 2, several types of computer processing are happening all at once, but the tasks can be roughly divided into two groups. One group consists of all the computations involving the simulation itself: these include aircraft performance, your position and that of other aircraft, interpreting your joystick inputs, and so on. The other group contains all the processing required to draw the view you see on the monitor screen. This view must take into account relative sizes and distances of objects, your visual perspective at that moment, the shapes, colors, and textures of visible objects, lighting, and shadow. Since both these tasks happen simultaneously, the computer processor must switch back and forth between the two. What this translates to for you is a slowing down of both processes and a jerkiness in the visual display. The faster the computer processor, the less of a problem this is. The best way to handle the situation is to take the bulk of the screen drawing tasks away from the main computer processor and give those tasks to a card dedicated to and designed for rendering graphics on screen. These cards are 3D graphics accelerator cards. A system with a 300-MHz processor and a 3D graphics accelerator card will probably provide a better gaming experience than a 600-MHz system without the card.

slots on the computer motherboard. AGP is a newer type of slot that is replacing PCI cards for video. An AGP card can exchange data with the main processor at a faster rate than a similar card running in a PCI slot. This translates into much faster and smoother graphics rendering on screen.

Some AGP cards and ports also support data compression that allows an even faster transfer of information. These are known as 2x and 4x graphics cards. For these faster systems to deliver their full potential, the card, the computer, and the game must be able to use the 2x or 4x protocol. Combat Flight Simulator 2 supports 4x acceleration. If your computer also supports 4x acceleration, a 4x card would work for you. If your computer only supports 2x, even a 4x card will only give you 2x results.

A computer has only one AGP slot; older computers don't have them at all. Check the documentation that came with your PC. It should say whether your computer has an AGP slot. If you can't find any of that documentation and you have a screwdriver handy, pop the computer open and take a look. The AGP port will be further from the edge than the PCI slots, and you will find only one.

Newer graphics cards also tend to have more memory on the card itself. More card memory frees the computer memory for other processing tasks. Most new AGP cards have 16 to 32 MB of memory on board. Anything less than 16 MB limits the level of detail at which you can play Combat Flight Simulator 2.

Note: *The graphics card is also the video card for a computer in which it is installed. If you install a new graphics card in your computer, you should remove your old video card and attach your monitor to the new card.*

Visual details in Combat Flight Simulator 2 can be rendered at 4x the resolution of Combat Flight Simulator, but these are drawn in real time only with an AGP card installed.

On the other hand, it is not necessary to get the best graphics card on the market to enjoy all the features of the latest game. Software usually lags about six months behind the latest hardware when it comes to taking advantage of new features. Buying the best card out there right now might not make much of a performance difference, as opposed to buying the second best. The difference in price could buy you a whole extra game!

Installation

When you open the package for Combat Flight Simulator 2, you will see two CDs. The first time you put disk 1 into your CD drive, you should see the Install screen with three buttons, two of which are available as options: Install and Web Connection. Web Connection will take you to the Combat Flight Simulator Web site. Clicking Install will lead you through the installation process.

Unless you have limited hard drive space, select Normal Install to place all the game files on your hard drive. If you have limited space, you can choose the Custom Install option, but any movies or data that must be run from the CD will degrade your game performance. Even if you install Combat Flight Simulator 2 without all the options, you can go back

Note: *It's not necessary to remove Combat Flight Simulator before installing Combat Flight Simulator 2. Definitely keep Combat Flight Simulator if you plan to import any of the aircraft or missions into Combat Flight Simulator 2.*

and add them later. The installer will check for available disk space and the right version of DirectX and then run the installation. When prompted, insert the second CD.

What Is DirectX?

DirectX is an application program interface used by software developers to simplify certain programming tasks related to working with game hardware. An abstraction layer gives programmers a single interface to many different hardware systems. In this way, a game can issue a command to play an explosion sound, for instance, without knowing what kind of sound card is installed. This is no trivial matter. If you were to program a computer to do a human task, such as opening the front door, you would have to tell it where the door was, what kind of doorknob the door had, where the knob was on the door, how to grasp the knob, and so on. DirectX takes care of these details, freeing the programmer to simply say, "Open the front door" or "Open the back door." DirectX is a suite of such APIs: DirectSound handles the game sounds. Direct3D handles certain graphics functions. (The "X" in DirectX is a variable that refers to all the various Direct functions.) Combat Flight Simulator 2 uses DirectX 6 or greater, which is installed automatically if your system needs it.

Note: *Although I do mention some game controllers by name in this section, these are for example only and do not make up a comprehensive list of available game controllers.*

After you have installed the software, you can immediately play the game. As with the original Combat Flight Simulator, Combat Flight Simulator 2 requires the game CD to be kept in a drive to play the game, even if all the data is running off your hard drive. After the game is installed, inserting the CD into the drive will give you three options: Play, Add/Remove, and Web Connection.

Game Controllers

While you can play Combat Flight Simulator 2 using only the keyboard and the mouse, the results are usually unsatisfying. A good game controller really makes the flight simulation experience work and is simply a lot more fun. This game controller can be a flight yoke or a joystick, but while many military bombers and transports did use a control yoke, all the fighter aircraft you can fly in Combat Flight Simulator 2 use a stick except for the P-38. If you already have a flight yoke, by all means keep using it, but if you plan to buy a new controller, joysticks tend to be better suited for flight simulation games than game pads. When selecting a joystick, a little planning beforehand will make the search much easier.

Force Feedback and USB

With so many new game controllers on the market, it helps to limit the field a bit by making a few decisions. One of the first choices is whether to get a stick with *force feedback*. Force feedback allows the game to send commands to motors in the joystick that make it move in your hand. The joystick can vibrate with the sound of the engine, jerk momentarily as the gear locks into the wheel wells, and resist movement as the airplane reaches its top speed. Force-feedback joysticks are significantly more expensive than some traditional joysticks, but you can still find one for less than $100. Two good examples of force-feedback joysticks are the Logitech WingMan I-Force and the Microsoft SideWinder Force Feedback 2.

Before you buy a force feedback stick, try one out in a store to ensure that you like the sensation. Many people find that force feedback adds immensely to the gaming experience, but some players don't like it. If you do buy a force feedback system, be sure it has a heavy base. Without something to hold the stick down, the forces can make the joystick jump around on the table. Also note that most force feedback systems have their own power supply, requiring an unoccupied plug near your computer.

Universal serial bus (USB) is a system for attaching up to 127 peripherals to a computer using a common bus. This system is simple to attach a joystick to. While USB provides faster data speeds than the standard game controller port on your sound card, the difference probably isn't noticeable while playing. USB cables are easily extended, though, so if the distance between your computer and the controller is an issue, USB might be the way to go. To use USB, you need a USB port, which most new computers have. USB is also hot swappable, meaning you can plug and unplug the peripherals without shutting down your computer. Finally, USB is cross platform, so if you want a joystick that also works on a newer Macintosh, USB is the best choice.

Features, Features, Features

Once you have a rough idea of what kind of game controller you want, the best thing to do is to go to a store and get the joysticks in your hand. The grip that fits one person best might feel awkward to someone else. You'll probably end up gripping that item pretty tightly when that Zero just won't come off your tail, so get something that's comfortable. The key is to find the control that works for you. In this section, I'll talk about some features of specific joysticks that you might want to consider.

Hat Switch Mania

A hat switch is like a minijoystick you control with your thumb. Unlike a joystick, which has an infinite number of positions, the hat switch has only four or eight positions, plus center. A good eight-position hat switch is key to effective combat operation. Two popular joysticks that include a hat switch are the Microsoft Sidewinder Precision 2 and the Logitech Wingman Extreme Digital 3D.

Buttons Under the Thumb and a Twist Control

The grip on most of the high-end joysticks, such as the Sidewinder Precision 2 and the Wingman Extreme Digital 3D, twists for rudder control. These controllers also offer multiple buttons under the thumb that allow you to program extra functionality into the stick. For example, you can program these buttons to fire rockets or to change views quickly.

Personal Ergonomics, Even for Lefties

The Saitek Cyborg joysticks are configurable for right or left-handed use—you can even switch the throttle control to either side. You can also adjust the hand rest on the grip to fit large or small hands. Saitek Cyborg products look mechanized and uncomfortable, but they feel and work great.

Cheap Analog Joysticks: Beware

Many computer stores have some really low-priced joysticks; sometimes they even give them away with computer systems. These joysticks are usually analog controls rather than digital and work poorly with the precision control systems used in Combat Flight Simulator 2. Get a digital joystick to take advantage of these features. The thing you'll find that limits a cheaper joystick the most is the lack of extra buttons and the lack of a twist grip for rudder control.

Throttle Quadrants and Rudder Pedals

Rudder pedal and throttle functions are critical items for game play, but having separate controls for them is more a luxury than a necessity. If you have to choose between the two, rudder pedals will probably add the most realism.

The twist grip joysticks work well, but real pedals work better. Rudder pedals go on the floor by your feet and let you send left and right commands to the rudder on the tail of the airplane. This system realistically simulates rudder pedals found on the actual fighter airplanes.

A throttle quadrant is a sliding control that more closely simulates the throttle on real airplanes. Most throttle quadrants have several extra buttons for user-assigned functions. The nice part about a throttle quadrant is that it allows you to have more buttons under fingertip control. If you do choose throttle control, having lots of buttons is key. When only one hand is on a game controller, the other can be standing ready at the keyboard. With both hands on controllers, the keyboard should be necessary only occasionally. A good example of a multifunction throttle controller is the Suncom SFS Throttle. It has two sliding controls and a plethora of buttons and hat switches.

> **Note:** *For an extra touch of realism, assign your guns in the Zero to a button on the throttle quadrant. Zero pilots fired their guns by squeezing a lever on their throttle that looked like a bicycle brake, instead of a button on their control stick.*

Adjusting the Controller Settings

If your controller doesn't respond the way you would like, try adjusting the calibration and sensitivity in the Combat Flight Simulator 2 Settings window.

There are only two things to adjust: sensitivity and null zone. Sensitivity refers to the distance the stick must move to get a certain input to the game. The more sensitive the given axis of control, the less control motion is necessary to get results. The null zone is the area in the center of motion that is considered zero input. The larger the null zone, the more you will need to move the stick off center to see *any* results.

Control Axes

Control axes refer to any control on the joystick that has a range of inputs. Every joystick has at least two axes, up/down and left/right. A twist grip or rudder pedals are a third axis; a throttle slider is a fourth. Hat switches are not considered axes. Not all functions in Combat Flight Simulator 2 can be assigned to an axis: You can assign the throttle to an axis, but you can assign the prop control only to a button—one button to increase RPM and another to decrease RPM.

Civilian Combat Flight Schools

If you ever have the urge to take your passion for combat flight one step further, there are several combat flight schools that offer half-day to two-day courses in combat flying using high-performance training airplanes. You usually don't need a pilot's license or any previous flight experience to attend. The course content varies from school to school, but most schools give you the opportunity to fly real airplanes in mock combat. There's nothing quite like feeling the g-forces and smelling the gasoline as you turn and dive through the sky. The real thing will be different from your Combat Flight Simulator 2 experience, but all your virtual flying will make a difference in how fast you learn in the real-world cockpit. Here's a list of some of the schools you could contact.

- **Air Combat Canada**

    Niagara District Airport, Highway 55, RR#4, Niagara-on-the-Lake, Ontario
    http://www.aircombatcanada.com/
    Training aircraft: Extra 300L

- **Air Combat USA**

    230 North Dale Pl., Fullerton, CA 82837 (800) 522-7590
    http://www.aircombatusa.com/
    Training aircraft: SIAI Marchetti SF260

- **North American Top Gun**

    270 Estrella Ave., Hanger H-4, St Augustine, FL 32095 (800) 257-1636
    http://www.natg.com/
    Training aircraft: AT-6 Texan / SNJ (Note: the SNJ was the advanced trainer for the Navy during World War II.)

- **Stallion 51**

    3951 Merlin Drive - Kissimmee, FL 34741 (407) 846-4400
    http://www.stallion51.com/
    Training aircraft: TF-51 (Note: Stallion 51 does not offer combat training, but they do offer flights in the TF-51, a two-seat version of the P-51 Mustang.)

- **Texas Air Aces**

    8319 Thora St., Hanger A-5, Spring, TX 77379 (800) 544-ACES
    http://www.airaces.com/home.htm
    Training aircraft: T-34

Reference Materials

There's a whole world of materials on combat flying covering tactics, history, simulation, and pilot supplies. To start your search on line, begin with the Combat Flight Simulator home pages on the Gaming Zone or on Microsoft's Web site. (See Chapter 14, "Playing Well with Others.") If you're looking for books and flight manuals, here are a few excellent resources to get you going:

Bergerud, Eric M. Fire in the Sky: The Air War in the South Pacific. *Boulder: Westview Press, 1999.*

Boyne, Walter J. Clash of Wings: World War II in the Air. *New York: Simon & Schuster, 1997.*

Shaw, Robert. Fighter Combat: Tactics and Maneuvering. *Annapolis: United States Naval Institute, 1985.*

Spick, Mike. Allied Fighter Aces: The Air Combat Tactics and Techniques of World War II. *Mechanicsburg: Stackpole Books, 1997.*

For pilot handbooks and training materials, you can contact these organizations:

*Aviation Publications, PO Box 357, Appleton, WI 54912-0357 (*http://www.hbs.net/gcc/index.htm*)*

*Historic Aviation, 121 Fifth Ave. NW, Suite 300, New Brighton, MN 55112 (800) 225-5575 (*http://www.historicaviation.com*)*

Index

....➤

Note: Italicized page references indicate figures, tables, or code listings.

Jeff Van West

Jeff Van West is a freelance writer, curriculum designer, and flight instructor. In addition to writing about flight simulation, Jeff has developed an international pilot training program for a new airplane design, and he has delivered workshops on aerobatics, tailwheel airplanes, and mountain flying. Jeff lives with his wife and child-to-be in Seattle, Washington.

The manuscript for this book was prepared and submitted to Microsoft Press in electronic form. Text files were prepared using Microsoft Word 2000. Pages were composed by Microsoft Press using Adobe PageMaker 6.52 for Windows, with text in Garamond and display type in Ultra Condensed Sans One and Helvetica Condensed Black. Composed pages were delivered to the printer as electronic prepress files.

Interior Graphic Artist
Joel Panchot

Principal Compositor
Gina Cassill

Principal Proofreader/Copy Editor
Holly Viola

Indexer
Rebecca Plunkett

Expert
advice!

Master the expert tips, tricks, tactics, and strategies for popular Microsoft games with the Microsoft Press® INSIDE MOVES series. This inside information comes straight from the game developers and isn't available anywhere else. Get these books to get the most fun out of these games!

- MICROSOFT® AGE OF EMPIRES® II: THE AGE OF KINGS: INSIDE MOVES
  ISBN: 0-7356-0513-0

- MICROSOFT AGE OF EMPIRES II: THE CONQUEROR'S EXPANSION: INSIDE MOVES
  ISBN: 0-7356-1177-7

- MICROSOFT FLIGHT SIMULATOR 2000: INSIDE MOVES
  ISBN: 0-7356-0547-5

- MICROSOFT COMBAT FLIGHT SIMULATOR: INSIDE MOVES
  ISBN: 1-57231-592-X

- MICROSOFT COMBAT FLIGHT SIMULATOR: WWII PACIFIC THEATER: INSIDE MOVES
  ISBN: 0-7356-1176-9

- MICROSOFT URBAN ASSAULT™: INSIDE MOVES
  ISBN: 1-57231-861-9

Microsoft®
mspress.microsoft.com

Get fast answers—
at a glance!

Here's the easy, *visual* way to find fast answers for using the Microsoft Windows family of operating systems and Microsoft Office 2000 applications. Microsoft Press® AT A GLANCE books help you focus on specific tasks and show you, with clear, numbered steps, the easiest way to get them done now. Put Microsoft software to work for you with AT A GLANCE!

- MICROSOFT® OFFICE 2000 PROFESSIONAL AT A GLANCE
- MICROSOFT WORD 2000 AT A GLANCE
- MICROSOFT EXCEL 2000 AT A GLANCE
- MICROSOFT POWERPOINT® 2000 AT A GLANCE
- MICROSOFT ACCESS 2000 AT A GLANCE
- MICROSOFT FRONTPAGE® 2000 AT A GLANCE
- MICROSOFT PUBLISHER 2000 AT A GLANCE
- MICROSOFT OFFICE 2000 SMALL BUSINESS AT A GLANCE
- MICROSOFT PHOTODRAW™ 2000 AT A GLANCE
- MICROSOFT INTERNET EXPLORER 5 AT A GLANCE
- MICROSOFT OUTLOOK® 2000 AT A GLANCE
- MICROSOFT WINDOWS® 2000 PROFESSIONAL AT A GLANCE
- MICROSOFT WINDOWS ME AT A GLANCE

Microsoft Press products are available worldwide wherever quality computer books are sold. For more information, contact your book or computer retailer, software reseller, or local Microsoft Sales Office, or visit our Web site at mspress.microsoft.com. To locate your nearest source for Microsoft Press products, or to order directly, call 1-800-MSPRESS in the U.S. (in Canada, call 1-800-268-2222).

Prices and availability dates are subject to change.

mspress.microsoft.com

Stay in the *running*
for maximum productivity.

These are *the* answer books for business users of Microsoft software. They are packed with everything from quick, clear instructions for new users to comprehensive answers for power users—the authoritative reference to keep by your computer and use every day. The RUNNING series—learning solutions made by Microsoft.

- RUNNING MICROSOFT® EXCEL 2000
- RUNNING MICROSOFT OFFICE 2000 PREMIUM
- RUNNING MICROSOFT OFFICE 2000 PROFESSIONAL
- RUNNING MICROSOFT OFFICE 2000 SMALL BUSINESS
- RUNNING MICROSOFT WORD 2000
- RUNNING MICROSOFT POWERPOINT® 2000
- RUNNING MICROSOFT ACCESS 2000
- RUNNING MICROSOFT INTERNET EXPLORER 5
- RUNNING MICROSOFT FRONTPAGE® 2000
- RUNNING MICROSOFT OUTLOOK® 2000
- RUNNING MICROSOFT WINDOWS® 2000 PROFESSIONAL

mspress.microsoft.com

up! Step Step

STEP BY STEP books provide quick and easy self-training—to help you learn to use the powerful features and tools in Microsoft Office 2000, Microsoft Windows Professional, and Microsoft Windows Me. The easy-to-follow lessons present clear objectives and real-world business examples, with numerous screen shots and illustrations. Put Office 2000 and Windows 2000 Professional, and Windows Me to work today with STEP BY STEP learning solutions, made by Microsoft.

- MICROSOFT® OFFICE 2000 PROFESSIONAL 8-IN-1 STEP BY STEP
- MICROSOFT WORD 2000 STEP BY STEP
- MICROSOFT EXCEL 2000 STEP BY STEP
- MICROSOFT POWERPOINT® 2000 STEP BY STEP
- MICROSOFT INTERNET EXPLORER 5 STEP BY STEP
- MICROSOFT PUBLISHER 2000 STEP BY STEP
- MICROSOFT ACCESS 2000 STEP BY STEP
- MICROSOFT FRONTPAGE® 2000 STEP BY STEP
- MICROSOFT OUTLOOK® 2000 STEP BY STEP
- MICROSOFT WINDOWS® 2000 PROFESSIONAL STEP BY STEP
- MICROSOFT WINDOWS ME STEP BY STEP

OWNER REGISTRATION CARD   *Register Today!*   0-7356-1176-9

Return the bottom portion of this card to register today.

Microsoft® Combat Flight Simulator 2: WW II Pacific Theater: Inside Moves

FIRST NAME   MIDDLE INITIAL   LAST NAME

INSTITUTION OR COMPANY NAME

ADDRESS

CITY   STATE   ZIP

( )

E-MAIL ADDRESS   PHONE NUMBER

U.S. and Canada addresses only. Fill in information above and mail postage-free.
Please mail only the bottom half of this page.

For information about Microsoft Press®
products, visit our Web site at
mspress.microsoft.com

ATTLE

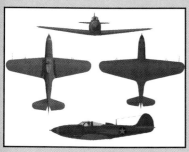

Bell P-39D Airacobra

Range: 600 mi.

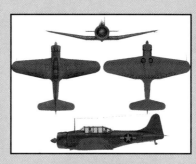

Douglas SBD-2 Dauntless

Range: 1100 mi.

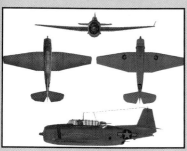

Grumman TBF-1 Avenger

Range: 1215 mi.

Use the ranges on this card to help design missions. Ranges for many planes can be increased by adding drop-tanks.

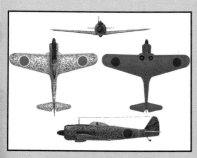

Nakajima Ki-43-IIb Hayabusa (Peregrine Falcon) "Oscar"

Range: 1095 mi.

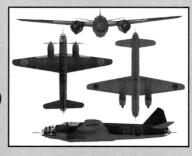

Mitsubishi G4M2 "Betty"

Range: 2982 mi.

U.S. non-player-flyable:

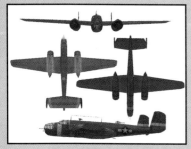

North American B-25D/PBJ Mitchell

Range: 1350 mi.

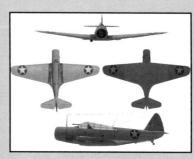

Douglas TBD-1 Devastator

Range: 716 mi.

Douglas C-47 Skytrain

Range: 1600 mi.

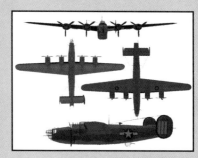

Consolidated PB4Y/B-24D Liberator

Range: 2200 mi.

Japanese non-player-flyable:

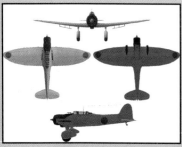

Aichi D3A1 "Val"

Range: 1131 mi.

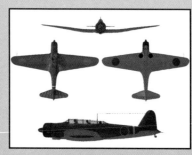

Nakajima B5N2 "Kate"

Range: 609 mi.

ENEMY

U.S. player-flyable:

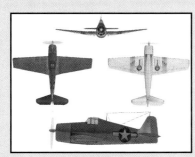

Grumman F6F-3
Hellcat

Range: 1090 mi.
V_c: 151 knots

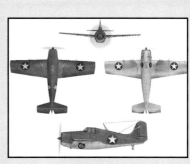

Grumman F4F-4
Wildcat

Range: 770 mi.
V_c: 178 knots

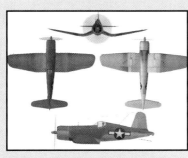

Vought F4U-1A
Corsair

Range: 1015 mi.
V_c: 219 knots

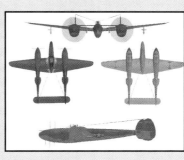

Lockheed P-38
Lightning

Range: 900 mi.
V_c: 192 mph

Japanese player-flyable:

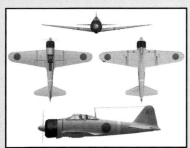

Mitsubishi A6M2
(Model 21) Reisen
(Type Zero Fighter)
"Zeke"

Range: 1160 mi.
V_c: 164 knots

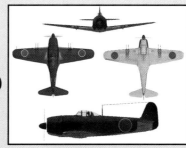

Kawanishi
N1K2-J
Shinden-kai
(Violet Lightning,
improved)
"George"

Range: 1160 mi.
V_c: 175 knots